We're Off To See The Wilderness, The Wonderful Wilderness of Awes

A hiker's 2000-mile adventure journal
of the Appalachian Trail

by

M.E. "Postcard" Hughes

2005

Library of Congress Number: 2005904979
ISBN :   Hardcover   1-4134-9821-3
                Softcover   1-4134-9820-5

This book was printed in the United States of America.

To order additional copies of this book, contact:
Xlibris Corporation
1-888-795-4274
www.Xlibris.com
Orders@Xlibris.com
28083

    That final look at the Weather Channel showed nothing but clouds with lightning bolts and rain for the next three days. As I strapped on my backpack, a tumbling thunder rolled across the sky announcing today would not be boring. The folks asked if maybe I should wait and start in a few days. "Somewhere between here and Maine, I'm going to be rained on. I might as well get it over with," I answered and handed them the car keys. One more hesitant look at the darkening sky and one more hug, and then I started up the Approach Trail. "See you in six months," I shouted back as I disappeared into the woods.

N
W · E
S

MAINE

Vt.

N.H.

New York

Mass.

Conn.

Pennsylvania

N.J.

West Virginia

MD.

Virginia

Tenn.

North Carolina

Georgia

☆ Springer Mountain
■ Harpers Ferry
★ Mt. Katahdin

YOUR COMPASS

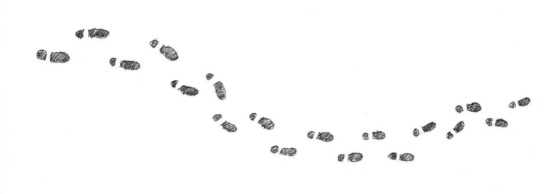

PREHIKE THOUGHTS AND FRETS

ZAG

I've decided to hike the Appalachian Trail. I've decided to seek out an adventure, to vanquish the rut of just working and sitting around the house and then repeating that monotony each day. Sometimes you have to stop and smell the evergreen.

It's a decision that requires countless other decisions. Decisions such as to not go looking for the next paycheck, but rather a cool mountain breeze. (I wonder which will give me the greater return on investment when the year is over.) It requires selling a house (which I just sold) and moving everything into storage. It's a decision that demands listening to one's own heart and having courage. Before a single mile is put behind me, I realize that the decision itself is part of the journey.

This is not the first time I've made this decision though, it's the third.

How does anyone really make a decision to leave everything they've known their whole life to spend six months in the woods? Do we run from something or do we run to something? Has life become so homogenize, so expectedly routine that watching TV each night is the most common activity? Is it any wonder why we all are getting spare tires and atrophied muscle? Have we lost the imagination to look at a horizon and consider the possibilities? Even if one did, is it even possible to have a true-life adventure in today's overly cautious guardrail, warning sign world? Has adventure become limited to the billionaires who can afford the around-the-world hot air balloons or the twenty-million-dollar rides into space? Can one seek adventure without seeking a headline? And if someone did get a wild-hare notion to go explore, where could you go to avoid the thousands of miles of strip malls? I can't remember even using the word "adventure" in the last decade. Adventure holds a romanticism and mystique, I know it did for me. Drawn by the irresistible pull of possibilities and pushed to escape the stagnant, boring life I allowed to find me, it was easy to embrace the Appalachian Trail.

You might be led to believe after reading the above that I have a boring profession. I don't, quite the contrary. My profession allows me to dream all day and play Connect the Dots with all sorts of interesting products. I'm a creative director. That's a person who thinks in words and pictures and music and color and design. For twenty-three years I've worked in the fun profession of advertising where I've created TV commercials and print advertisements for all kinds of products. I do this work with others in an advertising agency for clients who want you to consider their widget over someone else's doodad. I love doing it, and that passion has blessed me with success. Having had many opportunities to speak to young adults looking to find their purpose in life, I've counseled them to pursue what they truly love. When your profession brings you joy, you'll do it better and longer if need be than the individual who does it because it's their job. The person who follows their passion will have happiness.

When I began my career in advertising, I did so because I loved putting words and pictures together into new combinations. Although many will say that advertising isn't an art in the traditional sense, good, fresh advertising does require artistry. I have bookcases loaded with awards that I suppose say I have some ability at it. But when clients start to seek the mundane and formula replaces creativity, passion can quickly become a "job." Eventually you find yourself in the doldrums looking at your watch for the hour to head home instead of staying and hunting down that magic phrase or picture that would make the difference. You find yourself becoming more cynical and less positive, or at least I did. It was a place I was unfamiliar with, and it eventually led me to volunteering my name for a layoff. Life is too precious to waste it on work that held no value.

So with time on my hands and résumés in circulation, I remembered Bill Bryson's book a few years earlier about the Appalachian Trail. I laughed when I read it then; I also said when finishing it that I had absolutely no desire to subject myself to the pain and grief Bryson had experienced before he came off the trail after several very long weeks. But since so much in life is about timing, I was different now. I had few things in my life giving me joy. My job had turned sour, so it was ended. I was living in the city of Chicago, which I had moved to for the job. With a less-than-perfect relationship concluded some six months earlier, I was living solo again. Being single was becoming an unfortunate annoyance. I found myself for the first time in my life thinking that I was in a rut. Hell, I've never been close to using that word before either. Having grown up camping and experiencing the outdoors of Texas, the last twenty-odd years in New York's Manhattan and then Chicago, all that nonstop, big city energy had long since lost its appeal. I was looking for a change or maybe it's more accurate to say I was predisposed for one. So when I remembered the Appalachian Trail, I did so with the imagination I was blessed with. Immediately visions of adventure danced through my head, visions of escape from the doldrums. Maybe, just maybe it was where life was pointing me?

With a bounce in my step, I headed over to the bookstore to find something on the Appalachian Trail. I bought two books that evening and started reading. When I learned that most start hiking in March and April, which was a month away, I knew that the romanticism of adventure was calling. The clincher came the next morning.

Feeling obligated to the habits of society, I made a follow-up interview phone call and that's when an odd thing happened. With the passing of each ring came a growing hope that the person wouldn't answer. When I got their voice mail, I hung up without leaving a message; I knew at that moment I was no longer adrift. I would zag from all I knew and hike the Appalachian Trail.

Never one for small, bashful gestures, I called a friend who was a realtor and put my condo in Chicago's Gold Coast on the market. Where some might say this is a bit impulsive, I'd say guilty as charged. I've been this way my whole life. A vision finds me, the dots connect, and passion takes over. Is there any better time in life than when you find purpose and direction? It's so incredibly empowering. I was transformed from a slow, lumbering slug, back to my normal high-energy, optimistic self. I was going to leave all this baggage behind and jump into another era. I was going to make new footprints on the land and leap beyond the nine-to-five rat race. I would spend my year hiking the Appalachian Trail from end to end. It was a big, grand plan, and it was fresh thinking. To use an advertising phrase, it was a big idea. I would become the heralded "thru-hiker."

Trading the corporate climb for one more natural.

I bought more books and my first *Backpacker Magazine*. I was moving into a brand new world. It mattered little that I had never backpacked or climbed a mountain before; after all, I grew up camping. I was a capable man, one who had achieved success in the mountains and valleys of Manhattan. I was just twenty-two when on the second day after graduating college in California, I hopped on the red-eye and arrived in New York City at 6 a.m. I didn't know anyone. I carried one suitcase and one portfolio. I had one hotel reservation and one interview set up. It was at the greatest, most famous advertising agency in the world, and it mattered little that no one from my prestigious college had been hired there in over six years. At 11 a.m., I showed up for my interview in a ridiculous three-piece suit, where to my amazement they didn't hire me on the spot. I left dejected and low. I sat around my roach-infested hotel room depressed, unable to muster the will to call other agencies for an interview. Every other place was a distant number 3, 4, or 5. There was no desirable number 2. The next day though, I got a call from the agency to come back that afternoon; I told them I could be there in ten minutes, they told me to come at two. And so I started my career in advertising and over the years I grew to stand on the top step of the ladder. I had made it in New York; I could certainly make it on the Appalachian Trail. I was the master of my universe, and the AT would be my next accomplishment. (Apparently, the mountains of the southern Appalachians were far from impressed with my big city accomplishments.)

I didn't know what I didn't know. As the arrangements were made for this first time of packing up my life for storage, I read more books on the AT and started buying my gear. It was fun and exciting. Those last weeks before leaving Chicago, I set up my tent each night in my condo's great room and climbed in to sleep. The linens on my bed didn't get a wrinkle for weeks. Each morning I'd strike camp in my living room and pack up for practice. It was all so silly but terribly fun. I started taking six—to eight-mile hikes along Lake Michigan with a full pack on to get in shape. I read trail wisdoms in the books like the weight of your pack should be around 25 percent of your body weight, which meant that a fifty-pound pack would be my load. Every other day, I'd head off in the morning for my two-hour hike along the extremely flat Lake Michigan walking paths, always returning home a pool of wetness but feeling empowered at my strength. Surely carrying this load along the trail wouldn't be much different. Eight miles is eight miles, isn't it? Some of the books had suggested that doing practice hikes was a good idea, especially over similar terrain. But in Chicago, the only thing close to a mountain is a skyscraper, but few let strangers train in their staircases, so along very flat Lake Michigan was my training ground. The books also talked about depression and loneliness on the trail. It seems the isolation gets to many and really plays havoc. This was the one area I was convinced wouldn't be an issue. After all, I was still single. I was used to spending time by myself. Depression would not be a problem. (I would later write in my journal that when I was in the city, I was single. But when I was in the woods, I was alone.) As strong as I thought I was emotionally, the woods and mountains have a way of removing all the distractions and in turn revealing your frailty.

And so in mid-April of 2002 with the house still unsold, I gave the lawyer the power of attorney and loaded up the car to headed out to the folks for a short pit stop and then we'd all head to Georgia. I had determined April 18 as my start date, giving me six months to make it to Maine before the northern terminus normally closes due to winter conditions.

I share all this with you since the success rate of those who make it to Maine and complete their thru-hike is around 15 to 20 percent. And that's with it creeping up in the last couple of years. In the past, it was only around 10 percent or said another way, a 90 percent failure rate! Does anyone really go into a new endeavor thinking they'll be one of the 90 percent? Of course not, it's in our nature to place ourselves into the 10 percent of success stories. Especially in my case, it's practically impossible for me to look at anything half-empty. So my decision to thru-hike the Appalachian Trail two years earlier, like so many others each year, was made without understanding the endeavor. I would experience a baptism by mountain. This year, 2004, would be different. (Knock on wood.)

This decision helps me fulfill one of my life's goals to not wait until retirement to enjoy life and its many textures. I've been to all fifty of our states, but I've never walked through fourteen of them. I've been picked up by a tornado while in my car, but never have I rode out a thunderstorm in a tent. I can run six miles, but I've never known the strength and athleticism of a 2,000-Miler. I've stood frozen in the face of an angry African bull elephant but have never faced off with a rattler in the middle of the trail. I think its great that so many of my friends travel to Italy and France, but I wish they would try the splendor and awe of America's wilderness.

In today's society, when the only adventure most get are from their DVD of Indiana Jones or the designated "lands" of Disney, the Appalachian Trail takes us all on a truly grand adventure. By sheer necessity, we who hike it learn the difference between what is needed and what is wanted—a distinction that has long been lost by most living in metropolis. It's been said that the outdoor experience has been an integral part of America's history. And so on this, the bicentennial anniversary of our country's most famous journey of discovery, the Lewis and Clark expedition, I'll be on an adventure as well. My exposure to the AT gave me a new level of patience, humility, and a new sense of calm. I suppose when you've battled mountains, rain, hail, wind, heat, cold, snow, and the sounds that go bump in the night, new perspectives are likely to be gained. The more time I spent on the AT, the more my priorities found a new order. Not only will a new order bloom within my fellow thru-hikers of the class of '04, but so will the need for more of the AT experience. What may have started as an escape from something else two years ago has become for me a yearning to regain that sense of freedom, that simplicity. I'm choosing to start again at the very beginning, Springer Mountain in Georgia, and thru-hike my way to Mt. Katahdin in Maine.

Having an artist and writer's background professionally, I plan on drawing and writing my way to Maine. I hope to share a bit more of the whimsical and different sides of the Appalachian Trail as they bump into me—hopefully not too hard. Those who've attempted to thru-hike the Appalachian Trail have done so for the past thirty or more years under a trail name. The origins of the trail name are a bit fuzzy, but I'm sure escapism is a strong component. My trail name is "Postcard," and I intend to share my adventure with you through my postcard drawings and stories of the trail, and I'll do so in the format of my journal. So I invite you to come along on this grand adventure.

GREAT GOOGLELY MOOGLELY

The first look I got of the Appalachian Mountains was in Connecticut. They don't rise up to meet the sun like their powerful cousins of the West. Frankly, their modest elevation was far from impressive. But the first day I actually *saw* their drama? Well, that was two years ago in northern Georgia, the day before I would attempt my first ever backpacking trip, which in my typical fashion, was a thru-hike.

My folks, being retired, had agreed to take the drive down to Georgia and bid me farewell. They've always wanted to be involved with the lives of my sister and mine that way. Better parents simply do not exist.

Throughout my preparation, I read that of those who start a thru-hike, nearly 30 percent stop at Neels Gap, a mere thirty miles away. It was an action I simply could not understand. Thirty miles? What could possibly unravel these committed adventurers from their dreams after only thirty miles? But as I drove around that bend en route to Springer Mountain, I saw the answer to that puzzling question.

"Oh my god!" A visual memory from that first sighting.

There before us, as the trees dipped toward the valley, laid a vista of rugged, saw-toothed mountains. The spectacle extended beyond my peripheral vision and only then did the naiveté grow closer to comprehension.

This entire visual and many more like it would become my world for the next six months. The power, the beauty, and the enormity of this endeavor blinded me for the first time. At this moment the pleasurable romanticism of hiking in the woods was replaced by fear, anxiety, and apprehension. With some knee-jerk reaction of bravado, I remarked that it "looks like fun!" when "oh my god!" was what I was really thinking. I had never climbed a single mountain in my life, let alone with a backpack. Before me now was nothing but one rugged peak after another. I truly must be an idiot at times, for I had forgotten that I had never hiked a mountain before. How on earth does one forget that tiny fact?

Having grown up in the relative flat lands of Texas, where other than the occasional hilly golf course, my decision to hike the AT had put me face to face with a mountainous foe I was unfamiliar with. Nonchalantly, I said to the folks, "I hope the lounge at the hotel is open, I'm ready for a cocktail."

The next morning, after breakfast, my folks and I left the Amicalola Falls State Park Lodge and headed out on a series of roads, eventually finding the Forest Service Road that led to a trailhead, just a mere nine-tenths of a mile from the beginning of the Appalachian Trail. The trailhead allowed hikers to avoid the arduous nine-mile climb of the Approach Trail. That should have been a red flag, after all—why hike a bunch of miles that don't even count? Many skip over the Approach Trail as I did that year, but worrying about extra miles is one thing a thru-hiker just needs to let go of. Frankly, it has been estimated that when you add up all the distances walking to shelters, water sources, into towns and detours, a thru-hiker will cover a couple hundred extra miles. So fretting over the 8.8 miles to reach the copper plaque and the AT's first white blaze on Springer Mountain now seems silly. The Approach Trail is part of the tradition of the hike.

Nervous and apprehensive, I strapped on my behemoth backpack, a collection of fabrics and braces and foam stuffed to the zippers with loads of wilderness conquering doodads. It was a monster. And it was as heavy as a coffee table. If I let my guard down for just a moment, it would topple me off balance. Despite the nerves, enough adrenaline was being released that a little thing like fifty-four pounds wouldn't matter, until the first climb that is.

It was surreal saying goodbye to the folks and walking into the woods. One moment you're standing there with those who represent the foundation of your world, the next, everything becomes unknown as you disappear into the wilderness. Enthusiasm carried me swiftly along the gentle, mostly downhill first miles. Unaccustomed to backpacking, the AT, relying on water, and checking guidebooks, I walked myself right into a dramatic first day. First was the revelation that eight miles along Lake Michigan in Chicago with a heavy pack was not the same thing as eight miles up and down the mountains of the Appalachian Trail. The second was the shock of how incredibly hard it was to carry a pack *down* a mountain trail. Gravity magnifies each downward step, and your knees quickly let you know they're not happy about this need for adventure. (Couldn't the three of us, my two knees and I, take a road trip instead? In a car? Sitting down?) The third was I quickly learned that you must always drink water. Lots of water. I've never been too enamored with water, always opting for Diet Coke or wine or anything with flavor. Drinking anything was always done out of desire, not need. I understood little how important staying well hydrated was and how doing so avoids many evils. Not drinking is an invitation for disaster, which I'll now share.

I had planned to camp at Justice Creek, a 13.7 mile first-day trek. Since tenting would help me avoid the shenanigans of the shelter mice on my way to Maine, there was no need to walk the extra tenths to visit the shelters. (This would be my second error, the first was planning a 13.7 mile first day with a backpack as heavy as a steamer trunk.) Rest, who needs rest? I'm hiking the Appalachian Trail—gotta go, go, go. That's how I did things in the city. I don't need no stinkin' rest. I'm fit and virile; my body doesn't need to take it easy and get in trail shape. (You can see it coming, can't you?)

At eight miles I failed to check my guide book to find out where the next water would be. Amazingly, I was still working on my first liter of water, about one-third of it was remaining. Little did I know that it would be five-plus miles more to the water source at camp. And between water and me were the three nasty climbs of Hawk, Sassafras, and Justus mountains. With only a few ounces of water, it seemed that the only thing I had plenty of was ignorance. Behind me was a full, warm hiking day that had me running on excitement and adrenaline but not enough water. Without the proper hydration in me and muscles nowhere near ready to carry the fifty-four-pound backpack up and down three more mountains, they rebelled. Loudly.

On the way up Hawk, I felt a tingle in my right thigh and then *wham*, a huge cramp hit the muscle and hit hard. The pain was so intense it took nearly five minutes to massage it away. I took a small sip of water and shrugged it off as a one-time, odd occurrence and continued up. In another hundred yards I started to feel another tingle; this time, however, in my left thigh. *Wham*, it cramped. But this time it had company. *Wham* went the right one as well. With both in severe spasms, I couldn't stand and fell to the trail. Both legs were shaking with spasms and painfully locked. Wincing and wiggling the best I could to unlock the cramps, I lay grounded, just the ants and me. Three more times both legs would lock from these overused, dehydrated, heat cramp muscle attacks throwing me to the ground. Overshadowing it all was the ever-falling sun. With miles to go, my watch told me I had just over three hours till darkness would add to the drama. Only a week before leaving, I'd read a trail wisdom/ slogan that I was now living. I had inadvertently gone "too far, too fast, with too much, too soon." It took three hours to walk the last two miles into Justus Creek campsite, just moments before sunset. After a power chug of a few liters of water, it was all I could do to just get the tent up, eat, and go to bed. Exhausted beyond description, the journal writing would wait till another day. The leg muscles were so damaged from day 1 that it was hard to even walk slowly for the days that followed. It's moments like that which made me such an accomplished hiker now and why I want to help you avoid the comedic idiocy that can find you out on the trail. It's moments like that why I now carry several liters of water in a hiking bladder with a bite-valve drinking tube and drink liberally all day long. As the days went on, I found the weight I was trudging with had me walking with my head down and my eyes locked on the trail. I was slogging along without the least amount of joy. Then, on day 5, it hit me like a ton of Georgia boulders. I wasn't having fun. None. The whole idea of the adventure had been sweated out of me. A moisture-rich air that morning had loaded anything that had fabric with extra weight, bringing my load up to around sixty pounds. I was making the climbs, but I wasn't looking at the vistas. I was making the miles, but they felt unfulfilling. Upon reaching the Unicoi Gap road crossing at 50.7 miles, I got a ride into the town of Helen, Georgia, and came off the trail.

I had gone twenty miles farther than a third of those who try a thru-hike, but I was far from proud. My planning was way off too. I was carrying ten days of food because I thought resupply opportunities would always be rare; my mail drops were too far apart forcing me to shoulder too much food. The entire approach I'd worked so long on was completely wrong. Individually, the coffee-table-heavy backpack, a landscape I was completely inexperienced with, and all my mail-drop support planning being so out of kilter would have been quite a foe. But together, they ganged up on me to bring out an emotional weakness I had been suppressing. I couldn't fight the mountains and myself at the same time. Aside from injury, despair is the biggest reason most do not make it. It certainly was my undoing. It helped me to be more encouraging with others having a hard time of it. I see no need why other hikers have to learn the way I did.

There have been books written by brave souls who sought out the Appalachian Trail to heal from a personal loss. Frankly, I can't imagine tackling the AT and all it asks of you without having your "A" game. Only now, with the emotional upheaval in my past can I see that my thru-hike could have continued. But finding a positive perspective seemed outside my scope of ability then. Being able to adapt along the journey is vital, which was yet another aspect I didn't comprehend at the time. In an unexpected way, there was this underlying feeling that I had let many people down. Not one to hide my intentions, I learned early on that when a vision finds you, you should be brave enough to share it. To let others know and in turn, where possible, others will miraculously turn up to help you complete the dream or purpose or task. Coming off the trail was not a source of embarrassment so much as I felt others were embarrassed for me. Kind of like when I see a comedian bombing on stage, it makes me uncomfortable to witness it. I believe even some of my friends were disappointed with my meager fifty miles. All they knew was that I couldn't walk the talk. That's understandable. Any public acknowledgment of a grand vision will always make one vulnerable to snickering if not successful. So be it. It was to be my hike not theirs, I wanted it to be joyful, not drudgery because I might face embarrassment. Behold the turtle; it only makes progress when it sticks its head out.

Through it all though, despite my far from joyful introduction, the Appalachian Trail touched me. Its trees, views, and fresh air reminded me of the beauties of the land. The sense of freedom, although coupled with the insecurity of the unknown, liberated me from those years of city living compromises. The Appalachian Trail began to whisper to me deep down inside that we were not finished with each other. No sooner than getting behind the wheel to drive home, I knew I still wanted to be out there, that I still longed for the adventure of a thru-hike. But not the way I had just tried.

Not long after, I'd realize that I could still hike by doing sections. In doing so, I kept changing my gear and lightening my load. I was teaching myself how to hike and how to love the journey. Some days I'd push, other's I'd linger and take a nap in the middle of the day. Then in November of that same year, I did a nine-day 140-mile hike into Harpers Ferry, West Virginia. The experience was joyful each day. I knew then that I'd take another stab at thru-hiking as soon as time permitted. I ended up hiking nearly four hundred miles that rookie season, all of which taught me more than the eleven books I'd read earlier. Why, I've even learned how to have a cocktail at the end of the day, thanks to a tiny plastic flask of spiced rum.

The next year, with my affairs in order, I started down in Georgia to finish all that remained to Maine, about 1,800 miles. But after receiving news from home, I was forced off after one week. That was when I realized that, aside from the required physical and emotional strength, a bit of luck was also needed from those we care about to stay well.

It's now two years after that first thru-hike attempt, and there are only two more months before I leave Florida and head to Springer Mountain to reintroduce myself to a more beautiful side of this world. April 30, my foot hits the Approach Trail, between now and then, only a gazillion things to do such as packing up everything and moving it into storage. This is the second home I've sold to go thru-hiking.

Sixty-three days and counting down.

THINGS I'LL MISS

Any individual setting off on an AT adventure has to be ready for the barrage of questions that will ensue. Popular questions such as "How heavy is your pack?" or "How many miles a day do you walk?" Or the very common "Where do you go to the bathroom?" I remember the question put to me so frequently was "What do you think you'll miss most?" At the time, I could only guess and often replied that it would probably be something simple, something that we all take for granted every day—no, not my wife; still single (Gosh! Darn it!). It wasn't till I spent some real time out on the trail that those prized items of longing started to reveal themselves.

The first of these is one of the great inventions of the civilized world. The chair. If it weren't for the chair we'd still be sitting on the dirt or a tree stump. Oh wait, that's exactly what I will be sitting on. See how a chair helps? So much for progress marching forward. Naturally, being a bit of an aficionado on design, I favor the low-slung lounge chair with decadent ottoman. How glorious it would be to stride into camp after a big mileage day, take off the pack, and collapse into a slouchy, classic leather lounge chair and put the big throbbing dogs up. To make the moment all the more brilliant would be to have a nice Zinfandel sitting on the chair's arm!

My second item of massive longing was the humble piece of bread. Yes, give us our daily bread and let's say a smear of butter and I can go another ten miles. My bias of bread leans toward that of the Italians. Crispy, flaky, chewy crust with soft, puffy white texture. To turbo the bread, put the fixin's of a sandwich between two of those Italian beauties and attack—a rush of gastronomic proportions. Finally, do this from the slouchy, lounge chair and you've got heaven on trail.

When finished—a big, long swig of minty mouthwash—rinse and spit without ever leaving the nirvana of the chair womb. Sorry, got carried away there.

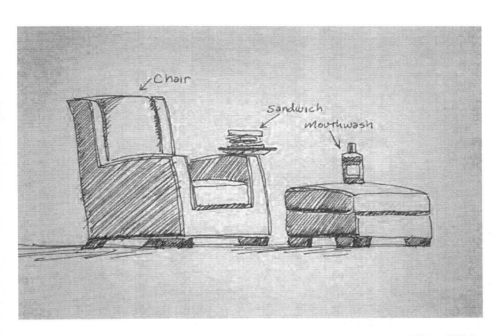

Things I'll Miss

Fifty-two days left to put my feet up.

THE APPALACHIAN TRAIL DIET

Although not as well-known as some of the more famous diets that make it to hardcover, the Appalachian Trail Diet just may be the most effective path to shedding those unwanted pounds.

The AT Diet allows you to eat anything and everything you want. Actually, it demands it.

Words like *sacrifice, deprivation,* and *denial* are replaced by *pig-out, gorge yourself,* and *AYCE* (all you can eat). Imagine putting an end to calorie counting or portion control? Say farewell to fat-free anything and hello to triple chocolate fudge cake. What diet routinely asks you to polish off an entire half gallon of rich, full-fat ice cream?

As a devotee of the AT Diet you'll lose your inhibitions that have plagued you your whole life. When asking for seconds once triggered a mental wrestling match, you'll now think nothing of visiting the buffet counter three, four, even five times. Why, you'll never cower from a carbohydrate again.

So magical is the AT Diet that as you move from main course to main course, you'll not only drop loads of pounds, you'll build muscle! A slimmer, fitter, more beautiful you is just one of the fringe benefits. Your skin will exhibit a healthy, sun-filled glow, and your lung's breathing capacity will double. Those days of listless energy and feeling winded from getting off the sofa will be a distant memory.

Amazingly, the AT Diet also lets its followers travel. Big sky mountain vistas and cozy meandering trails engulfed by the spicy scent of evergreen will be there to greet you. Yes, a heaven of culinary gluttony awaits you, and all you must do is don a backpack and walk! How easy is that!?

So say hello to the AT Diet. Who wouldn't want to eat any and everything one wants while still losing forty pounds and seeing the world? Those thirty-inch waist trousers and that size 2 dress are just over the mountain.

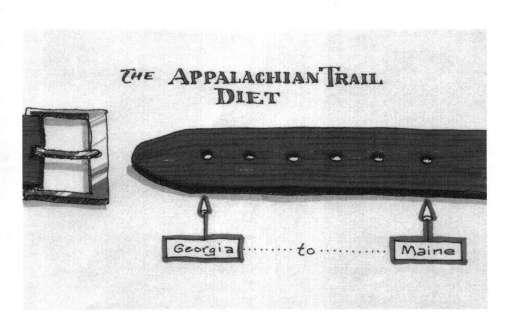

You'll come to love the phrase, "all you can eat."

Eat up, only forty-seven days remaining.

What We Carry

A tent or a tarp? A water filter or drops? A frown or a smile?

Its been said that the disposition we wear today will carve its creases in our face tomorrow. For me, moving north will be about both latitude and attitude. I have to remind myself that it's not the weight of my gear but my outlook that determines so much. Confucius said, "Fall down seven times, get up eight."

It's a fact that people have made it end to end with gear exceeding sixty pounds while others who carried only twenty-five pounds came off the trail. Although not as fanatical as some, I am a champion of hiking with lighter gear. It's basic common sense and the least we can do for our legs and feet. My bathroom scale says my stuff is thirty-two pounds which includes five days of food (7.5 lbs) and two and a half liters of water (5.5 lbs). Of course I have a fairly archaic bathroom scale so it could be thirty-five! The gear will lighten by several pounds when the cold weather stuff gets sent home. But I also mean lightness that goes beyond stuff. The simplifying of my life has been underway ever since the AT revealed some of its less tangible beauties.

My recent short-lived move to Miami was a great opportunity to give the old worldly processions a clean sweep. Purging myself of all the clutter, all the accumulated junk— well, most of it anyway—makes me feel I'm living smarter.

During the 1990s, multitasking Americans discovered that having time had become the new luxury. After pushing for success and achieving it, many found themselves with literally no time to enjoy it. So they got a nanny, a dog walker, a housekeeper, a gardener, and countless modems and wireless objects just to help them keep up. In the process, I believe many lost touch with the genius of going light.

I'm starting to feel that what could evolve into the new luxury of this decade may be simplicity. One thing I won't be carrying on my journey to Maine is an appointment book. I won't need to remind myself of the 8 a.m. meeting before the 9 a.m. meeting to decide if I should fly at 1 p.m. to follow up on yesterday's 3 p.m. conference call. The wheelers and dealers of the world would benefit from some time in the woods. Anyway, simplicity is one of the great lessons learned on the AT, and it appears to be an agreeable lesson for most.

Unfortunately, simplicity doesn't just happen; it seems to take a deft touch and some tough decisions. I think it's hard for some to see the beauty in simplicity when they're so consumed with having more. The desire for having more and more is the proof of how stuff is far from fulfilling. And in an odd way, the more exposure to simplicity I had, the greater the desire for seeking it out. Do I dare quote "less is more"?

Some say the Appalachian Trail with all its challenges serves as a condensed version of our journey through life. And the equipment, despite all the recent advancements, is still just equipment. No matter what stuff we surround ourselves with in life or hike, it is all a weak alternative to the greatest thing we can carry— common courtesy, a sense of humor, and, most importantly, a positive outlook.

After all, what else can get you to put on those cold wet socks yet again?

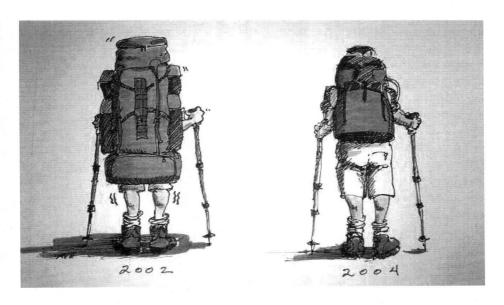

The joy of the journey can be found on a mountain vista, but it's the simplified load that can get you to that summit a lot more joyful.

Thirty-three days to simplicity.

NIGHT ZERO

In the activity of backpacking, there is the principle of the golden triangle. It states that when one sleeps in bear country, one should take some extra precautions to not sleep where you cook and eat. So imagine a large one-hundred-foot triangle. Your tent would be at one corner with your bag of culinary delights hung in a tree in another and your cooking and dining room in the final corner. Just in case you spill your turkey tetrazzini on the ground, it would be nice not having it at your tent's front door. Need I remind you that your tent walls are no thicker than the fabric of your underwear, which you are sure to soil if such a confrontation took place. All of which reminds me of a story.

Night had come and a cool breeze was blowing, my home was at the southern tip of the Appalachian Trail in an open-air lean-to called the Springer Mountain Shelter. Even though I've read the stories about how annoying the congregation of mice around shelters can be, I'm here. But others, who have also heard the courageous antics of these brazen mice, felt less comfortable and decided that tenting would be a better option for their journey. One such hiker traveled under the trail name of Kingfisher.

I took a liking to Kingfisher right off since his backpack equaled mine in size, weight, and stupid decisions. Having read the principles of the golden triangle, he had set up his tent and cooked and hung his food bag in a way that would make a park ranger proud. But not everyone who hikes reads, apparently. So even if you do all the right things, others may not take the same precautions, and that's how the comedy begins.

It wasn't long after hikers' midnight—that is what sunset is called and the ensuing darkness—that this true story gets interesting. At about this hour, short of journal writing, there's not a whole heck of a lot to do except sleep. And God knows we all need the time out from underneath our coffee-table-size packs. So having finished his first dinner and triage performed on countless blisters, it was headlamps off and into his mummy for a good night's rest.

For some reason, early in the hike, the darkness alone can be pretty unnerving for some, and that doesn't count what's wandering around out in it. As Orion slid across the sky and the hour of real midnight came, Kingfisher awoke. A bit disoriented at first, trying to remember that he was on top of a mountain in the middle of the woods came *snort, snarl, snarl, snort* not but a foot away. As his pupils dilated and his sphincter contracted, there was nothing but darkness, a paper-thin fabric of false security and more *snarl, snort, snort.*

Petrified with horror, he was quickly drenched in a cold sweat. The black bear was breathing him in and deciding on whether he was the entrée or the desert. Kingfisher had his beautiful new backpack just outside the tent with all its wonderful little bear toys in it. True to form and curious as a cat, Mr. Bear started spreading it all out for a better look. And doing so while leaning against the tent that Kingfisher sat paralyzed in. Just as thoughts of poking it through the fabric were ruled out, the beast caught the aroma of his food bag bounty. Off the lumbering monster went to consider the entire area's dining options. Not terribly worried about being silent, the sound of snapping branches and twigs under the bear's massive weight heightened the terror. Although Kingfisher had hung his food bag in textbook fashion—that is to say at least ten feet off the ground and at least eight from the tree's trunk and a good four feet below the hang limb—black bears learn. And this one was a model student. It realized that the bag was unreachable from the host tree, but the clever, hungry bear climbed an adjacent tree where it could get its claws on the hang limb. With a few mighty swats, the limb was broken off; and all of Kingfisher's provisions lay helpless on the ground. For the next hour, it was nothing but tearing, ripping, and snarling. The ferociousness of the sound was horrific. Everything Kingfisher had to eat was being devoured, and his hopes for starting his hike being swallowed. *Well, better my food bag than a body part*, he thought.

The mayhem continued for a very long hour, until the fading sound of snapping branches said that the midnight marauder was moseying off. It was at that moment the thought of collecting the damaged remains occurred, if any, but he thought better of it. One just never knows what else may be waiting in the dark.

By 2 a.m. Kingfisher's pupils had found their normal size, and he was moderately calm again; but any idea of sleep was far from happening. The hours went by, and peace returned to the woods. Near 4 a.m., as the edge of sleep started to overpower his paranoia, a distant *snort, snarl, snarl* started moving his way. *Holy shit!* Maybe it was time for his arm to be desert? Or maybe it wanted a hiker drumstick? As the sound of the snapping twigs grew, it was moment of truth time. Everything Kingfisher had bought and planned hung in the balance. *To yield or not to yield, that was the question.* With headlamp on head, Kingfisher jumped out of the tent in unlaced boots and underwear, grabbed a hiking stick and a nearby rock. This would be a battle of titans. An angry, terror-induced, screaming hiker on one side against a smelly, hungry black bear on the other. (Frankly, I liked my decision to hang out with the mice about now.)

The towering Kingfisher courageously braced for the coming clash as the bear's advance grew from the darkness. As he yelled and screamed hoping to make the bear rethink its plan, he heard the sounds of the snapping branches stop. A dead silence fell on the moment. Just out of the reach of his illuminated headlamp, the sounds renewed, but this time moving to his right. It was now circling him in the dark. Oh how the terror grew and the time slowed. The standoff continued for an interminably long five minutes as the bear check for a geographical weakness. Still yelling and throwing everything he could into the dark abyss, Kingfisher heard the sounds finally recede and disappear into the vast sea of night.

As 6 a.m. came around and a glow on the horizon started to emerge, Kingfisher fell asleep. A restless nap was all he could muster, so it was off to see the food bag. There on the ground, were the shredded remains of his "bear-proof" food bag. It was as if someone had run over it with a lawn mower. Foodless and rattled, he came to the shelter to compose himself, where all he found was a bunch of smiling, well-rested hikers. We had heard nothing of all the shenanigans that night. However, it was revealed that another hiker, who'd tented as well, had left a gallon of Kool-Aid outside his tent and may have started the frenzied feeding. Thanks to the generosity of a couple of overnight hikers heading home, Kingfisher was able to get enough foodlike objects to log a real honest-to-goodness mile on the AT. Now most of us would probably call it a hike right then and there but not Kingfisher.

So without a single official mile trekked on the AT, Kingfisher put his first night behind him and moved north, vowing to never tent again. It would be shelters and mice forever. Or so he thought.

Relative to last night, the day was completely absent of drama. As many find, hiking eight miles in Georgia is not like hiking eight miles on flat ground. The hikers quickly start to understand why counting ounces is not fanatical but practical. Tonight would be an early dinner and a spot on the floor of the shelter with the other hikers. Everyone was bushed. Without the physical exercise of hiking to keep you warm, everyone retired to his or her sleeping bags as hikers' midnight came, that's when a resident family of field mice sprang into action. The mice, hoping to catch a rookie hiker off guard, had visions of sugarplums and energy bars dancing in their heads. It's fascinating how such a small, cute, furry creature can give the heartiest soul the willies.

Out they came to scurry along the rafters and around the perimeter of the floor to search for a dropped crumb here or a candy bar that failed to get hung in the food bag. These little bundles of joy will chew right through a pack pocket to get at a misplaced morsel. Trail experience teaches you to leave all your pack pockets unzipped so they can get in and out without consequence. Throughout it all is the constant, soft patter of little mice feet against the wood. As Kingfisher lay wide-eyed in his mummy trying to ignore their sounds and the fact that one had just ran over the foot of his sleeping bag, a terrible crash came from a falling glass. One of the little creatures had knocked it from its resting place up in the rafters. The impact shattered the glass as well as Kingfisher's nerves. It was now midnight, and the show showed no sign of letting up. It was maddening, and enough was enough.

He got up and yanked his tent out of his pack and set it up right in front of the shelter. Within fifteen minutes, Kingfisher was back inside his mummy bag and protected from the varmint gymnastics. That's when he heard it. *Snort, snarl, snarl, snort.* Mr. Bear had come for dinner. *Shitdamnfuck!* was all he could think.

He jumped out the tent and with poles in hand started yelling, which woke the troops and everyone joined in. True to form, Mr. Bear hung back just out of the range of everyone's wimpy headlamp and circled again. But the odds were different tonight, and it wasn't long before it moved off to find a quieter place to ransack. The conquering hikers celebrated openly. But as each returned to their bags to sleep, the sounds that go bump in the night presented each hiker with a silent chill.

All just part of the AT experience. As for Kingfisher, it might be motels forever more.

Nineteen more nights till the start of the journey.

Homage to Being Last

We can't always be first in our endeavors.

Occasionally you have to become comfortable with being last. Actually, sometimes being last is favorable to not being at all. Even though I will be one of the last to leave Springer Mountain and head north, I might be the most appreciative member of the class of '04 for having the chance.

What would first be without last?

Already this season, many have started before me and are rackin' up significant miles before the summer heat. Some began while the AT was still in winter's grip—Mt. Katahdin will be theirs by August. But for me it will be the colorful display of the fall foliage—my favorite time of the year. Those who started first have faced numerous southern snowfalls where the going was slow. It may be a similar fate we late starters might face up north.

But they're really not first, and I'm really not last. We are all just "middles." Many have come before us. Hikers like Earl Shaffer, the AT's first thru-hiker in 1948 and Ed

Garvey, whose thru-hike in 1970 led to a popular book. Hmm, now there's an idea. Amazingly, the numbers of completed hikes remain below 750 from 1937, when the trail first became a continuous footpath till 1980. In the year 2000 alone, more hike completions were reported (429) than in the first forty years. And many more adventurers seeking a fellowship with the wilderness will come after. Of course, let's not forget all the SOBOs (southbounders) who have yet to begin up in Maine and head toward Georgia.

No, being last is no scar on my character. Quite the contrary, in track and field, the last person on the relay team is known as the "anchor." And if I remember correctly, every time the Chicago Bulls basketball team was introduced, the last person was some guy named Michael Jordan. Hmm, being last doesn't necessarily say you're least.

Naturally though, those who go first receive great accolades and parades. Young maidens hanging from high windows will wave, and gallant gentlemen in carriages will be poised to carry them to wherever the town may be. All this and more because they were bold, brave, and had zero-degree sleeping bags.

Einstein said it's all relative, and the AT experience is no different. Yes, they may have the glory of leading this train of humanity, but what engine would feel truly complete without its caboose? So I say to the class of '04: move with confidence and security because Postcard's got your six. Oh, and leave some blueberries up north for me.

Eleven days till I start chuggin'.

Hello I Must Be Going

My departure date has been the source of some angst. Although I consider myself fit and ready to face the Appalachians, I can't overlook one immovable fact—five months and two weeks from when I begin, I must be at Mt. Katahdin in Baxter State Park in Maine. The park service has deemed October 15 as the date they close down the park.

Since January, I've been training and pumping iron to increase my muscles and stamina. With my pack weight manageable, I find I'm starting to entertain some potentially disastrous thoughts such as pushing hard on the miles early on to get ahead. Fortunately, I have just enough AT experience to recognize the folly of such thoughts.

One cannot conquer the Appalachian Mountains; they're not to be trifled with. In a recent study of our lands three great long-distance trails, the Pacific Coast Trail and the Continental Divide Trail were deemed less tough despite being longer and over taller mountains. It was the Appalachian Trail with its endless elevation gains for every mile that has labeled it the toughest. These mountains will ask us to show them the full measure of our physical strength on their ascents and to use our patience in slowing our momentum on their descents. It seems going downhill is the hidden demon that so many cannot comprehend in the beginning. It is the source of many knee injuries and hike-ending pain.

These occasional fretting thoughts about starting late will serve no helpful purpose and only tarnish the splendor of the journey. To head into the mountains focused on the inner *ticktock* of the clock can only push me closer to misery than to Katahdin. I must keep a handle on these thoughts and not let them steamroll me. From all I've read and experienced on the AT, one does not slay the dragon; but rather, one must learn to walk along with it. Even a dragon can enjoy having a new friend.

Just five more days—everything changes on April 30.

> Ticketty tock, it's time to walk.
> Some go swift. Some go slow.
> If it's Maine you seek, then go, go, go.

Making a friend of the mountain.

Just five days more.

Traveling Companions

Many have been asking if I'll be traveling alone. The answer is, "sort-of." Other thru-hikers are out there, and some are indeed hiking solo too. But that doesn't mean they or I want to hike by ourselves. As far as I'm concerned, absolutely not! Still others are in pairs—or couples—or threes and fours. Families are usually out each year as well.

Once thru-hikers start seeing the same faces each night around the shelters, we all start to understand each other's pace and temperament. Two singles of similar pace may form up and start meeting each night at the same destination—a partnership is formed. Others will come upon the new twosome and join if all the vibes are good. Eventually, "tribes" will emerge. This organic process will ebb and flow as individuals take "zero days"—that is a day with zero mileage hiked on the trail. Generally, zeros are taken in a town. If the others continue up the trail, the partnership loosens. However, as the others take their zero, the tribe is reunited.

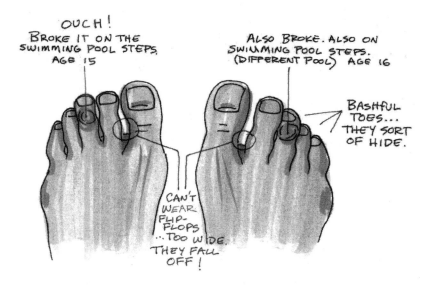

Now some traveling companions are more important than others. Case in point, my ten buddies in the picture will be with me every step of the way, hopefully. When I walk they'll walk—duh! When I sit, they'll . . . well, throb, I suppose. And when I eat, they'll most likely still throb.

They've got some mileage on them and some of life's texture too. They were with me when we outran the neighborhood bully in football at age ten—which made me famous with all the kids on Crest Cove Circle. Unfortunately, it made me less popular with the bully. They walked me up to the podium at all three of my graduation ceremonies. No, I don't have a PhD. My first ceremony was actually a cap-and-gown graduation from first grade. I swear it was the only picture my late grandmother had up on her wall of me! And they accompanied me across the hardwood stage in front of three thousand people at Lincoln Center in New York City when I won my first TV Clio Award for the best food commercial. Yep, these dogs are my good friends, and they'll help us meet many more new friends as we move north. We may even meet "One Leg Wonder"; he has one ordinary leg and one very special computer bionic one. So that'll be cool.

As you can probably understand, my companions are not very fond of swimming pools. Why just a hint of that evil chlorine aroma and they cramp up. Anyway, they're looking forward to crossing thirteen state lines, but it wasn't without some negotiations. They've promised to not yell or scream too terribly much if I promise to rub them each night with Bag Balm and treat them to a new fluffy pair of hiker socks each month. All quite reasonable I thought. I didn't dare tell them that some of their nails might fall off—who knows what they might do.

Three days more and then I walk the talk.

MY STARBUCKS

My Starbucks coffeehouse has been the source of much entertainment. It seems I can't stop laughing at the fact so few people walk anymore. Many of my neighbors here—on this my last day in south Miami, Florida—will tolerate terribly long lines which move slower than a one-legged turtle with a leg cramp just to avoid getting out of their cars and walking. My Starbucks has a drive-thru.

Even if it means getting the hot mocha-nocha-pocha with soy and whipped cream ten minutes sooner! Do I think these people are lazy and crazy? Yes, I do. I get the impression that some would choose root canal over having to park and walk. Heaven forbid ever considering leaving the "park" part out of that statement and simply walk somewhere. Anywhere. Why, others might stare, or worse, run you over. I'm sure this makes me sound greater than thou, which is wrong of me, but it is definitely odd seeing so many opposed to walking as I'm about to embark on a two-thousand-mile journey on foot. I would have to submit that some of America's many obesity issues are woven into this mind-set.

For me to have this point of view shows another one of the subtle beauties of the Appalachian Trail. The reintroduction to walking and an attitude that empowers me to move unmechanized is way healthy. I can only imagine that every walk to a mall or a store from the farthest parking space out will add up and up and up; and someday when I'm eighty, I'll still be fit, vital, and looking at women.

But the benefits don't stop there. One can see much more when one is on foot. Many of us look, but few see. Being a painter, I witnessed this increase in visual comprehension firsthand. And with the longer time frame of foot travel, patience is also heightened in all the other daily activities—which I've already spoken of.

I think a drive-thru is a great idea, especially when it's raining. But it's sunny most of the time here in Florida.

Hey, can someone pass me the cinnamon? I don't want to get up.

Finally, I'm off to see the wilderness.

Location:	The Approach Trail
Today's Miles:	11.3
Total Miles:	2.5 *(Actual AT miles)*
Date:	Friday, April 30, 2004

And so it begins.

The Approach Trail is as much tradition as it is a way to get to the start of the Appalachian Trail or AT. It is the beginning of the misery and comedy that can be your hike. Said to be one of the toughest sections along the 2,174.1 mile length of the AT, it has turned many a dreamer into a defeated, demoralized backpacker. People who've planned for years to thru-hike the AT—that is to say hike it from end to end in a single season—have had their optimistic bubble burst in those tortuous first 8.8 miles that don't even count.

The Approach Trail is not the steepest ascent we face on our quest; it is only the first. As the thru-hiker wannabes arrive at the visitors' center to sign in and confirm their intentions with a quip or hiking mantra in the register, the butterflies flock to the stomach. It is an inner battle of anxiety and excitement, fear and fun. We offer our fully loaded packs to the official scale there to face the truth. As the needle pivots, the pupils widen! Many will flashback to the countless decisions made about gear. If the scale has failed to get our attention, the Approach Trail surely will. For it starts as we exit the door. For the rest of the day, it is up, up, up, up, up, up, up—you get the idea.

Despite training in gyms or taking various practice hikes, most face this climb with naiveté, ill-fitting boots, and muscle fiber not yet accustomed to ups. It's very common for we adventurers to have loads of journey enjoying gear. Can you blame us? After all, a thru-hike will take about six months. So naturally we'll need to take along a half year's worth of stuff, right? But since we cannot possibly pull a U-Haul, a backpack will have to suffice. Unfortunately, most have no idea of how important those gear choices are before they start. No matter how many times I heard it two years ago, it just seemed too fanatical to count ounces. Really now, what's the big deal about something that weighs a measly eight ounces more than something else? And that's how the folly begins. But oh, how we learn. One achin' step at a time.

Another tradition exists for those who live near Amicalola Falls State Park, the home of the Approach Trail and Springer Mountain, the southern end of the Appalachian Trail. This one doesn't involve carrying stuff but rather picking it up. It seems the locals know that when the core group of dreamers start showing up in March, one can find all kinds of free goodies that have been tossed in hopes of lightening their horrific burden. Things like a gallon of Coleman fuel; that saves ten pounds. Maybe a nice camp chair or a tent big enough to sleep a small village. And my favorite that I've heard about—a Dutch oven. A Dutch oven is one of those fifteen to twenty pound cast-iron pots the cowboy chuck wagon driver would cook in. Not only are they terribly heavy, they're as big as a kitchen sink. Crazy, just crazy.

So like the swallows return to Capistrano, the locals arrive each season to partake in the cornucopia of free trail goodies. Remarkably, there's not a single piece of brand spanking new gear, regardless of its price, that isn't beyond being chucked if it means a lighter backpack. For me though, having already been there, done that, I make it up with my "lightish" load and get my photo taken by a day hiker at the beginning plaque and the AT's first "white blaze." It will be these 2 x 6-inch white rectangles that will guide us for the next six months, some 57,000 has been the estimate.

In honor of another tradition, I reach down and pick up a small rock to carry on my journey. I'll place it on the northern terminus cairn atop Mt. Katahdin in Maine.

So I'm off to see the wilderness, the wonderful wilderness of awes.

A simple copper plaque atop a rainy Springer Mountain proclaims,
The Appalachian Trail—For Those Who Seek a Fellowship with Nature

Location:	Gooch Gap Shelter
Today's Miles:	13.2
Total Miles:	14.7
Date:	May 1, 2004

Day 2 and the sun has finally made an appearance—thank goodness. If only it wasn't at sundown. It seems the trail is testing our resolve—others and me. It has been nothing but cold rain, cold fog, cold wind, and no views.

Georgia is waking up from winter, the hills are covered in chartreuse ferns, and the trees are in midleaf. The rocks, however, are omnipresent on these rugged mountains. Here with me on this trek to Maine is "Belle." We met yesterday at the Stover Creek Shelter, only then her name was Ann. As we headed out today, I kept hearing the *ding-a-ling* of a Christmas bell. It seems Ann's mother gave her the little noisemaker to scare the bears away—they hear you coming and hopefully run away. So yours truly suggested the trail name of "Belle." I said she was the beauty, and the trail is the beast. (Yea, I'm a flirt.) She accepted her new trail name that was inspired by her mother's gift.

The origins of the AT trail name is foggy like the weather, but it's been in practice for many decades now. You can name yourself or wait to see if circumstances present you with one. Many times it will be the other hikers that will bestow you with your new identity—not always a good thing. But most take it in good stride. In the case of my name "Postcard," it was revealed to me before beginning when I had decided to draw aspects of the adventure and write about its full texture other than just what mountain I had to climb. Then these pictures and words would be posted at my Web site, thus, sending "postcards" from the Appalachian Trail.

There's been a nice community of section hikers—someone who is hiking a piece of the AT—out here too. The company and conversation has been awesome.

A word about the Approach Trail yesterday, although demanding and having an infamous reputation, I didn't find it to be the monster I was dreading. In fact, today's 13.2 miles was much more a beast than the Approach. However, I did find sweaters and tarps and electronic devices and even a cast-iron frying pan! Good grief!

Thunder boomers have been forecasted for tonight, but as of 8:40 p.m.—maybe not. The real threat I suppose is all the bear activity that's been around. Apparently, last week at this shelter, a hiker had hung his hiking boots on the bear cables near the shelters, which we use to hang our food on. Why he hung his boots I can't imagine. Maybe he read how up north if you leave your boots out at night in an easy-to-get-to spot, the porcupines would eat on them because of all the salt that's accumulated from your sweat. Anyway, sure enough that night a black bear started swatting at the cables to bounce the food bags off, only they didn't, but the boots did. And that was all she wrote as they say. The hiker may have lost his boots, but he gained a trail name— "Bootless." He then had to backpack fifteen miles in flip-flops to the first area of services where he decided that was enough and came off the trail.

Yep, there's a lot of texture on the AT. Tomorrow may be a bigger day to grab a shower. I'll see how I feel, there's no reason to rush so early in this long journey. So I'll say good night from the Appalachian Trail, hikers' midnight has come, and my mummy is calling!

(It's not called *quitting* out here, but rather *coming off the trail* since one can continue their hike at any point in their life to earn the official 2,000-Miler Patch. That's what many section hikers are working toward.)

Location:	Walasi-Yi Center, Neels Gap
Today's Miles:	16.0
Total Miles:	30.7
Date:	May 2, 2004

Well, the weather forecast did not lie. The winds picked up at about 10 p.m. which was nice, then at 12:40 a.m. the first crack of lightning sounded its arrival. But we were all tucked in snug at a great shelter called Gooch Gap. At one point during the hardest rain, I sat up to look out toward the inky night. That's when a big bolt of one-hundred-thousand-degree light hit, giving me that wonderful afterimage of all the trees.

And in true form, by morning it was still raining then pouring then raining then misting then cats-and-dogs deluge. At one point as I climbed Big Cedar Mountain, it was raining so hard that cats and dogs were joined by monkeys, buffalo, and giraffe. Naturally when it rains that hard, your shoes and socks yell uncle. The crazy thing is despite the gully washer, when you come upon another hiker, you stop and chat!

At the start of the day, I was planning to only hike ten miles to the next shelter. But since I was feeling strong, I decided to take on Blood Mountain—the highest mountain on the AT in Georgia—and try to make it here to hikers' paradise. It's called Mountain Crossings at the Walasi-Yi Center, and it has everything a thru-hiker can dream of having. I'm bunking tonight here in the hostel and joined in the group that headed into town for AYCE (all you can eat) dinner. Gee, all I had visions for was a sandwich, but tonight I had turkey and stuffing and fried chicken and a strawberry sundae for dessert. Yep, an unplanned culinary extravagance.

The added benefit of pushing on today—aside from dinner, a shower, and laundry—was I'm a day ahead of my plan; and I finally saw a wonderful view coming over the far side of Blood Mountain. It was my first view in three days of rain, fog, and clouds. With all my necessary resupply packing from my first mail drop done, I'll be ready to head out early in the morning to yet another forecast of—wait for it—*rain*!!!

(A mail drop is a box of provisions that's mailed to yourself in care of general delivery to a post office or an establishment that accepts them along the trail. They usually have most everything one needs to get to the next mail drop. When I was planning my journey, I "guesstimated" that I'd need twenty-seven mail drops to get me to Maine. So before the start, all the boxes were loaded with dehydrated camping dinners, energy bars, batteries, vitamins, etc., and mailing labels attached and dumped into the hands of my support staff—my parents. God bless them. Then based on that guesstimated plan, they're mailed up the trail so they're there before I am. It's a behemoth of a planning project. And then some hikers plan nothing and just hitch into towns to resupply when they run out of food. I'd have to have a lobotomy before I could go so carefree. *Hike your own hike* is the mantra of the Appalachian Trail; it helps everyone to deal with everyone's differences.)

Day 3 and finally a view! Of course it lasted only ten minutes before it started raining again.

Location:	Low Gap Shelter
Today's Miles:	10.6
Total Miles:	41.3
Date:	May 3, 2004

No rain today. That deserves repeating. *No rain!*

I headed out of Neels Gap at nine this morning, it was thirty-six degrees. *Brrr.* The colder temperatures seem to really be cutting through me which was puzzling until I remembered that only a handful of days ago, I was in eighty-degree Miami.

I've yet to have a good night's rest. Sleep deprivation had definitely put a shadow over me. I was yawning so frequently in the first two hours that once I reached the spectacular rock vista on Cowrock Mountain, I plopped down, leaned against my pack, and took a thirty-minute nap in the sunshine. Now I have to admit that a problem or maybe I should refer to it as an oddity is developing. I seem to be talking out loud to myself. Yea, crazy—I know it—and with so much life left. Well, I suppose one never knows when one loses their mind. What? Who said that? Me! You? Who are you? (It's going to be a bit crowded in this mummy bag tonight. I think I'll get in first and hope the other "me" goes away. Wish me luck.)

Location: Tray Mountain Shelter
Today's Miles: 14.9
Total Miles: 56.2
Date: May 4, 2004

Here at Tray Mountain Shelter for the night. Since it was a long day with some really difficult miles, there was plenty of time to think about that bear that took the hiker's boots last week.

HIKER SHOE

BLACK BEAR PAW
(From VISUAL memory)

FIGURE A

How exactly do you think it's going to wear them? Figure A clearly suggests that it would be anatomically impossible. I don't believe there's a shoehorn made that could assist the furry individual. Of course, there's always the possibility that the bear could do some customizing, say tear the boot apart and lay the sides over and hope—oh hope—the laces will still reach. I suppose the bear would need to cross its paws on that—if bears think of the concept of luck.

Maybe it's considering wearing them over its ears. But I'm sure the other bears would make ridiculing remarks. Not let it join in any of their black bear games. Gee, almost makes you feel sorry for it. It's all quite puzzling. The best reason I could come up with was the most obvious one. The reason the bear took the shoes is because it was most likely a sow. A she-bear. After all, everyone knows how much females love shoes.

Well, another wilderness riddle solved. Tomorrow I'll try to solve that whole bumble bee—impossible to fly thingy. And of course, it's on to the next mountain!

Location:	Muskrat Creek Shelter
Today's Miles:	11.6
Total Miles:	78.4
Date:	May 6, 2004

I made an unscheduled detour into the town of Hiawassee and the hiker-friendly Hiawassee Inn; it turned out to be just what this hiker needed! Yesterday, the fifth of May, my day 6, had me feeling low. Why or how the loneliness throws this fog over you out here I cannot figure out, but it seems to happen frequently to me around the fifth or sixth day. It's happened to me more than once. So yesterday just when I was hitting bottom emotionally, I ran into Derek and Yaicha with their Border collie named Willow. Our connection was instant and our chemistry effortless. They were out of food and heading into town for supplies. As soon as they said Hiawassee, I was in! When we got to the road, I pulled out my handmade "Hiker to Town" bandana and attached the Velcro corners to the Velcro pads I placed on my hiking poles. Stretched out like a minibillboard, this was its maiden usage. Well, in no more than a minute a load of cars came along and much to my amazement, they drove by! Hmm, maybe the sun was in their eyes. It wasn't but another minute and the van that had driven by turned around to come back and pick us all up. He said he saw my sign and couldn't resist. Score!

Ron and Sam are the proprietors of the Hiawassee Inn and are really turning up the hospitality—a definite recommendation from us three.

We all hit the Dairy Queen next door first—a banana split for them and a double bacon cheeseburger for me. Then we took showers, did laundry, and went grocery shopping before dinner. Naturally we ran all our errands on foot, it was the first town stop of what will be many over the next many months.

With a later-than-normal start today and then countless ups, we made it here to this high mountain shelter by six. The altimeter on my watch says we're at 4,600 feet above sea level. But what's more important than that is to say, "Hello from North Carolina." Georgia is behind me, but the state line crossing wasn't what any of us had expected. What happened is as follows.

As the afternoon temperatures rose, so did the anticipation of crossing that very first state line. It was at the foot of Bly Gap that we spotted a wooden plank mounted to a tree. Crossing the first state line is a milestone by anyone's measure and should be reason for a joyful bounce in one's step. However, when we looked upon the plank and the simple engraved initials NC/GA we were disappointed in what we saw. Scrawled in black ink was the signature of a hiker a few days ahead of us. The defacement was the sophomoric pronouncement that "so and so was here." Didn't one stop doing that at age twelve? We couldn't believe another thru-hiker would show so little respect to the trail and for the rest of us who would prefer to not have this moment tarnished. To say nothing of the disrespect it shows to all the volunteers over all the years who built and made this miracle trail possible. Nor does it show any respect to the mantra of the outdoors: leave no trace. But I'm sure the hiker who scrawled the vitally important message that they "were here," evidently felt respecting the trail and all those involved with it were secondary. I am of the opinion that a thru-hiker can be an ambassador of the trail. A shepherd if you will, who can set a positive example to all those we meet on our way to Maine. Do any of us enjoy going out into the beauty of nature and seeing the graffiti associated with urban decay sprayed on a rock? I suppose I associate those defacements with "towners," youthful individuals living large and making their mark. A thru-hiker, however, as an ambassador of the Appalachian Trail should live large, have fun, hike with joy, but they should also hold themselves to a higher standard; and its been my experience that nearly all do. I only hope that not-so-old dogs can learn new tricks.

We all talked about crossing the state line and put our disappointment in others behind us and started the arduous climb up Bly Gap.

The Hiawassee Inn.
Hikers, put your thumb out and treat yourself to some southern hospitality.

Location:	Carter Gap Shelter
Today's Miles:	12.5
Total Miles:	90.9
Date:	May 7, 2004

My two new friends have gotten their trail names today. Yaicha and Derek have become Dharma and Greg. Seems for some time they've referred to themselves to others as Dharma and Greg from TV fame in explaining their families and contrasts. Of course, I didn't know this, but today at lunch on Standing Indian Mountain, I suggested the new trail names since I was picking up on the similarities to the TV show. It stuck!

Everyone has turned in, and I've been listening to the distant calls of coyotes by the campfire. Joining the coyotes in this wilderness experience are white-tailed deer, Eastern screech owls, barred owls, and one hauling-ass whitetail bunny rabbit I scared a day ago. The sky is an inky black canvas, and the stars are bright. The big dipper is high overhead, and a slight mountain breeze is freshening the chill.

Our hike today was much easier than yesterday's, which we were all thankful for!

I've been doing a lot of thinking about confidence, overconfidence, and arrogance as they pertain to the AT. Often I meet another hiker and they'll ask, "Where you headed?" Most times early on I'd say, "Maine, I'm thru-hiking." The question is, does saying that imply an arrogance or lack of respect to the enormity of this endeavor? Does saying I'm hiking to Maine trivialize this colossal physical and emotional challenge? In some ways I think it most certainly does, while in other ways it acts as a positive commitment to completing the journey. Confidence would most likely have me saying, "The plan is to hike to Maine"; and overconfidence would push me to, "I'm thru-hiking." Each is valid, but now that I'm once again truly in touch with the bigness of the land and it's demands, I'm taking the confident approach.

Additionally, an amazing change is starting to take place within me. No longer is Mt. Katahdin important to me or its distance to get there, but rather the idea of hiking for many months in the wilderness. Yes, I'll be moving north, but this new mind-set is helping me to stay in the moment as well as helping me to "let go." It's this letting go that I sense to be the most important change that will indeed get me to Katahdin. Somehow, it releases me from the go, go, go city mentality that casts doubt and makes us vulnerable by giving us the false feeling we're in control. Control is something which most seek and we would like to believe we have out here. But you can't control a mountain's elevation or the power of the weather. You can only walk with each and try to enjoy the journey.

With everyone already asleep inside Carter Gap Shelter,
it's just the coyotes and me howling at the moon.

53

Location:	Winding Stair Gap
Today's Miles:	15.9
Total Miles:	106.8
Date:	May 8, 2004

I hiked solo today since Dharma and Greg were moving kinda slow at the junction. The older you get, the easier it seems to be to get going early. That and the fact I can hear John Wayne as a cowboy in those cattle drive movies bellowing out at the top of his lungs, "We're burning daylight."

I climbed Albert Mountain and got my picture taken. A task infinitely easier said than done since Albert Mountain starts moderately difficult and then gets worse. The brutal climb finally emerges out of a snarling mass of mountain laurel delivering me to the summit with a lone, abandoned fire tower. I collapsed on the rock cliff and enjoyed the victory. I could see for a hundred miles and that's when I heard it. It was soft and melodic; it seemed to move on the breeze—a Native American flute. It was beautiful and tranquil in its tune. Whoever played it must be somewhere hidden. The moment grew all the more special with that haunting melody. But that's when I started to second-guess myself as to its origins. Maybe it was the breeze through the fire tower structure or maybe the mountain laurel branches. I can't be certain other than it was real and there. I wondered if Indian spirits from times gone by were offering me a gift in celebration of my summit. My very own haunted serenade. Wow, it was worth the climb.

I pushed on to the next shelter and that's when I met the angel of the AT. She walked around a corner of the shelter and I said, "Hi, I'm Postcard" and she just started laughing. She is Barbara and mentioned that she was waiting for her son who was doing a section—a big twenty-three-mile section! I mentioned that I was thinking of either going into Franklin or on to the next shelter. "I have a car," Barbara replied. *Well, a gift from heaven.* While we waited for her son and husband, she brought out apples, sandwiches, and homemade superdelicious trail magic chocolate chip cookies! Naturally, I had to eat some—it would be impolite not to. I then met Dave, Barbara's husband, and we all chatted and waited for Steve their son to show. When I realized that Franklin had an outfitter, the prospect of getting a new backpack emerged.

(Sidebar: Both of my shoulder straps on my backpack broke away from the pack two days ago. I "McGyvered" a rig that was holding up, but it forced me to use my hip belt as a stomach belt. Not terribly comfortable, but the rig worked; and I got out of the woods, so to speak.)

So we all headed to town with the arrival of Steve with them insisting on swinging by the outfitters before they closed. While en route, Steve was shocked and yet puzzled at his mom picking up a complete stranger—me. We then went to their motel where I got a room and a shower. Yeehaw! That's two in under a week! They of course asked this homeless hiker to dinner where the conversation was wonderful. Upon returning from dinner, Barbara forced more of her awesome cookies into my hands. I couldn't stop her, really. I tried, sort of! Moving around all that cookie dough has given her some mighty stout arms.

This morning we all went to breakfast before heading back out to the trailhead.

Their names are Barbara and Dave Fishback, and they are humanity at it's finest!! Thank you, both, as well as to their son, Steve. You filled my heart with joy, and it carried me the sixteen miles to Cold Springs Shelter and beyond!

BARBARA FISHBACK's "TRAILMAGIC" COOKIES

Coyote

I never actually put an eye on one, but like many of the birds I heard, the ones with the best sound rarely were seen. It was back near the Georgia State Line that a nice pack sure added to the wilderness experience, howling their moonlight sonata during that first week. Normally they hunt at night, which is when their prey is out to feed as well. You'd think that howling would scare everything away though. Maybe it's a victory cheer.

Barred Owl

A large puff-headed woodland owl. The hooting is emphatic, may sound like a barking dog. Usually eight hoots in two groupings: hoohoo-hoohoo, hoohoo-hoohooaw. The aw at the close is its signature. A few live near Cold Spring Shelter in North Carolina. They gave us quite a symphony one night at 2 a.m.

Location:	Cold Springs Shelter
Today's Miles:	15.8
Total Miles:	122.6
Date:	May 9, 2004

Despite the many ups today, my continuous motion with few, if any, breaks had me the first to arrive at this older, tiny shelter. Others would straggle in before dark, and everyone had the same thing on their minds. Tomorrow would be twelve miles, mostly all downhill, to the Nantahala Outdoor Center and their mighty restaurant. How the heck am I going to get to sleep with visions of cheeseburgers dancing in my head? Three Tylenol PMs of course.

Trying to get the wet hiker clothes to dry on the antimouse food bag hangers.

The contraptions hanging from the shelter keep the mice from having their way with your food. By tying knots in the middle of a rope, an empty tuna can sits suspended, but very wobbly. A twig is knotted around the end, which allows us to loop our food bag cords over it. As the mice come out to explore after sundown, they crawl down the rope and upon stepping on to the tuna can—which teeters beneath them, they fall to the floor (and onto you and your sleeping bag.) Hey, at least the food's safe.

Location:	Nantahala Outdoor Center
Today's Miles:	11.5
Total Miles:	134.1
Date:	May 11, 2004

Saigon. Still in Saigon. Oh, wait, that was Martin Sheen. Nantahala. Still in Nantahala. Arrived yesterday late morning and decided to get a room and kick back with a "zero day." That's a day with no miles accrued on the AT. It's been eleven straight hiking days and even though I'm blister and pain free, I thought it would be nice to give the body the extra rest before I push them over the Great Smoky Mountains some two days away. Known as the NOC, the Nantahala Outdoor Center is a white-water Mecca. The AT crosses right through the complex over their bridge. They also cater to thru-hikers with lots of services and large portion meals.

Tomorrow when I leave, we all face an uphill climb of eight miles and 3,500 feet of ascent. The last time I did a hike like that was climbing out of the south rim of the Grand Canyon. I couldn't walk the next day. I had no idea we had that many muscles in our ass to make sore!

But I'm much more fit, and the big leg muscles are powering up these climbs. In some cases, I climbed some of these same mountains I did last year, a whole hour faster. Things that pounded me other times are but a bump now. I don't want to sound cocky, but all the gym training is paying dividends.

Some of the earlier hiker faces I met have reappeared with this zero. Belle showed up, hadn't seen her since day 3; unfortunately, she lost her bell. No *ding-ding* as she walks now. I don't know where Dharma and Greg and Willow are. And with my pace, I've met many new faces and ate a few meals with them yesterday.

About five days ago my backpack self-destructed under the weight and terrain, seems the shoulder harness straps completely tore loose from the main pack. I had to do some fancy "McGyvering" with some Velcro straps I had, and it got me here. So I bought a new, hopefully tougher backpack for all that awaits me and this adventure.

My outlook is really positive. I'm here to have fun and see the trail and all that surrounds it. If I have fun tomorrow I'll see another day and so on. Everything is getting easy. Walking, laundry, unpacking, packing—it's all falling into a rhythm of simplicity. I'm guessing I've dropped ten pounds while building up a lot more leg strength too. The journey is becoming the activity. Everything that was different and new is becoming the familiar. As a result, I'm settling into a new way of life. Just going and hearing and seeing, it's very interesting and profound. However, this bed is still awfully nice and realizing that every night doesn't have to be spent in the woods seems to agree with me. If the town presents itself, great, but no bother if not. All is good, and I hope you all are finding this adventure fun to read. I picked up the book *The Tao of Pooh* yesterday which was fun to read. I'll most likely read it again on the trail. Nothing like Winnie the Pooh philosophy to help you capture purity. Enjoy your day, everyone, that's what it's for!

The AT crosses the bridge here at the Nantahala Outdoor Center. One can get food, a shower, food, laundry, food, and a bed. My first zero day.

Location: Brown Fork Gap Shelter
Today's Miles: 16.0
Total Miles: 150.1
Date: May 12, 2004

We hikers have rituals out here. There's the unpacking-every-night-and-the-packing-every-morning ritual. There's the hanging of the wet shirt or other clothes to dry at the end of the day and slipping into the dry stuff at camp.

For me, there's the unlacing of the boots and sock strip-off at the end of the day; that's then followed by me smearing the old dogs with Bag Balm to soften and sooth, and then it's on with the camp shoes. Camp shoes are lightweight sandal-like slip-ons that are highly breathable—the feet need some airing out after sixteen miles.

But I'm forming a plan that involves two new rituals that may catch on, particularly the one involving sandwiches. From now on when I'm in town or have access to a restaurant, I'm ordering a sandwich-to-go with my order. I pack it out on the first day and have it for lunch. Or in some cases, as Pippin and Mary from *Lord of the Rings* would say, have half for second breakfast and possibly the other half for the second lunch or first dinner. Either way, it's a nice and easy way to stretch "normal" food from town to the trail. Others are picking up on my doing this and are starting to think of doing it themselves. Hikers cook a lot of Ramen noodles out here because they weigh so little, less to carry. The drawback is that's what you eat, which is completely underwhelming to my taste buds.

The other new ritual—when in town with a motel room—is to clean the equipment that spends its entire day in the dirt. The hiking pole tips! I mean heck, I'm cleaning the clothes. I'm cleaning myself. And by simply taking the poles and standing them in the "john," there's no fuss, no muss, and in no time all is clean and shiny. It's the least I can do for the equipment that has twice already prevented me from crashing down onto the trail. As the old adage says, "take care of your gear, and it will take care of you."

Frankly, I think they rather like it. It's sort of their own private pool.

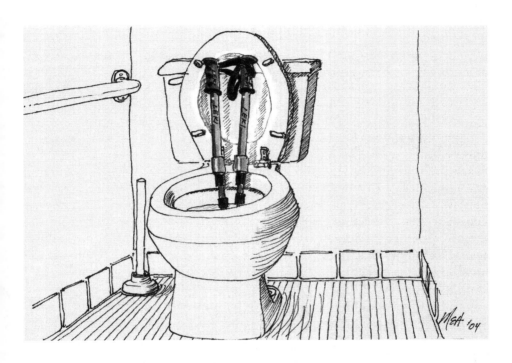

Just soak and flush. The thru-hiker way to shiny hiker pole tips.

Location:	Spence Field Shelter
Today's Miles:	17.8
Total Miles:	179.5
Date:	May 14, 2004

My first day in the Smokys, and I was greeted by many individuals much shorter than I. First, there are the countless centipedes of various colors. Every morning since starting on the Approach Trail I've eyed them. They're mostly black with yellow dashes and legs. I've seen them with yellow-and-black horizontal stripes with yellow legs too, which number about fifty I guess. The most beautiful centipedes I've seen have alternating white and black stripes with hot pink legs. Very graphic! I've only seen them three times where the yellow ones I've seen in the hundreds.

Now the newest critters I've spotted are the dull burgundy millipedes. They're about six to seven inches long with about a gazillion legs. They're so cool! I find them fascinating, especially their dull chalklike finish.

The Smokys are unique for having many little creatures that can only be found here. The snails are even unique—their shells are not vertically oriented, but rather angled on a diagonal. Much more interesting to my eye, and they're quite long. I spent most of the day doing the creepy crawler two-step to avoid hurting any of them. It seems that I'm visiting their home and, I should do my best to tread lightly. But inevitably, one step might miss—or should I say mooshhh! Oops.

With their incredible lack of speed, I couldn't help imagining one of the slimy sloths might react to my passing as an old codger yelling, "Slow down, you're moving like a bat out of hell. Damn hikers."

The Smokys' AT section rises pretty steep out of the dam area and then evolves into mild inclines—just perfect for me to climb without a great deal of effort. They're smooth and flat, mostly, and feel much better than the many miles of trail behind me. I believe it was yesterday in preparation for entering this part that I became aware of the oddest thing. The Smokys is spelled without the letter *e*! At first I thought, *Oops, misspelling on the maps—but sure enough, no* e.

Anyway, it was a lot of miles today, and a cold front has moved in with a roaring wind. The result is the mummy will be fully zipped tonight. Say good night, Postcard. OK, good night from the Great Smoky Mountains National Park.

The Creepy Crawler Two-Step.

*Since entering the Smokys, I've spent a lot of time looking down
so as to not smoosh my new trail buddies.*

Black-Throated Blue Warbler

An active bird, usually smaller than a sparrow with a thin needle beak. It has a beautiful and unusual song, almost electronic sounding with an echo. Days before a day hiker enlightened me, several of us kept hearing what sounded like someone's cellular phone ringing from inside a cave. Later upon hearing it, one of us would yell out, "Answer the phone!"

Lady Slipper

A rare, showy flower. Orchid like. The pink is in the majority when I saw them at all, but I did see two yellow ones side by side—an even rarer sighting from what I've been told. It's also been mentioned that each flower is worth a tidy sum. Only I believe they're protected, so don't even think of picking them. Capture them on film and let the next hiker see their splendor as well.

Location:	Silers Bald Shelter
Today's Miles:	11.8
Total Miles:	191.3
Date:	May 15, 2004

Ain't it always the case? You say something nice about the gentleness of the trail in the Smokys and *baam!* The next day turns nasty, steep, narrow, angled, pitched, contoured, rutted, lumpy, rocky, and altogether unpleasant for anything resembling a human foot. Then add the fog, drizzle, and 30 mph winds, and you have the perfect recipe for a turned ankle. But no whining. Three Extra Strength Excedrin and some lunch and I became a transformed hiker.

This morning in camp a buck strolled in and at lunch, in a different spot, three does wandered around. They almost seemed tame, although I wasn't going to try petting them. I've seen those TV commercials selling those *When Animals Go Mad* videos. Later on I almost planted my hiking stick on a woodchuck, or at least I think it was a woodchuck. It's possible it could have been a groundhog or a marmot, but then I wouldn't have been able to recite that famous tong-twister. As you can imagine I started vocalizing, "How much wood would a woodchuck chuck, if a woodchuck could chuck wood?"

A red squirrel was also part of the fauna today as well as a beautiful butterfly. It had black edges with an unusual sea-foam green color with red spots at the rear—saw two of them—the butterfly I mean. Although a sea-foam green squirrel would be a heck of a sighting—any things possible out here.

At one point when I was pushing hard up a hill, my legs were pumping and my mouth was open pulling in deep breaths, I inadvertently *hoovered* in an annoying gnat. The sucker hit the back of my gullet with such force, I'm sure it thought it was hitting the singularity of a black hole. One swallow later, I had some extra protein, and I'm almost sure my pace picked up a bit! All in all, another great day here on the trail.

Location:	Ice Water Springs Shelter
Today's Miles:	15.5
Total Miles:	206.8
Date:	May 16, 2004

Today was spectacular and full of texture. Wind, fog, and sun led the day, and then followed by rain, sleet, and sun again! The trail went over the highest mountain on the entire AT—Clingman's Dome. It stands right at the halfway point in the Smokys at 6,648 feet. As high as it is, the climb really isn't a difficult one due to the fact that since entering the park, we've been climbing. It seems the Smokys' mountain peaks all rise out of a very high ridgeline. So the ascents aren't very formidable. The climb led me into alpine terrain where the dominant impression was the sweet-smelling aroma of wet spruce. Oh, how I love that evergreen scent. Joining them were short needle pines and possibly some balsam fir. But the fog lay heavy on the mountain, and no views could be found until the other side of the mountain. As the sun came out and the spruce edged in tighter, I thought many times of the forests that Frodo and Sam traveled through.

At one point the spruce became so thick, I couldn't help thinking of a fairy-tale-enchanted forest with Christmas trees everywhere. It was quite magical!

The Appalachian Trail though turned into the Appalachian Trench. As much as a foot or more deep at points and no wider than a hiking boot. When the rain began, again, the Appalachian Trench transformed into the Appalachian River.

By early afternoon I reached the heavily traveled tourist area of Newfound Gap. Shamelessly I admit to wanting to try my hand at *yogi-ing*—that's a term used out here for getting free food from the car-driving visitors—you folks. No sooner did I have my pack off, when a young couple asked me if I was a thru-hiker and if there was anything I might want. Naturally, I said, "I'd love a sandwich!" Without missing a beat, the man turned, a particularly more difficult move since Holly was riding on his shoulders. Holly said she was his backpack today. Anyhow, Otter returned from the car with a huge black Angus roast beef sandwich with sautéed onions and honey mustard. *Wow*, I was stunned! Otter thru-hiked in 1995 and still likes to return the generosity he received.

Some of the other thru-hikers by now had joined me; and we, in someway, became a most interesting visual entertainment for the parking lot crowd. Carp, as in the fish, is another hiker out here who has a pace similar to mine. Well, Carp started eyeing my huge score of a sandwich. I could feel him trying not to stare, but was failing miserably. Before he put any more of that sad puppy in his eyes, I asked if he'd like a hunk. A bigger smile has never been seen on the Appalachian Trail. He later reciprocated with a cream-filled Little Debbie Oatmeal Cookie in gratitude that he yogied. Sweet! Wow, it was practically Thanksgiving in May! My hunger is starting to get just a little more aggressive. This is day 17, and I can feel the stomach is not fully happy about the menu of this adventure. Without a weight scale around, I can only guess that I've lost fifteen pounds already. The legs are becoming superstrong, but the stomach likes to remind us all, that unless its demands are met, we aren't going to be going anywhere!

It's a full house here tonight. Joining me on the shelter floor are Belle, Doosie, Pop Up, The Rev, and a whole bunch of hikers out for a weekend. Unfortunately for them, this is a wet weekend.

Tomorrow may be a 20.3-mile day, followed by a short 8. Why? Well, at the bottom of that short 8 is the end of the Smoky Mountains and a place called Mountain Momma's—who serves *gigantic* cheeseburgers! Can you say, "Yea baby!? I'll take two please—one for breakfast naturally."

Good night all!

Location:	Cosby Knob Shelter
Today's Miles:	20.3
Total Miles:	227.1
Date:	May 17, 2004

Today I hiked the Appalachian River. But before I go into that and rock hopping over the Appalachian rapids, I want to discuss my disappointment with some of our feathered friends.

Knowing it was to be a long day, I headed out early just behind Belle. I caught her about twenty minutes out, and we talked and hiked together for some time. I've been feeling amazingly strong, so after Belle took a breather, I pushed on and cranked it up a gear. I reached thirteen miles by lunch and had a snack at the Tri-Corner Knob Shelter. It was a glorious day with lots of sun and blue up above. But I had 7.3 more miles to go before camp, and I was unaware of the dark looming cloud formations just over the ridgeline.

As I climbed up to another summit, the rumble of thunder said, "Hello, hiker." Despite the gathering storm and disappearing sunlight, I continued up into the darkening mess. Why? Because all the birds were singing their happy birdsong—chirps and tweets and warbling and *who-whos*.

For some idiotic reason, I was under the impression that if the wrath of the heavens were going to unload, our feathered friends would be silent! Boy did I figure that one wrong. Crack went the lightning one thousand feet over my head. Down came the rain and sleet like water pouring from a bucket!! It was at this moment I knew I had been duped by those evil birds. I believe what they were doing was signaling each other to sing me right into harm's way. "Here comes another one of those humpback wingless knuckleheads."

Anyway, back to our hero who is up on a ridgeline in the middle of a thunderstorm. As I crested the summit and started down—where do you suppose all that rainwater went? Why, down the Appalachian Trench, of course—I started hiking down the shoulders of the trench or should I say river, moving from one side to the other as momentum and turns and bends required. At one point my stride was left then right then rock hop then left side and right side and so on. I'm glad there wasn't another hiker behind me; my spread-eagle style of striding could have been confused for a severe case of rash. But on I went and on it rained. By 4:30, my first twenty-mile day (20.3 to be exact) was behind me, and I was well poised for the short eight miles tomorrow morning which will take me out of the great foggy, rainy, windy Smoky Mountains National Park. I am thru-hiker, hear me roar!

The Cosby Knob Shelter sits in a small, dark hollow. Although still up at 4,700 feet, it's secluded I guess I mean. The night was void of moonshine and starlight; it was a dark one. Everyone had been asleep for hours when I awoke. It's common for me to get up and visit the woods at night; we do consume an awful lot of water out here. Only this stirring in me wasn't that. It was something else. Half awake, I felt the strongest urge to roll over and look out into the blackness in front of the shelter. There, low to the ground, I witnessed moving light—thin wisps of a luminous nature. They moved around for ten to twenty seconds and then, as if it *knew* I was watching, it vanished. It wasn't eerie so much as magical. Well, maybe it was a bit eerie in a ghostly way. I had heard of such phenomenon, a vague memory at best. There's a cluster of mushrooms here called Jack-o-lantern, which can emit a nightly glow from bioluminescence. Few organisms on Earth have this ability to generate light. But they have more a glow in the dark quality, not a moving wisp like a ground hugging aurora borealis. I'd also heard the phrase foxfire, but other than a flower of the same name, I don't know much about it. Whatever it was, it was something you'd expect to find in an enchanted forest.

A knife-edge trail walk. Spotted this beautiful dwarfed spruce—very bonsai.

Location:	Mountain Momma's
Today's Miles:	8.0
Total Miles:	235.1
Date:	May 18, 2004

Four days and three hours and I finished the Great Smoky Mountains. Not too bad for a middle-aged guy! Other than a bleeding big right toe, all is great and pain free. Mountain Momma's is true old south Americana. Aside from having hand-lettered signs up everywhere to answer every possible question you could ever think of asking, which they'd apparently prefer you wouldn't, the place has no shortage of cars lying around the lawn. The biggest profit maker here must be cigarettes, just boxes and boxes of them take over the entire end wall of the place. I figure that must be one of the more popular pastimes around these here parts.

I arrived at Mountain Momma's at 10:30 this morning and immediately attacked her famous *giant* cheeseburger. You should have seen it. I almost couldn't get it in my rather large mouth. It was nirvana. I've been told that calorie deficit should kick in around week three. Maybe then I'll start eating more, but for now, I have little desire for the food I'm carrying. It just isn't pleasing me. I followed up the burger with a BLT just two hours later and yet another burger two hours after that—so much for not having calorie deficit I guess. Well, I'll say good night from the porch here, good buddies. Ya'll take care now, ya hear!

Location: Groundhog Creek Shelter
Today's Miles: 9.6
Total Miles: 244.6
Date: May 19, 2004

Packed a burger for lunch today out of Mountain Momma's. Throughout the long, long climb, I wasn't focused on the constant ascent but rather the burger for lunch! I was the first one to the shelter; and as I ate, thunder started booming just over the ridge. It'll be another eight or nine miles to the next shelter so I tried to figure what to do. I sat there listening to the booms and gathering gray sky and basically gave myself a brain cramp. I finally decided that maybe a short day was best. So I unpacked and called it a half day.

The shelter only held six, but since we all knew each other, seven of us snuggled in. We got a campfire going, and laundry was hanging on twigs and branches all around the warm glow drying out the sweat. Tomorrow has a couple of big ascents, but it also has real town food just over the horizon. I just may make a big day of it.

Location:	Hot Springs, North Carolina
Today's Miles:	26.2
Total Miles:	270.9
Date:	May 20, 2004

Just arrived here in Hot Springs, North Carolina. This is day 21, three weeks finished, and 270.9 miles. If I average in the Approach Trail, it nets out to just less than fourteen miles per day, which is a strong average since it includes the early conditioning stages. Today was a milestone since I hiked longer and farther than any other time in my life. 26.2 miles over two whopper-size mountains. Max Patch was truly unique because it is a "bald." There's not a tree in sight, nothing but grass—quite unusual. As I climbed, the wind speeds continually increase until they were pushing 25 mph, and my head was in the clouds. Yet again the views were limited as they were through the Smokys.

Despite the big mileage day, I'm not sore and still blister free. The true boss of this adventure—my stomach—has been fed not once, but twice already. I wrangled the last bed here at Elmer's Sunnybank Inn—a nice Victorian with eccentric rooms here and there. My room is over the tool shed, which I enter and then climb a near vertical ladder through a trap door. Then it's through another bedroom to my attic room! It has a gabled roof with its own window, bed, and desk. I like it despite the bathroom being through the other bedroom, down the ladder, out the tool shed, across the porch, in and out of the kitchen till I reach the hallway and the bathroom, which several others share. Just part of the AT experience.

Tomorrow, it's laundry, eating, and conversation with familiar faces and meeting new ones. Also a visit to the outfitters for a new bite-valve water tube—mine is growing mold! Oh, and most importantly, body rest. It will be my second zero.

Hot Springs is a small valley hamlet sitting at the convergence of several mountains. If the building architecture were a tad more alpine, it would pass for a European destination.

With only the one real cold night back in Georgia, as well as the date being so close to June, I'll be mailing out my winter gear and swapping the sleeping bags. This should drop my gear weight by three pounds! There's a really good chance my pack weight with food and water will hover in the high twenties most of the time now. With that kind of reduction and my newfound leg strength, my boots will have wings!

One of the more joyful little pleasures about town stops is having a bed rather than the 5/8-inch thick, 3/4 length sleeping pad. But it's not the softness or the bounce that brings me smiles; I'm rather comfortable on the shelter floors with my pad. No, what brings me joy is the fact that I can roll over on my stomach and let my feet hang down over the end—ahh, simple bliss!! Do it in the shelter and your imagination will conjure up all sorts of monsters to grab you by the ankles and haul you away into the woods. Do it in the security of a closed room and its sweet, sweet dreams. Anyway, I'm having a blast and getting buff in the process!

Hanging ten on a town-stop bed. Elmer's Sunnybank Inn—an awesome thru-hiker stop.

The next day, I spent the majority of the time hanging out on Main Street. There's a terrific outfitters there with Internet access and the Paddlers' Pub just across the street. It was a sunny, warm day; I definitely think sending home the winter stuff will be OK. That night at the pub, I found Carp holding down the bar stool closest to the draft pull. We bought each other a celebratory brew on our terrific progress. I met and introduced myself to so many new faces there, at one point Carp started laughing. "What?" I said. He asked, "Are you running for office?"

This is just too much fun.

Location:	Hot Springs, North Carolina
Today's Miles:	0
Total Miles:	270.9
Date:	May 21, 2004

An unusual phenomenon is starting to emerge. It seems that as my mass continues to reduce—now nineteen pounds lighter than just three weeks ago—but without any reduction in my height, my body density is increasing. Anyone familiar with just a smidge of science knows that with this scenario, the result is a stronger gravitational force. Not unlike the physics of a supermassive black hole where the gravity is so immense, light cannot even escape its clutches.

What I've been noticing in the past few days is that flying insects have been going into orbits around my waist and head. As I walk they are making hula-hoop orbits that can continue for a minute or more. Try as they might to reach escape velocity, many fail and go crashing into the fabric of my clothes or worse, my face. This has happened with bumblebees, horse flies, and even tiny gnats. Once they stray too close to my ever-increasing gravitational force, they unfortunately face a dizzying fate.

But a lucky few do escape. Gee, I wonder if my new hiker aroma is luring them into these flying orbits. Nah!

Location: Little Laurel Shelter
Today's Miles: 19.6
Total Miles: 290.5
Date: May 22, 2004

For the last hour I've been holed up here in the shelter near the top of a mountain. Outside are lightning, thunder, hail, and driving rain. *Flash. Crack.* Oh, excuse me, I just jumped off of my sleeping pad. The lightning is hitting all around us here—it's almost as if we're up inside the thunderhead. *Flash. Crack.* Yikes, so much for counting the seconds in between the flash and the crack. Up here they're happening simultaneously.

I got here at 4:30 and ate by a campfire even though it wasn't dark yet. Off toward the horizon were the distant rumblings of this now nasty weather. *Flash. Crack. Boom.* I got out my drawing pad and started sketching it; little did I know it would become tonight's entertainment. Mother Nature can sure offer up some good theater!

I am here ⤴

Location:	Jerry's Cabin Shelter
Today's Miles:	6.8
Total Miles:	297.3
Date:	May 23, 2004

With nasty thunder and lightning going on all around, plus heavy rain, I decided it was a good day to take a midday nap. I'm cold with all the moisture in the air, and the best way to warm up would be to start making miles. But I just don't hike happy with all the rumblings in the sky. I'd rather sit and be anxiety free. What a bummer of a day.

I don't mind walking in the rain—well, that's not entirely true—but I hate having to do it when lightning is about. It's not safe.

Location: Bald Mountain Shelter
Today's Miles: 24.7
Total Miles: 322.0
Date: May 24, 2004

Yesterday was a wimpy seven miles. The thunder was popping up every hour the whole day, so I took two naps and practiced being a slug. It might have been the shortest day so far.

Today, however, was a different story. Blue sky made an appearance with a nice breeze and zero humidity. Belle's ankle was really bothering her last night and not much better this morning. We walked together the first hour until I got her to promise she'd hitch a ride into Erwin, Tennessee, and let it rest. Once that was settled, she insisted on me hiking my normal speed. It's hard for me to not look out for the friends I've made. She just doesn't want anyone to make a fuss over her, so I said I'd see her either tomorrow or the day after at Miss Janet's House, which is a hiker hostel.

I put the legs into another gear and started making some miles. The nice weather sure does make a difference on your attitude out here. In no time at all, I had powered past the first shelter and was at the second one at 1:15 p.m. for lunch. If I didn't linger too very long, I could make another ten miles before 6 p.m., which would make this my second longest day with 24.7 miles. By doing so, Erwin, Tennessee, would now be within reach tomorrow with a smooth sixteen miles. And of course, we all know what that means. *Real food*, not camp food. Yummmm!

Location:	Erwin, Tennessee
Today's Miles:	16.9
Total Miles:	338.9
Date:	May 25, 2004

For the last week my left leg has been walking in Tennessee, while my right leg has been in North Carolina. But being here in Erwin, sort of, officially now, puts me across another state line. As I descended from the high mountain ridgeline toward Erwin, the views of the Nolichucky River and the vista beyond were wonderful. The trail comes out of the woods near a hiker oasis called Uncle Johnny's, where I walked straight into its store, bought two bottles of apple juice and four Ding Dongs, and savagely consumed the bounty in no short order.

I moved on to a hiker hostel that's been gaining in popularity—thanks to its hostess and owner, Ms. Janet. Miss Janet's House as it's known has become a hiker Mecca where there's bodies in bunks and sofas, kitchen, and porch. This body feels like its been transported back to college days—or college daze—and thus, I'm going to move on over tomorrow to a motel. Sometimes it's just nice to have "Postcard" time. The highlight of today, other than the spectacular view, was going with Belle to the outfitters to help her completely regear. Seems she's prescribing retail therapy for herself. In an effort to help her ankle pain, she decided to buy all new gear to drop the pack weight she's been luggin' around. In the short time of knowing her I can confidently say that this gesture was on the grandest scale. For a self-proclaimed cheapskate, to drop a grand gives you a glimpse into the near-fanatical goal to reach Maine. So now when her ankle feels better instead of carrying forty-five-plus pounds, she'll be walking with a scant twenty-five! Sometimes you just have to pull the old wallet out and bite the bullet. Bravo, Belle.

So who is Belle, really? What I know is little, but on the trail that's OK.

We had a bond. Maybe it was because we were the first other northbounder each of us had met, maybe it was our first-day jitters, or maybe it was clear that she needed someone to take her under their wing for a bit—not that she knew it at that time. Whatever it was, we had a bond.

It was only a little more than three weeks ago, I sat alone in the shelter on that first day wondering what the journey would hold. Her slender form came walking out of the mountain fog with three other hikers out for a section. Introducing herself as a thru-hiker, she was the first and only other person attempting to make it to Maine I'd met that day. Frankly, they were the only other hikers on the trail that miserably wet, cold day. I paid attention to her in particular since she seemed to be carrying quite a load. When it landed on to the shelters picnic table, it spoke volumes.

Glad to have some company, we talked about our big plans for hiking the entire Appalachian Trail. Before Belle earned my respect with her grit, never-quit attitude, she made me laugh. Not from a joke-telling talent, but by her approach to gear and food or lack there of.

As we spoke, despite her confidence, there was a real naiveté about the journey to come—a childlike simplicity that came from a lack of real trail experience. Being an extremely adventurous person, she's traveled the world by herself. She had decided to thru-hike after reading Bill Bryson's book *A Walk in the Woods.* So with zero backpacking experience, Belle set off on this gargantuan odyssey with the impression that it would be a simple walk in the woods—hmm, sounds familiar. She'd left her home in the sunny vacation town of Key West, Florida, to do battle with the lingering winter's chill of the southern Appalachian Mountains. Aside from riding her bike back and forth to work, not much physical preparation had been done.

Gifted by a complete lack of ego, Belle, who was Ann at that time, informed me that her pack weighed in at forty-eight pounds. Belle was at best 110 pounds, and that was only if you caught her after third helpings on Thanksgiving Day. Feeling like I could help, I offered to go over her gear to possibly lighten the load for which she embraced.

Belle's short-term preparations mimicked mine just two years earlier. She crammed for the fast-approaching hike by reading countless hiking books to learn what to bring, buy, use, and eat. Working against her was her pronouncement she was a cheapskate. In fact, within the first hour of ever meeting this stranger, she boldly informed me she was a cheapskate seven times as we talked about what she was carrying.

Little did she know that I was one who'd drop $100 if it meant lightening just six ounces! But I had the benefit of knowing what carrying weight up and down a mountain felt like, a lesson she'd learn soon enough.

Here's how Belle displayed her charm. She didn't know what her backpack empty weighed; she chose it because it was yellow. Yep, I kid you not. Although I didn't admit this to her, I too made the same silly decision on a backpack two years earlier. Only mine was for the color blue.

She didn't know what her sleeping bag's temperature rating was, just that she had a nice big pad to put underneath it.

An allergy sufferer, she was carrying enough pills to last her several months without resupply. Just hundreds and hundreds of pills.

Ambitiously, she sewed a custom bug suit. Pants, gloves, and a jacket complete with an enclosed hood. Unfortunately, the hood top being fully enclosed had no means of a hole anywhere for the ability to drink water. But I was impressed at her resourcefulness. And she said she made it "cheap."

She carried no water pump or purification drops and told me that if she needed them she'd just borrow someone else's—which got a huge raised eyebrow from me. To thru-hike all the way to Maine means being prepared for the unexpected. To think that water was always going to be available without treatment was, well, quite risky. And let's not even get into the borrowing thing; every thru-hiker must be self-sufficient.

She carried no stove. Had no mail drops planned. And didn't have a single map or guide book. What she did have, which we'd laugh about in that first month, was three very large Ziploc bags of food. The first was stuffed to the zip with Captain Crunch cereal. The second bag was packed with several dozen Ring Dings. They're a chocolate-cream-cupcake-like object. And finally, the kicker, was an enormously big, heavy bag of trail mix, sometimes called Gorp, she proudly said she made herself. This thing alone weighed seven to nine pounds.

"Wow, that's a lot of Gorp! Did you like Gorp before the hike?" I asked.

"No, never have, but the books say that everyone brings it along," she replied.

"Listen, if I were you, I'd go dump that far out in the woods somewhere for the bears," I counseled and asked, "So just how long is all this stuff for? How many days of food is this for?"

"I don't know," Belle answered.

Well, all righty then. I thought I'd better become big brother and quick. In all her naïve enthusiasm was her charm and a zest for life. She laughed at herself when she revealed that upon reaching the beginning plague on Springer Mountain, she started walking south down the Approach Trail instead of north. Without having any guide books, she didn't know that starting at the forest service road actually meant a short back track to begin. It was there that the other three section hikers from Iowa found her and pointed her toward Maine. She was unflappable. Not the rain or fog or cold winds soured her optimism. However, there was this phobia of bears.

Trying to be big brother, I didn't dare share that "Night Zero" encounter in the prehike section of this book. On that first night, apparently my occasional snore was enough to startle her several times that indeed a black bear was coming toward the shelter.

The exact moment when Belle realized that a dinner of dry Captain Crunch cereal didn't hold quite the appeal she imagined.

We woke that second day to morning rain and fog and cold winds and no views. Not knowing her plans, I said farewell and wished her luck. But like a tenacious turtle, she appeared that evening at the same shelter. Good for her, I was impressed. Whether she was moving on pride or joy remained to be seen, but she was where I was and by carrying nearly twenty-five pounds more than me. And so the bonds from the trail began to form as they do with many. Shared distances and nightly stops unite us, and friendships grow.

I wasn't planning on taking a zero day here in Erwin, but I need some different supplies and since the day sort of slipped by gear shopping, I'll take tomorrow off and then push seven big days into the legendary trail town of Damascus, Virginia. But for now, I'll rest here in this rocker on Ms. Janet's shady porch and listen to the soothing sounds of her many wind chimes.

Location:	Cherry Gap Shelter
Today's Miles:	16.3
Total Miles:	355.2
Date:	May 27, 2004

Just when you've got the fire blazin' good and its sending its glow up on the towering trees that stand all around you—where the only sound is a distant Eastern screech owl and the hissing moisture of the wet logs—in comes a crowd of hikers. In twenty-eight days I've not had a single shelter to myself and now, apparently the string will continue. With darkness nearly upon us all, they all swing in to the essential camp chores. *Mayhem* might be a good word to describe it!

Everyone loved the fire I made and then to my surprise, marshmallows miraculously appeared to bring even more warmth to the moment. Some of the hikers had no idea how to roast the little fluffy white gems. Smack in particular, who I first met that last full day in the Smokys, who got her trail name there when we discovered she wouldn't spend the extra few pennies to buy Ramen Noodles and opted for the cheaper, unknown brand of Smack Noodles! She's a person with a huge heart and a smile that travels for hundreds of miles. Turns out Smack is quite the athlete having been a college basketball star! Anyway, she didn't know bubkiss about toasting marshmallows. So yours truly took charge and demonstrated the art of the char and pull then repeat. Great fun!

Although the sky is clear and the moon and stars bright, a quick listen to the radio predicts a thunderstorm after midnight. At around 1 a.m. the winds started increasing and in came the storm.

This morning (5-28-04) the winds were howling and rain was still pelting down. But when I realized that the rain I heard on the shelter roof was only water being dislodged from the wind blown trees, I got motivated. The others laid zipped deep in their mummies as they planned elaborate excuses to tell themselves so they wouldn't have to go out in the nasty weather. Sometimes, you just don't want to go to school I suppose. Once I informed the group that it wasn't actually raining, the zippers began to move. Man, kids these days!

A clear night. A half moon. And a campfire's golden glow.
The AT, how sweet it is.

Location: Stan Murray Shelter
Today's Miles: 20.0
Total Miles: 375.2
Date: May 28, 2004

Déjà vu is the only way to describe today's hike. The morning winds blowing all the nights rain from the trees, the fog, and dampness had me thinking I was back in the Smokys. The AT also had me climbing the third-highest mountain of the journey, Roan Mountain. Unlike Clingmans Dome in the Smokys, the AT's highest, which you continually climb over several days, Roan Mountain is one big fast, steep, leg-up-on-rock-then-leg-up-on-root climb. Well over 2,200 feet of rugged ascent, made all the worse by the drizzle, stiff cold winds, and 40 mph gusts. The summit was totally socked in clouds as I climbed up into them. Actually, the only good thing about it, other than it being behind me now, was the spruce Christmas tree forest at the top. What an awesome aroma those evergreens produce. Even though the day was filled with yucky weather, it did have a wonderful silver lining.

Since leaving Springer Mountain back in Georgia almost a month ago, I've seen only one red-orange newt. (Heck, it may be a salamander or something else, I'm not a slitherologist). If you've never seen them you're missing something, they're quite striking in their beauty. Anyway, today's hike had me see forty-six of them! It was a day that I spent mostly looking down on the trail for them, I didn't want to hurt any of them. It was so cool; I couldn't believe how many had come out to the trail to hike. Well, maybe they weren't actually hiking—at the near—snail's pace which they move, I'm not sure they could reach Mt. Katahdin in their lifetime. Regardless of whether they were hiking or just poking around, I counted forty-six, beautiful red-orange newts/salamanders/whatevers. It may have been a lousy day for weather, but it was a stellar day for seeing critters!!

It's now about 9:30 p.m.; and there's only one other hiker, Mello Mike, sharing the shelter tonight. We're both in our mummies since the dampness and cold winds has it pretty darn nippy—come to think of it, we're still fairly high in elevation as well. At over 5000 feet, and factoring a 2 to 3 degree lower temperature for every thousand feet of elevation, it's going to be in the upper 30's tonight. This thirty-five-degree bag will get a fair test! *Brrr*, and I thought it was almost June. It's a world gone mad.

Location:	Campbell Hollow Road
Today's Miles:	13.8
Total Miles:	389.0
Date:	May 29, 2004

What a difference a day makes, as the saying goes. I woke to blue skies filled with golden morning sun. A nice change from yesterday. With only a short ten miles to the next shelter, the pace was relaxed. The trail led up over two "balds" and upon reaching the first, memories of Julie Andrews and *The Sound of Music* flooded my thoughts. At the top of the second, Mello Mike and I dropped our packs and plopped down on the sun-drenched grass to soak up the rays. Glorious, just glorious!! I wish I had a kite.

The plan for the day was a bit sketchy since the first shelter was at ten miles and the next after that an additional eighteen. I hadn't planned on having a twenty-eight-mile day. So what to do was on my mind, but finally a plan revealed itself before the first shelter appeared. Mello Mike arrived just after me, and I proposed a way to celebrate my one month trail anniversary—one day early.

Just a half mile up the trail was the road US19 and a half mile to the right sat King of the Road Steakhouse. Then later, after we were fat and happy, we'd hike back to the trail and put a handful of miles in before we'd both tent for the night. Making the next shelter just wasn't a reality. So that was the plan, and Mike liked it too! Even though they wouldn't open for serving till 4 p.m., we decided to get there early and hang out. The owner spotted us waiting for the place to open and let us come in and start eating at 3:30. I had a rib-eye steak with all the fixin's, followed by apple pie a la mode. And of course, we both ordered *two* cheeseburgers to go for the next day—gotta love that town food. Everything was delicious, and we both felt like kings as we saddled on our packs and headed back for the trail!

It's now past hikers' midnight, and I'm snuggly zipped inside my tent in a grove of hemlocks and pines. Happy anniversary to me!

I sure hope it doesn't rain tonight; I'd like to avoid a moisture-heavy tent tomorrow. Our plan is for three high mileage days, which will deliver us into the town of Damascus and over our third state line—Virginia. Staying in the tent tonight is introducing me to many new sounds; it will take a little getting used to. I can hear critters walking around outside as well as the occasional field mouse; I think it's a mouse. It could also be an eighty-foot anaconda looking to devour a nice hiker.

Overmountain Shelter is a huge barn.
A cool place to stay unless it's a breezy, chilly night, then it's a cold place to stay.

(Drawn while waiting for the King of the Road Steakhouse to open.)

Location:	Kincora Hiker Hostel
Today's Miles:	20.2
Total Miles:	409.2
Date:	May 30, 2004

We rolled up our dew-wet tents and were on the trail by 7:30 a.m. Our goal was to do 22.1, a very doable distance since our profile maps seemed to show a fairly tame contour. Wrong!

The only way to describe today is up, down, up, down, rain, rain, up, down, up, down, up, down, rain, rain, up, down, up, down, stop. Twenty miles of it! Kincora Hiker Hostel has a wonderful reputation and since the trail passes so close and being two miles shorter than the shelter, well, Mello Mike and I said "detour."

Unfortunately, the rain kept many hikers from leaving today—hikers have become squatters. The result is there's no room at the inn. So we're crashing on the owner's porch tonight in our mummies. We did, however, participate in their shuttling of this whole hiker hoard to town for all-you-can-eat Chinese. It's nice to have some different flavors for a change. Bob People's, the owner, is one of the AT's chief volunteer leaders for trail maintenance and upgrades in the region. Anyway, it took two vehicles to carry everyone and that was with thirteen hikers stuffed into his pickup. Yea, thirteen, it wasn't a typo.

I believe today was either my seventh or eighth twenty-plus-mile day. To do another tomorrow, Mello Mike and I will most likely move ahead of all the squatters that are still here tonight—many who started a full three weeks before me. That's hard-core! But as good as that is for pace, there are still a handful who are pushing even beyond us—the young punks!

Even though I'm sleeping here on the porch, I still was able to do laundry. My rain gear has been smelling like ammonia. Everything is now back in its proper stuff sack ready for an early start. Damascus is within two long days or thee moderate ones—at which time I'll consider taking a double zero. I've basically worked every day for a month with only three days off. Why I'm not even getting this Memorial Day off!

Location:	Vandeventer Shelter
Today's Miles:	17.5
Total Miles:	426.7
Date:	May 31, 2004

The porch was interesting last night. Yet another thunderstorm rolled in, this time at 3 a.m. putting on quite the display. Fortunately, the overhang and wind direction kept us from scrambling. I just love the drama nature can put on. I do not love how the moisture-rich air loads itself onto every surface of stuff we carry, thus increasing our gear weight by five pounds in some cases, and it just makes everything sort of clammy!

I was the first out of Kincora, everyone else other than Carp wanted to avoid the rain that was still falling. I can't blame them, but as the saying out here states, no rain, no pain, no gain, no Maine! So I walked again in the rain for half the day.

At Watauga Lake, I lunched on my two-day-old cheeseburger. "Yuk" did I hear you say? Out here, it's a fine delicacy to be savored! Afterward, since my final destination was only eight more miles, I hopped up on the picnic table and took a nice snooze. Crazy, isn't it? Sleeping on porches and picnic tables, eating several day-old food and loving it. Is this the same guy who's run advertising agencies?

Laurel Fork Gorge and a dramatic riverside trail.

Location:	Damascus, Virginia
Today's Miles:	34.1
Total Miles:	460.8
Date:	June 1, 2004

A day or two ago, Mello Mike had mentioned that there was a sort of AT Challenge that existed from the Vandeventer Shelter. The challenge was to do the entire 33.1 miles into Damascus in a single hike.

As I woke to the rain and dew soaked everything, again, the clouds had been blowing straight into the shelter all night; I really had no intention of taking the challenge. Mello had lingered at the lake for a party that interested him the day earlier, while I hiked on. The cold dew and wind had the three others in the shelter that morning hiding deep in their mummies. But, as usual, I packed up and was off by 7:30 into the foggy soup.

The weather was definitely bumming me out. When I got to the first shelter, I squeezed about a liter of water out of my socks. I ate a little something that has long ago lost any taste-appeal for me and wrote an entry in the shelter register asking about where the sun-drenched strolls in the woods had gone to.

Like magic, the sun made an appearance and chased the pewter skies away. My mood immediately started to move north and with it, my pace! As I reached the second shelter, I pulled everything out of my pack into the sunshine to dry and lighten up. When I pushed on, my pace was even faster; and in record time I was at the third shelter—and then it was game on! "The challenge" was within my reach, and I'd knocked out 23.1 miles in only eight hours. With only another ten to Damascus and the clock reading 5 p.m., I gave the boots a fresh lacing and powered on! I covered the last ten miles in two hours and fifty-five minutes and entered the "friendliest town on the trail" while the sun still hung in the sky. Some 34.1 miles had been covered in eleven hours of hiking with a thirty-pound pack on my back, that doesn't suck! And amazingly, I feel awesome! The feet are still a bit soggy but not sore. After checking into a nice B&B and getting a look at myself in the mirror, I may have lost another ten pounds today alone.

Oh, have I mentioned I just crossed another state line? Welcome to Virginia, everyone. We will be hiking here for the greatest number of miles of the fourteen states the AT travels through. To celebrate, I tried out Sicily's and one of their large pepperoni pizzas. Yea, finished the whole thing.

Reaching Damascus is a huge psychological boost for us thru-hikers. It sort of says that if you can make it here, you've got a good chance at making it to Harpers Ferry, an even bigger milestone. I'm going to treat myself to a double zero, not that I feel I need it. I just want to be proactive and impose body rest as a strategy to keep myself strong.

Damascus, Virginia
Known as the friendliest town on the AT.

Each year, in the middle of May, the town hosts a three-day celebration of the Appalachian Trail and its hikers called Trail Days. This annual festival hosts a parade where past thru-hikers march together in groups according to the year they hiked. A town tradition of a water balloon fight between the "towners" and the hikers follows the parade. A talent show, free food, and gear manufacturers all join in the silliness. Over twenty thousand showed up in 2004.

Ruffed Grouse

A large chickenlike bird. It's usually not seen until it flushes with a startling whir, scaring the Gatorade out of you. Its call is a drumming that sounds like a distant machine gun which starts slow and then speeds up, bup,. bup, bup, bup, bupbupuppppppp. I met hikers who got chills from hearing these little thumpers—I told them it was an escaped silverback gorilla from the zoo.

Eastern Hemlock

Also known as Canadian Hemlock, this member of the pine family has a strong presence from Georgia to Maine. Some are rather large oweing to the difficulty of the terrain that made logging them too tough. Thank goodness. These older growth stands are dark with shade and echo a feeling of greater isolation. Maybe Germany's Black Forest is comprised of Hemlocks. One also notices how these areas seem to be quieter, void of distant planes and township life that the trail coexists with.

One-star Bathroom, Five-star View

Enjoying my second zero here in Damascus and with all my necessary errands completed yesterday, I thought I'd share some of the colorful texture that is the AT.

On the trail, this structure is called a privy. You'd know it better as an outhouse.

Most shelters along the journey have one, and each is different. Some have windows, one even has curtains; some have translucent roofs for light, while others are as dark as a cave. Some are new, clean, and smell free; and some aren't. Most have doors and then some, like the one above, doesn't. Without a door, embarrassing moments are avoided by looking to see if a pair of legs is in view, very simple, very functional. But this privy at Deep Gap Shelter does, however, have something most do not—an outrageous front-row seat to sunrise. For only here can one find a sunrise and a full moon living in harmony.

The mighty Carp and his 80 lb. load on Blood Mountain. He'd hesitantly whittle it down to a meager 60 lbs, where it would remain for the journey. He's a stronger man than I. With all its easy to reach stuff sacks hanging and dangling, it reminded me of a one-man band. All Carp needed was a pair of cymbals between his knees.

Location: Damascus, Virginia
Today's Miles: 0
Total Miles: 460.8
Date: June 2, 2004

Today I'm saying hello, from the shady porch of the Apple Tree Bed and Breakfast, where I can watch the world go by from this rocking chair!

The sky is awash with blue, and a small breeze is bringing the wind chimes to life. It is a peaceful moment here in small town USA—all we need is a squash festival with cotton candy and children giggling while waving sparklers!

Taking a page out of my multitasking city-living days, I headed uptown to the Laundromat to put a different kind of sparkle back into my duds while sitting on their stoop writing postcards. Yea, I am a multitasking powerhouse, am I not?

With it being a sunny June 2, kind of the unofficial start of summer, Belle hobbled her way over from the Place (a hiker hostel) on crutches, so she could have a good view of the town's energy. While we sat and talked and watched everyone rush here and there from the porch, Carp came hiking into town and dropped his pack to chat. *Thud!* His pack is quite heavy, but then again he was ten years in Australia's special forces! Carp somehow thinks that things like his half-a-pound gunshot, gash bandage just might be needed someday out here. Ahh, yea right, maybe if a squirrel attacks you.

Belle and I went to hang out at the outfitters where a couple of folding camp chairs out front had our names on them. No sooner after having sat down did I catch wind of the most horrible smell. Did I step in something? "What *is* that smell?" I asked. Just then a hiker walked out and reached behind us both to grab his socks he laid out on the window seal. "So that's what we're smelling, your socks. We thought a possum had died. Have you ever actually washed them?" He looked up with a slow grin and that's how I met Goose. "Hey, I'm Postcard." He answered in his slow Virginia way, "Hi . . . I . . . m . . . G . . . o . . . o . . . o . . . o . . . s . . . e" and walked on up the street, out of smelling range—thank goodness.

By six, both Belle and Carp returned to test out one of the porch rockers and enjoy some red wine before we moseyed over for dinner. But we had to enjoy the wine in stealth mode, its not acceptable in Damascus to do such racy things in public. The three of us all get along effortlessly, so the food and conversation were great. Then in comes Pop Up, which is how he got his trail name, he just seems to pop up when no one knows where he is. Then Mello Mike, Butterfinger with her hiker buddy's, London and Greybeard and the Reverend Yukon Jack. It was as if a tour bus of hikers had just landed! See how a zero day reunites you with those you know. Anyway, it was a wonderful, peaceful day—a perfect zero!!

Location:	Lost Mountain Shelter
Today's Miles:	15.8
Total Miles:	475.6
Date:	June 4, 2004

After two wonderfully restful sunny days in Damascus, it was time to make some miles again. So naturally, it was raining. I was moving fairly slow after last night's libations with the tribe on my B&B's porch. Everyone had brought something, from red wine to donuts to good dispositions. We laughed at each other's stories and our own trail goofs. Later we all relocated down to the mill for a nice dinner, but afterward we all had to say farewell to Belle. I'd be hiking out the next day while she'd still needed to nurse the injured ankle. Achilles Tendonitis can't be taken lightly. We encouraged her to continue to jump up the trail to rejoin us when she was finally able to walk without the crutch.

Anyway, back to the rain.

Beth, the owner of the Apple Tree B&B had my breakfast ready at eight. I'll admit that when I saw the rain I wanted to rethink hiking out. But as a thru-hiker, you just have to move despite the weather. It takes true grit at times.

On went the rain gear and pack cover; and up main street, I went to find where the white blazes leave the town and disappear into the woods of America. Earlier in the hike, knowing the physical difficulty I'd face for the day would trigger some angst—but this has been slowly vanishing and transforming into just moving north— I believe the confidence of knowing what has already been tackled, all those miles and mountains that are to my south are empowering me. It's a feeling that whatever lays ahead is no longer worth fretting over; I will handle it, move over it or around it. That's what I do. The only thing at issue is whether I desire to do it. It's not a question as to if I can, I am. Now it's much more about if I want to hike all the way to Maine. And that issue all comes down to enjoying the journey, which I most definitely am.

Virginia provided a nice stroll today even in the rain. The coolest part of the hike came in the afternoon when the AT joins the Virginia Creeper Trail on an old railroad bed—the kind from the steam engine days. It then moves over one of those classic wooden railroad bridges over a deep gorge. The whole thing had been converted to a footbridge, which was so high up that you could gaze down *onto* the forest canopy— a refreshing change from walking underneath it. As I walked across I counted how many steps it took—221. It was a really interesting piece of architecture and fun to cross. Good trail texture.

Many were already here at this nice shelter when I arrived. Short days seem to dominate the hiker crowds on yucky days. Unfortunately for them, it means making slow progress. Most likely that's why I'm now meeting hikers who started a full month before me. Oh well, "hike your own hike" is the AT mantra.

It's chilly tonight; and the rain has everything dark early, maybe I'll hit the mummy and warm up. Hmm, some music might cheer up the dreary weather.

The AT joins the Virginia Creeper Trail north of Damascus to cross over a converted old wooden railroad bridge.

Location:	Old Orchard Shelter
Today's Miles:	23.2
Total Miles:	498.8
Date:	June 5, 2004

They're called the Grayson Highlands, and they are indeed named properly. The entire area harkens back to my time in the highlands of Scotland. Thankfully, I didn't have haggis on tonight's dinner menu. Haggis, for those who haven't had the dubious pleasure of this Scottish standard, is a chopped mixture of heart, lungs, liver and onions, oats and herbs, packed into the stomach lining of a sheep and boiled or deep-fried. Now doesn't that sound delicious? (No wonder those people talk funny.) For centuries, the Scots have eaten odd things long before the TV show *Fear Factor* was ever conceived.

"Hey, Angus, insteads of tossin' those innards away, what say we eats 'em?"

"Yea, I's think you gots something there Shivas. Sounds yummy!"

Great groves of Rhododendrons in bloom throughout the Grayson Highlands.

It was quite gray with low-level clouds clinging to the mountains; but as morning was edged out by midday, the sun started to assert itself. It would toy with us the rest of the day. Joining us were just herds and herds of weekenders to enjoy the beauty on this fine Saturday—especially since we were able to leave the rain gear packed up. Yes, I know it's hard to believe, but today saw no rain. Truly amazing.

Most seem to be out for a weekend camping adventure where they could use all their camping doodads and adventure whizbangs. By my count, I guess there must have been over four hundred weekenders. Not exactly a wilderness experience. Tents were everywhere, some in clusters resembling outdoor cities.

It was a tougher-than-normal twenty-three miles because so much of it was rock. At one of the midway shelters, Goose and I met Dave Underfoot who ask if we'd like some hot chocolate. "Sure, that sounds like a great way to warm up. Thanks." (With the sun playing hide-and-seek behind the clouds, the cold finds you fast while it's off hiding. Especially when you stop walking and everything you're wearing is wet from sweat.) And that is how we three met and came to hike together for a week or two. During lunch, a doe wandered in to look us over. "No food to spare, sorry." By afternoon, I hiked up upon a family of five who are attempting a thru-hike as well. Mom and Dad and their three children travel as the "Garland Five." The kids are thirteen, eleven, and nine; and each carries their own pack, set up their own tent, and take turns with camp duties. Real nice folks, and the kids love to take charge of making the campfire, which is usually something I do. So tonight I'm just sitting back being a slug and gazing into the fire. Most thru-hikers don't bother with having a campfire since they're tired or don't want to go to the bother, but I just love the ambiance it creates. When you turn in and the glow of the flames flicker on the shelter and woods, it's pretty darn cozy. Frankly, having a campfire has always been one of the highlights for me early on when I first started camping in life. Like them so much do I that down in Miami, I included a sunken fire pit area in my backyard landscape. Campfires have a hypnotic quality, its hard not to drift off into Neverland in the middle of a stare. Stress relieving and primal in many ways, a campfire says escape and wilderness. It says adventure.

The long mileage today had a purpose—if you've been following my journal then you may have an idea as to the motivation. By hiking 24.7 miles tomorrow, I'll be sleeping at one of the newest shelters that even has running water and a shower! But as good as both those conveniences sound, they can't surpass the fact that the local pizzeria will actually make deliveries to the shelter!! So there it is. Tomorrow will be a big mileage day to a large pepperoni pizza. Yum!

Location:	Partnership Shelter
Today's Miles:	24.7
Total Miles:	523.5
Date:	June 6, 2004

To celebrate crossing through the five-hundred-mile mark, Mother Nature granted me blue skies, light breezes, and glorious sunshine. The feet are a bit sore from the two-day fifty-mile distance. But I'm letting them rest now as they have served me well and deserve time off.

I arrived here early, and Goose and I have already ordered pizza for Dave and ourselves, who should be here in another hour or so. I'm writing as we wait for the delivery person to show up with all the delicious bounty. Eight hikers and one dog descended on him the moment his motor turned off. And what had been one nice pepperoni pizza sitting in front of me a moment ago has disappeared into the ever-deepening abyss called my stomach. A nice reward for a near—twenty-five-mile day! Which is a new topic of thought. Should I be pushing my mileage into the twenties so often? It does garner certain benefits such as getting to towns earlier than my original plan and thus allows me the luxury of taking zeros without falling behind. I believe that can still be accomplished without twenties each day, but if I do continue to do a lot of them, I'll be in Harpers Ferry in under a month, some five hundred miles. This feat would eliminate any worry about getting to Katahdin before they close Baxter State Park on October 15. I suppose, however, doing twenties is the same as hiking in general. If it's enjoyable to do them, then I should do them. If not, don't. How's that for profound thought? Frankly, I didn't know I had it in me to bang out so many. One thing that is increasing on these twenty-plus-mile days is my hunger. You see, I just had a whole pizza pie and now I'm ready for a whole apple pie.

Today completed five full weeks on the trail in addition to passing the five hundredth mile. Lunch and dinner are becoming all the more important as well as *what* those meals actually are. My five-hundred-mile pepperoni pizza was my finest hour for a trail dinner—and having it in the woods, all the more memorable. The last couple of days I've been hiking with Goose and Dave Underfoot—that's his trail name. Dave Underfoot has been a major volunteer over the last ten years in the actual building of the AT—and he isn't even American. He's Australian. The third Aussie I've met now; Carp and K Bear being the others. In fact, he took a week off from his thru-hike just a couple of weeks earlier to help on a new *relo*. That's short for relocation, and it happens when the ATC (Appalachian Trail Conference), the governing body of the trail acquires new, permanent land for the trail. Or when an older route can be improved by using switchbacks to ease the climbs, which was the case in his week of volunteering. Anyway, together we've been planning big miles; we all seem to be similar in daily ability. Goose lives here in the area and has extended an offer to Dave Underfoot and me to hike and hang at his house each night for the next couple days. That means laundry, showers, and normal food!! *Goose rocks*! Yea, baby, how good is that! Why, I might even be able to sneak off to a cinema to catch the new Harry Potter movie? Wouldn't that be something, thru-hike and pop culture! You gotta love America.

THE 500 MILE PIZZA

The celebratory pizza for crossing the five-hundred-mile mark, which gets delivered to the shelter.
Now that's my idea of camp food.

(The pepperonis don't actually spell out the mileage, but it was delicious nonetheless.)

Location:	VA 42 Road Crossing
Today's Miles:	23.4
Total Miles:	546.9
Date:	June 7, 2004

It was a day filled with variety and trail magic. Goose and I seemed to keep a lot of the crowd at Partnership Shelter up with our dueling nighttime symphony; its not our fault they don't have ear plugs after this long on the trail. Anyway, we sort of got out of there extra early before the grouches woke up. Heck, we slept well.

The trail led us over streams and into dark hollows, beneath sun-filled summit trees and across huge hay fields where the temps might have been pushing ninety degrees. It was good that our purpose today was hiking and not fishing. The heat had all the cows lying down in clusters under the shade of the trees. Anyone who grew up in Texas as I did knows that when the cows are lying down, the fish aren't biting.

By 11 a.m., twelve miles were done and then the AT did something miraculous. It exited the woods directly across the street from a Dairy Queen. Score! We stayed for over an hour—lunch was the first priority or was it the strawberry sundae? Goose had prearranged a pickup with his folks farther north, which meant another big chunk of miles. So we reluctantly left DQ and all her dairy delights. The variety to the trail continued as we climbed three ridgelines, then dropped at a knee-busting pace to a raging river— and all the while, climbing these A-frame ladders called stiles over numerous fences. It was like a boot camp since we must have gone up and over a dozen.

I met Steve, Goose's father at VA 42; and off we went to their home where Betsy had the most amazing home-cooked dinner all ready and waiting. We did, however, first desmell ourselves with a shower; it wouldn't be polite to subject Steve and Betsy to our charming stench. Hey, I'm not unreasonable; it was the least I could do. For dinner there were fresh vegetables and secret recipe mash potatoes. Chicken and applesauce, fresh rolls, and a rhubarb strawberry bread pudding! Oh, did I mention to-die-for brownies? If that wasn't enough, their warmth and generosity rated an eleven on a scale of ten! In the morning, they naturally made an equally amazing breakfast then drove their son, with me tagging along, back out to the trailhead so we could hike and do the whole thing over again. Yes, they are special people! I only hope I can think of a drawing worthy of all the favors they've done for me.

I'm not entirely sure Steve and Betsy knew what Goose had offered us (myself and Dave Underfoot), but like true champions, they swung for the fence on the first pitch and hit a two-thousand-foot home run outta the ballpark! Two nights of nirvana here at the Cardwell's trail magic home, but tomorrow, it's back out to the shelters where with some determined miles I can have myself in Pearisburg for a zero. We've already knocked out 104.1 miles in the last 5 days. With another three days to go before then, a zero day may not be a choice but a necessity. I'm not as young or as rambunctious as Goose.

Virginia hay fields, we aren't always in the woods or on a mountain.

Location:	VA 623 Road Crossing
Today's Miles:	17.3
Total Miles:	564.2
Date:	June 8, 2004

I saw my first black bear today.

As I came around a bend, Goose stood frozen in the trail with his finger up on his lips, I was puzzled. He had walked right up on a momma bear and her three cubs, which she was protecting. I never saw the cubs since they moved down off the ridge, but the momma stayed put, grunting and scratching the ground. Not exactly a welcome posture. We all looked at each other during an awkward couple of minutes. Goose had on full leather boots, so I thought I had a good chance of outrunning him if the bear attacked. If I couldn't I was willing to use my hiking poles to trip him up so the bear could find a quick satisfaction. Yuk, yuk. Eventually, there was sufficient room to move up the trail away from her. I got going while Goose stayed to temp fate for a Kodak moment. It's a scary thing to come up on a mother and her cubs! Not the scenario I was hoping for, but it was quite thrilling! No sooner did I get some distance on the situation, the damn trail made a hard U-turn and headed right back to where the momma had backed off. Jeez. I started hitting my hiking poles together yelling out, "Hey, bear" so I wouldn't surprise her. I wasn't in the mood to have one of my body parts becoming a snack. Thankfully, the trail took another hard U getting me the heck out of there for good.

Other thrills came in the afternoon as Goose, Dave Underfoot, and I made the long climb up Chestnut Knob Ridge. Being a pseudobald, it was really beautiful with great views of Southern Virginia. However, the surrounding thunderstorm clouds were keeping me from truly appreciating it. After our quick lunch at the shelter on the top of the ridge, we made a hasty exit to get to our meeting place where Goose's father would be picking us up. As quick as we were, we couldn't avoid the inevitable. But I won't complain, there's been about four days of sunshine, the rain was due. It's amazing how cold you can get when you're wet from head to toe the moment you stop hiking. Or maybe I should say it's amazing how warm you can keep yourself when you are. The human motor is quite the heater. The shivers can happen very quickly, so you tend to put on and take off a wind shirt or fleece frequently. If the shivers are more dramatic, your only course of action is to change into your dry stuff you keep in a Ziploc inside your clothes bag. Fortunately this afternoon, we were able to step inside Steve's car and out of the chilly wind, and then we were off back to their house for another feast. Despite being in the car, the shivers found me. I tried to focus my concentration to stop the shivering with sheer mental strength, but it was useless. I for one was terribly glad to be out of the woods and out of the wet world, trying pathetically to get my soggy clothes dry! When we arrived back at their house, I got out of those clothes faster than a couple of newlyweds.

Then it was more trail magic from Steve and Betsy Cardwell, maybe the friendliest family on the trail!

Goose, Dave Underfoot, and I hiking up into harm's way on Cosby Knob Ridge.

Black Bear

You can't outfight them. You can't outrun them. So be thankful they don't want anything to do with you. They do, however, love your pack of goodies to eat. I witnessed four sightings—three in Virginia and one in New Jersey. But black bears are in every state the trail travels through. Unlike a grizzly, you don't play dead if attacked. Black bears don't fall for that ruse; with them, you have to fight for all your worth.
You might call them cute from the security of your home, but I call them formidable, especially since I'm out here in their woods with only my "spork" eating utensil.

Location:	Helveys Mill Shelter
Today's Miles:	17.6
Total Miles:	581.8
Date:	June 9, 2004

A beautiful sunny day in Virginia! We got a late start but were able to make the miles fast—thanks to forgiving terrain.

At one point I crossed one stream twelve times. Each time meant rock hopping, and I remained totally dry until the last stream and the last rock, which teeter-tottered on my right foot giving me a boot of cold mountain water. Oh well, almost perfect!

Sittin' and sunnin' and snackin'.

I haven't known many people from the great state of Virginia. I've certainly never hiked with any of them before now. I'll obviously need to seek out more of these great individuals if Goose is any barometer of their good qualities. That is if you overlook his very stinky, unwashed hiking socks. Or at very least, always keep upwind of them.

I really came to know Goose on that first rainy day after leaving Damascus. He had arrived at the shelter before me and had been lying down to take a prebedtime nap. Only he drifted off with his stuff and himself right down the middle of a shelter space for two people. Another hiker came in later on that wet day seeking shelter space out of the rain. There was room, but not until Goose woke up to scoot over. After an hour of Goose lost in slumberland, someone gave him a few nudges to wake him up. Unfortunately, due to his deep sleep, he woke up with complete confusion. He asked what time it was. When he heard it was eight o'clock, he assumed it was a.m. and started to make movements to pack up and head out. Without any of us comprehending Goose's disorientation, we too became a bit puzzled why he didn't simply just scoot over instead of getting up. One of us finally did say 8 p.m., that is, once we stopped laughing. Poor Goose, he was obviously quite tired. He had barely taken two minutes off since leaving Springer Mountain.

Posing with Goose near his hometown of Rocky Gap, Virginia. (Steve and Betsy, you done good.)

For the next couple of days, Goose and I had the same planned mileage, so we started trail bonding. It didn't hurt that Goose was a hard sleeper; he claims to have never heard me snore. Goose on occasion had a nice nighttime symphonic talent himself.

It didn't take long for Goose's generosity to come out. We were nearing the mountains and valleys of his hometown. With his folks and home cooking getting closer each day, Goose extended the offer I mentioned earlier to Dave Underfoot and I to meet the folks and devour some of their awesome home cookin'. The only thing that needed to be done was to match Goose in his daily trek of big mileage. The next three days would see us kick out back to back midtwenty-mile days. At this pace, the infamous "Virginia Blues" would hardly be able to catch us. (The Virginia Blues is a phrase relating to a malaise that finds most thru-hikers at this time. With having more AT miles than any other state, Virginia's never-ending distance can put some bad mojo on the thru-hikers' mental strength. Many will leave the trail from depression or loneliness or monotony.)

I've found a real pride in doing more aggressive mileage during this time. And it was refreshing to actually hike the day with someone instead of only hooking up with them at camp. Goose started the trail as an athlete, mostly due to his involvement in bike racing. He simple transferred his racing stamina to the slightly slower speed of the trail. After a week or so hiking together though, Goose would leave Dave and I to honor obligations concerning a friend's wedding. He'd be taking a couple zeros to dance with young maidens and hopefully catch the bride's garter. I'm sure once his hangover goes away, we'll see one other again; it's a long journey to Maine and the Goose knows how to motor.

Location:	Wapiti Shelter
Today's Miles:	24.0
Total Miles:	605.8
Date:	June 10, 2004

It was one of those mornings that fill you with smiles. As I packed up the gear over on the Brushy Mountain ridgeline, the sun started to show its rays. The terrain was rocky but relatively flat and was giving up some fast miles—a good thing since the plan was to do twenty-four miles. This would get us into Pearisberg the next day for a zero. It would be the first day off in the last eight with a sizeable mileage tally.

By 1:30, we came to Kimberling Creek and its large suspension bridge. Dave Underfoot took a dip while I sat on the bridge checking the maps. That's when I discovered that just a half mile to the left was a store/restaurant/pizza place. It took only two little words to get Dave to commit to the detour—ice cream. So we had a pizza and soda, then each of us polished off our own pints of ice cream—strawberry for him, Cherry Garcia for me. We followed that up with a cheeseburger and a tallboy Budweiser to go. I really shouldn't let my journal become so focused on food detours, although it does reveal what is happening to my body and needs. Burning five to seven thousand calories every single day will do that I suppose.

Right on cue, the skies were becoming dark, and the rumbles started to make there presents known now that it was midafternoon. We hiked the last eight miles hard and fast, and despite getting caught by a three-minute cloudburst, we made it to the shelter only a tad moist but not soaked.

Two nice events did take place that should be noted. The first was hiking right upon a wild cherry bush. Dave pointed it out, so we stopped and ate handfuls of the sweet red fruit. My first time. The second happened just 1.8 miles after the pizza-cheeseburger-beer stop. The event involved hiking over our six hundredth mile. Dave and I stopped, shook hands in congratulations, and continued to haul butt to beat the rain.

When we arrived, all new faces and trail names greeted us. I suppose this last week's pace had taken us into a whole new tribe of hikers—lots of new fellowship! However, I'm not sure we made a good first impression after we unpacked our still-cool Budweisers and toasted our great day of unplanned town food in front of them.

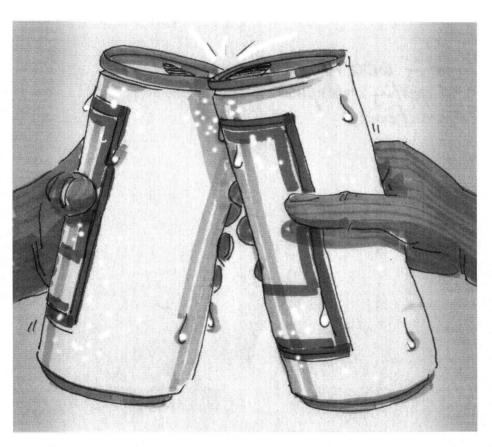

An after-hike cocktail.
Toasting our six hundredth mile on the Appalachian Trail and loving it.

Location:	Pearisberg, Virginia
Today's Miles:	16.2
Total Miles:	622.0
Date:	June 11, 2004

The trail brought us right to the edge of a couple rock cliffs with just amazing views. The first was a vista of clouds hanging low to the valley with the mountains rising out of them during the morning sun. The second came before we would start our descent down into Pearisberg; it was a sun-filled valley of farmland sprinkled with trees and rooftops here and there. I really love those moments just as you begin the last miles down off the ridgeline into town. It always feels like the end of a chapter in a book with the arrival in town as the last sentence.

I checked into the motel at the base of the mountain and ordered Italian food for delivery square away. Veal Parmigiana, salad, and cheesecake arrived in a flash and disappeared even faster! I got my laundry started so that tomorrow I could have no worries other than getting a new backpack. Oh, yes, did I mention that my second backpack, the one that's only a month old, has had the same shoulder strap rip-out problem?

I called the manufacturer and was given a full reimbursement when I informed them I was a thru-hiker. Those are magic words to the makers; they know we know our stuff and talk to one another. Then it was a call to those great people at Mt. Rogers Outfitters in Damascus and spoke to Jeff. With two packs failing by the same manufacturer, I decided to try a new tack. A company called ULA (Ultra Light Adventure) makes a real top-notch thru-hiker's pack, so that was my choice. And most importantly, Jeff actually got up the next morning at 5 a.m. and arrived at my motel by sunrise to not only hand deliver it, but to masterfully fit me to the correct size. Jeff coming personally to fit me was a gesture above and beyond, Damascus may be the *friendliest town on the AT,* but Mt. Rogers Outfitters may be the best outfitters in the country.

Anyway, after we spoke and I knew that the replacement pack would arrive the next morning, I did what any thru-hiker would do. I called the Italian place again and ordered another Veal Parmigiana, another salad, and another cheesecake. Oh, and a ham-and-cheese sandwich, just in case! It seems in the span of two hours I had consumed two days' worth of dinners. Only on the AT.

So now, I'm on backpack no.3 and at the post office tomorrow, I pick up hiking shoes no.2. Gee, it's almost like starting a new hike, only I have a 622-mile head start!

Location:	Pearisberg, Virginia
Today's Miles:	0
Total Miles:	622.0
Date:	June 12, 2004

As I mentioned yesterday, Jeff from Mt. Rogers Outfitters started my day for me at 6:30 a.m. to fit me and deliver my new ULA-P2 pack. As you can imagine, I would highly recommend them to any hiker who values an expert staff who know their stuff.

With Pearisberg all spread out, I decided to run errands with the new pack on and hiked up the road for breakfast, then to the post office for my boxes, and then finally moseyed over to a hiker hostel to see if Belle was there. The trail scuttlebutt said she had arrived there from Damascus only a day earlier. Sure enough, Belle was there. Her ankle injury—an Achilles tendonitis—had improved, but she still needed to be off it. Dave Underfoot returned from doing laundry to the hostel and invited us to come hang with his friend who runs the Appalachian Trail Conference's central division out of Roanoke.

I had suggested that we all go see either the new Harry Potter movie or *Shrek 2*. Sounds like a plan, so we all hopped into her car and headed over to her hometown of Roanoke and the cinema where two of us saw Potter and two of us saw *Shrek 2*—loved it. Loved it.

Afterward, we headed over to the local church where an all-you-can-eat fish fry fund-raiser was taking place. Six bucks later, we were loading on the tarter sauce and waded into the first of several plates. At the deep fryers were the men, and spreading the icing on the cakes and pouring the lemonade were the women folk. It was a true slice of America!

The last stop was to Kroger for hiking groceries and then we headed back to Pearisberg. It was a great zero with nice new friends. Dave and I will both head out tomorrow but not together. The plan is to meet tomorrow night at the shelter.

Back at the motel, I spread out the grocery store food along with my mail drop provisions; and using my maps, figured out how many days it would take to get to the next bed—I mean town. Oops!

Location:	Pine Swamp Branch Shelter
Today's Miles:	19.6
Total Miles:	641.6
Date:	June 13, 2004

It was a good zero. I feel rested, and my stomach is smiling—can they do that?—with all the calories I shoveled into it. And I got some pop culture from the normal world with the Harry Potter 3 movie.

So now that it was time to hike out of town, guess what happened? Yea, it's been rain gear all day, but I'm here early after a near twenty-mile day. It's called Pine Swamp Branch Shelter, which is odd. There are no pine trees, and the nearest swamp may be back in Florida. There are, however, lots of branches lying on the ground everywhere. Go figure. The other thing that's missing is Dave Underfoot. He didn't show. Hope he's OK.

Rice Field normally has nice views here from the summit. Or so I've been told.

Location:	Laurel Creek Shelter
Today's Miles:	18.5
Total Miles:	660.1
Date:	June 14, 2004

I've spoken of the kindnesses of those who've taken me to town while filling my hands with homemade cookies or those who picked us up each day after hiking and gave us dinner and breakfast before returning us to the trail.

But I've failed to share with you the smaller yet wonderful trail magic gestures that have found me. About a week ago on the way to Bland, I started a climb through a thicket of mountain laurel when I happened upon a large Styrofoam chest with the magic words *Welcome Hikers* written on it. When I opened it, a treasure trove of fruit juice, sodas, and V8s were revealed. I've been craving fruits and their sweet natural juices for the last week. The weight of fruit makes it less feasible to carry out of town. Like a kid in a candy store, I grabbed and quickly vanquished an apple juice.

There has been five-gallon buckets suspended from rope pulleys a month back that were stuffed with peanut-butter-and-jelly sandwiches, lemonade, and fresh strawberries.

Today as I crested the steepest climb of the day and was trying to catch my wind, two ice chests sat near a log with those magic words again. Off went the pack and down went my very tired ass onto the log to savor a Coke and cookie—a chocolate cream cookie no less! It was left by a hiker-turned-trail-angel named Super Dave. I wrote a thank you in the journal he left. The bounty had been there for several days by the time I reached it, but there were still plenty of sodas.

It's these kindnesses that make the whole AT experience so memorable. It's the constant generosity of others shown to us, complete strangers, that renew my faith in humanity so frequently out here. These are people who make a difference. Thank you for your big hearts!

Trail magic along the trail is like a Christmas present.
The kindness lifts the spirit and fills more than the soul.

Location:	Pickle Branch Shelter
Today's Miles:	22.3
Total Miles:	682.4
Date:	June 15, 2004

In 1704, a hundred years before Lewis and Clark would start their own great adventure, a small seedling began to rise in a quiet valley. It was situated in a land that a hundred years later would be known as Virginia. Sheltered from nature's harshness by the surrounding trees, it weathered summer's drought and winter's cold during its most vulnerable stages. As a youngster of some four feet tall, it found itself between a hungry coyote and a tail-raised skunk. Although it didn't see it as a blessing at the time, the little black and white's aromatic spray hit it. A silver lining lies behind every cloud, and the aroma kept the local grizzlies and black bears from scratching up against it.

Seventy-odd years later, it witnessed the frontiersman becoming minutemen rushing to arms to battle others in red coats. By chance and circumstance, its quiet hidden valley spared it from the ax—and so it grew. As the years passed, it began to outpace its neighbors; thanks to a small hollow that funneled even the most meager amount of water to its roots. And so it continued to grow even in the dry years. Another hundred years brought uniforms of blue and grey to battle over the rights of all at its field. Its ever-widening canopy of shade helped to cool the wounded, while its thick branches became the last thing some of these fallen warriors would ever see.

Fifty more years would see it used as a marker, a property line. This, once again, would keep the ax and saws from touching its bark. Young lovers would meet and picnic, it would see much that others would not.

It is now 2004, some three hundred years from that fragile beginning and a thru-hiker named Postcard walks up to admire its massive trunk and majestic limbs that seem to defy gravity. Its wide-stretched limbs remind him of the welcoming arms of a loving parent.

Now, an old growth landmark, this magnificent white oak looms over all its neighbors. Known as Keffer Oak, it is one of the miracles of this planet and one of the wonders of the Appalachian Trail.

The massive Keffer White Oak.
The AT brings its hikers directly to this three-hundred-plus-year landmark.

Location:	Catawba, Virginia
Today's Miles:	11.9
Total Miles:	694.3
Date:	June 16, 2004

My hands look like raisins and my feet like prunes. Both pairs of socks are wet as well as all my hiking clothes. The trail is a boggy, mushy mess from the nonstop rain. The rocks, which are numerous, are now also slippery. The rain pants I switched to in Damascus have helped, as well as the watertight second pair of hiking shoes; but with rain falling at one inch an hour, everything just gets wet! Its days like these why my sleeping bag is in two water-resistant stuff sacks and why my fleece and long john bottoms are sealed in a Ziploc inside my clothes bag. It is imperative that those articles stay dry. Despite it all, it hasn't dampened my spirit. For the last four days, I've been moving north solo. My past companions either are still behind me or were delayed. Four days of rain does test one's emotional endurance, not to mention slow one's pace.

By lunchtime, I had completed the 11.9 AT miles to the road crossing that would take me to Catawba. There I'd pick up my mail drop as well as find the Down Home B&B. As the hard rain turned into a deluge outside, the people at the post office called the B&B for me to see about a vacancy. Yea, I swear. Small towns seem to help one another.

All my stuff is drying out now. I've showered and shaven, feeling clean and human! It will be no damp, cold, wooden shelter in the rainy woods for me tonight but rather a bed with linens and a movie on TV. It's so nice to relax, it's been a trying four days and an expensive one.

My digital camera died when moisture worked its way through *two* Ziplocs sending it to the land of worthless toys. My watch, which gives me the time so I can monitor my mileage, tells me the barometric trend, serves as my alarm clock wake up, informs me of my elevation and is my compass, also drowned and was unable to be revived. Both items are used every day, which is a good trail rule of thumb for what you carry and what you don't, and so will need to be replaced quickly.

Tomorrow I'll receive breakfast and a ride back to the trailhead, then its about twenty miles to Daleville and a zero may be in my future!

There are so many wonderful aspects about the Appalachian Trail;
this, however, isn't any of them. Four days of rain.

Pileated Woodpecker

This is a large, powerful borer of holes. It can pound away at a tree like a jackhammer, the sound of which travels far through the forest. Both sexes have that spectacular red crest.

Location:	Daleville, Virginia
Today's Miles:	19.6
Total Miles:	713.9
Date:	June 17, 2004

It may be one of the most photographed vista overlooks on the AT—it is called McAfee Knob. The rain had moved off last night leaving clean air and long views. A youth group out for a few days snapped a photo of me there, and then I snapped about ten or eleven shots of them, each with a different camera. A few miles later came Tinker Cliffs where I laid my pack on its side and plopped down using the pack as the back of a chaise lounge—and drifted off for a thirty-minute catnap. It is a good thing I don't sleepwalk considering where my bed was. Oh, the freedom afforded by the AT!

The sunshine was glorious all day, what a change. The only low point was finding out that the Mexican restaurant was closed for renovations. *Rats!* Here in the Howard Johnson's—newly acquired from Best Western—it's the first HoJo's I've stayed in since my buddy Gary and I went to Ft. Lauderdale, accidentally on spring break week back in the 1980s. What a zoo! It felt like we had time traveled into that older movie *Where the Boys Are* with Sandra Dee.

Location: Daleville, Virginia
Today's Miles: 0
Total Miles: 713.9
Date: June 18, 2004

Zero days are what weekends are for all of you. This was my seventh day off in the last seven weeks. By hiking into town after a full day, I get to enjoy two nights of showers, laundry, and easy food that I don't have to carry. However, I would not say that a zero gives me a more normal life. For me, normal does not mean hanging out in Laundromats or walking to stores where cars are whipping past me with nary a consideration for right-of-way. Its safer out with the bears in many ways.

I walked into a bank today and picked up on a defensive, apprehensive "May I help you?" because my clothes were not normal, I had a pack on my back, and that my face wasn't familiar. I suppose that's sort of OK. You can imagine how the clerk's opinion soured all the more easily when my credit card's computer rejected my request for an advance. The clerk was dismissive to me not willing to try it again. I nudged her to dial the 800-customer service number. Hesitantly she did and she learned to her surprise that it was for my fraud protection, she also learned that my credit did not merit her apprehensive looks. I continued to be polite, despite the chilly reception, and explained that I was hiking the AT and was not homeless. By the time I left, I feel the clerk and her associates had learned a page from the "don't judge a book by its cover" school of thought. Why they even wished me a safe journey!

Next it was on to find the post office to pick up my mail drop, but before I located it I found a salon. It's been a month and a half since my last haircut. I've been shaving every town stop, but the hair definitely needed some attention. When I walked in, a very chilly reception greeted me. I asked if they took walk-ins. A slow up and down look at me was then followed by a slow hesitant "Y . . . e . . . s." "Great," I said. I introduced myself using my real name and started chatting with the ladies of the salon. It seems that although this miracle of a mountain footpath was at their doorstep, none knew anything of it. In no time, ladies on the edges had moved over to ask questions and join in the laughter. There I was getting all neat and trimmed while entertaining the ladies and helping them, maybe just a bit, not to judge too quickly. When I finally left the salon, the ladies all waved and wished me well on my journey and had me feeling that I was an AT ambassador. I suppose that is true, isn't it?

My errands today hopefully helped to show a few people that all things are not what they seem—and I too reminded myself to be more patient with others. It was a zero day that turned into a ten.

Just me and the ladies of the salon in Daleville. Sharing stories and changing first impressions.

Met a different sort of fellow today while hiking out of town. He was heading south, and I naturally was heading north. We stopped abruptly and stared at one another for a moment, and then I said, "Well, hello there, little fella."

"Who you callin' little?" he answered.

"Umm, I didn't mean to—"
Then he interrupted saying, "You two leggers—jeeze!"

Trying to make amends, I asked if he was trying to hike the whole trail.
"No, just a section," he responded, and then asked, "You?"

I said, "Yes, my plan is to go all the way to Maine."
"Maine? Where the heck is Maine?" he asked.

I just simply replied that it was a fair piece north of here and then asked about how far of a section was he intending to hike.
"To that tree over there. Should be there in an hour or two, I'm quite fast!" he said proudly.

"Oh," I said, "Do you have a trail name?"
"Doesn't everyone out here? They call me Rocket."
"Hi, Rocket, I'm Postcard"
"Listen, Postcard, it's been a little slice of heaven," he said and added "but I don't mean to be rude, you think you could get those big honk'n feet of yours out of my way, I've got feet to make today, and I'm burning daylight."

"Ummm, oh, yea sure. Pardon me. Have a good hike."
"Yea right," he replied.

Met someone new today.

Location:	Thunder Hill Shelter
Today's Miles:	23.6
Total Miles:	756.0
Date:	June 20, 2004

Today was maybe one of the nicest days since leaving Springer Mountain. A cool front moved in last night bringing with it some chilly forty-degree temps—good sleeping weather! It also vanquished the near 90 percent humidity we've all had to hike in for the last two weeks. The bright sun and clear skies put me in a wonderful mood. I'm a bit confused as to if today is the first day of summer or tomorrow the twenty-first. The reason being that the first day of summer is Hike Naked Day, which I didn't, nor did I intend to. But a male hiker named Bilbo did know that today was indeed the first of summer, just hiked into camp butt naked except for his backpack and a strategically placed bandana since he was approaching the shelter. Great. Why couldn't it have been Heidi Klume? Oh, and guess who caught up and passed me during my Daleville zero day—The rambunctious Goose. Bummer, but I'm sure the trail will reconnect us.

Came to the most interesting landmark right at the end of the day. It's called The Guillotine, and it is a bit unnerving to walk underneath which you must since there's no other way. You try to not let it get to you, but it does—with some double-time, quick stepping I got through with my head still attached, so I won't be joining Nearly Headless Nick anytime soon.

Location:	Punchbowl Shelter
Today's Miles:	25.1
Total Miles:	781.1
Date:	June 21, 2004

This whole section between Daleville and Waynesboro has had me a tad confused on how to hike it. With needing to get to one town for a mail drop, shelters, and the terrain, none of it seemed to present me with the ideal plan—until tonight.

It was another big mileage day just so I could do another tomorrow and still not be where I'd want to be. See what I mean? Of course, the new plan involves town food with a motel followed by reaching my Montebello stop the next day and more town food! Now that's a good plan! Things are lookin' up.

I had a cool deer encounter this morning. The doe was standing across the trail looking at me when I saw her. I stopped to look and hopefully not spook her. She didn't seem scared at all, so I began to say hello and talk to her. She'd twitch her ears at my various words while raising her nose to smell me. She moved a bit off the trail to nibble some plants, which allowed me to move slowly by. As I continued to talk to her, she did something that none of the other twenty-six deer I've experienced so far on this adventure have done. She walked back onto the trail and started following me at about twenty feet back. I'd stop and turn back to talk to her, and she'd stop too. I'd walk on, so would she. It was so cool—quite special! I'm not sure why I didn't think I'd see this many animals beforehand, but I see so many every day. It's all very magical in a way!

Location:	Buena Vista, Virginia
Today's Miles:	10.9
Total Miles:	792.0
Date:	June 22, 2004

Last night I had to remind myself that it's not the miles we do that are important but the journey! By deciding earlier that when I reached the road crossing I'd hitch nine miles into Buena Vista, I got to experience another piece of texture.

I opened the "Hiker to Town" bandana I made, and the second vehicle to drive up quickly stopped to pick both Waker and me up. I met Waker about a week ago, and our pace has had us at the same place, so now we're hiking together. (It was the same day that Dave Underfoot didn't show up, and I still don't know where he is.) Anyway, no more than thirty seconds had elapsed since reaching the road that we had our ride!

Waker and I were then treated to a wild and fun ride down the mountain in the back of a pickup. The driver was good and his right foot heavy. The mountain was curves on curves on curves, but with his driving skill the ride echoed that of a roller coaster—and all because we chose to go to town. Part of the fun of the AT is all that surrounds it and how we negotiate our way through it!

Location:	Montebello, Virginia
Today's Miles:	16.6
Total Miles:	808.6
Date:	June 23, 2004

The disaster of a week ago—the hard rain that killed both my watch and my digital camera—has now been fixed. Unfortunately, it required buying new of each, and today as I reached the Dutch Haus B&B, my new digital camera was here waiting. This one is a waterproof Sony, so let it rain.

Here at the Dutch Haus, I've met more new faces that have shared more news of hikers who've come off the trail. The numbers are reducing, but to me, it still seems a lot are moving north. My pace has me meeting new hikers almost daily. Lunch today was by a river where I gave the feet a soak in celebration of the coming of summer.

Did you notice the total miles section? I crossed through another landmark. Whoa, that's a lot of miles!!

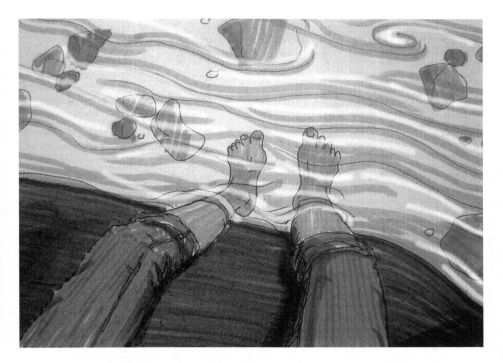

One of life's truly great pleasures. The AT's countless streams to sit and soak.

Location:	Maupin Field Shelter
Today's Miles:	18.2
Total Miles	826.5
Date:	June 24, 2004

The Appalachian Trail teaches its travelers many things: patience, staying in the moment, and honor.

Having played golf for some time now, I can say the lessons learned are the same. Honor being the greatest of these! With no one other than you to count your strokes and then mark your scorecard truthfully, that's all about honor.

Today the AT gave me a little test of honor when I least expected it. The story begins with a wonderful sunny, low humidity day—hiking out of Montebello and its Dutch Haus B&B gave beautiful views all day.

Midway through the hike, I came to a trail sign that said my destination for the night, Maupin Field Shelter, was 8.8 miles farther north. Now, all 8.8s are not created equal, and this 8.8 was rock on rock with steep, lung-exhausting, leg-weakening climbs! It would be a long three-thousand-foot ascent over Three Ridge Mountain. It was everything the profile maps showed it would be—tough!!

As I reached the second of three ridges and upon another trail sign, it pointed out that a side trail could be taken to the left reducing the distance to Maupin Field Shelter to only three miles. The sign also indicated that the Appalachian Trail continued straight to the same Maupin Field Shelter with another six to seven more miles—and knowing the AT, that routing would take me up the toughest part of this steep mountain.

I stared at this crossroads trail sign and weighed the options. Go left, avoid the summit, and be at the shelter in an hour or so, or go straight following the AT another six or seven miles along a steep, rocky ascent.

Come October, when I finish my journey in Maine and all 2,174 miles of the Appalachian Trail, I can submit a document to the Appalachian Trail Conservancy, the governing body of the AT, stating that I have completed its entire length. They, in turn, note the achievement in some logbook and then send me a small piece of fabric, a patch. It has a number and a word embroidered on it in gold thread which says, *2000 Miler*. That is the simple designation given to those who claim to have hiked the AT's full length. It doesn't matter whether you do it in one season or twenty, just that you've done it all. And it's all on the honor system.

I continued straight.

Sleeping here at the Maupin Field Shelter with its resident six-foot rat snake assures you of one thing—no mice. Waker, Trail Dawg, and I had the shelter to ourselves since four other hikers opted for tenting.

Location:	Waynesboro, Virginia
Today's Miles:	21.1
Total Miles:	847.6
Date:	June 25, 2004

The last twenty-four hours have been considerably black and white. Back at last night's shelter, Waker and Trail Dawg—a hiker I met the day before—show up late from Montebello. Trail Dawg is holding his pack rain cover out in front of him, a bit unusual. He lays it down on the shelter floor and opens it to reveal a small twitching nose. Out came the tiniest of young skunks! Although the size of a grapefruit, it kept raising its tail to spray—which was of the amount of an angry eyedropper. Of course, I had all my gear out on the shelter floor while Trail Dawg's stuff was still in his pack. The others there quickly suggested that he must return it to where he found it on the trail if it was to have a chance for reunion with its smelly kinfolk. Cute, unusual, but not shelter broken. We all hoped the little fella good luck and safe passage!

With the forecast calling for—wait for it—rain, I moved swiftly all morning hoping to cover as many of the twenty-one-plus miles into Waynesboro before it began.

I was flyin' low as my mother would say. I had all twenty-one miles done by 2:15, that's quick. But just as I neared the end of the distance, my eye caught a big black piece of something, about one hundred feet up the trail. At first I thought it was another hiker's pack cover, but that was quickly made clear when it turned around onto the trail facing me, it was a large black bear! I stopped, froze, thought, then yelled, "Hey, bear" and started hitting my hiking poles together. The bear thankfully turned and ran up the trail out of sight. It was big, and I was alone, so I continued to yell, "Hey, bear" while hitting my poles together as I moved slowly up to where it had been—had no choice, the vegetation was too thick, the trail was my only route!

Bears don't like human contact, mostly; I hoped I wouldn't face the exception. Nothing else happened, and I made it to the road and the day's destination. It was thrilling to be confronted by so large a black bear while by myself, but I'm glad this story lacks any further drama.

4 ounces   400 pounds

Close encounters of the animal kind.

Fawn—White-tailed Deer

Deer have been the most plentiful large species I've encountered. Whitetail specifically and it brought a smile to my face each and every time. But in the Shenandoahs I got to see two fawns with their mothers. My Disney upbringing had me thinking of Bambi. They are so frail and as pure as innocence can be.

Luna Moth

A fantastically colored giant pale green silk moth. Adults can have a wingspan from three to eight inches. Their antennae are featherlike, similar to a two-sided comb. With its green-brown "eye" on each wing, its soft long-haired body and the long sweeping lower tail-wings, few flying objects can match its exotic beauty. Unfortunately, this beauty is fleeting. Adults live only for a week. Bummer.

Location:	Blackrock Hut
Today's Miles:	20.0
Total Miles:	867.6
Date:	June 27, 2004

All of us since starting have heard constantly about "Wait till you get to the Shenandoahs." Meaning that the terrain becomes gentler, and you'll be able to make bigger miles. The only issue with this statement is that the more miles you do, the less time you get to be in the park. As it is, my plan is to exit the entire length of the Shenandoah National Park's one hundred miles on the morning of the fifth day. But that's getting ahead of it, I've just entered the park; and yes, the terrain is gentler.

Shenandoah National Park has something the other parks don't—wayside grills with real town food. These grills even have wine and beer in the next-door camp stores. But today's hike only started the park; tomorrow will take me to the first of these waysides. It will be far from a primitive existence. The other thing you hear about is how tame the deer are since hunting isn't allowed, they get used to you so they're not as skittish. I saw five today, bringing the number up to thirty-five meetings thus far. I will admit to having black bear a wee bit more on my mind since the other day's encounter. And this park has a whole bunch. Let's go see what we can see, it should be exciting.

Entering the Shenandoahs.

Location:	Hightop Hut
Today's Miles:	21.4
Total Miles:	889.0
Date:	June 28, 2004

Despite the wonderful wayside restaurant which cooked up a nice double breakfast for me and meeting the hiker with the computer-operated artificial leg named One Leg Wonder, one thing was causing me much angst. It seems the calendar—Harpers Ferry post office hours of operation, available motel rooms, and the big July 4 holiday weekend—are all at odds with one another. It seems upon looking deeper into it, my suspicions are correct. If I continue to do midtwenty-mile days for each of the next five days, I'll arrive in Harpers Ferry the late afternoon of the third. The post office will be closed by then, so I'll be stuck in town for two and half days. I'm guessing that a room as well will be hard to come by. But what's most important to me is getting my picture taken by the ATC for this year's book files. I'll call them to see if they'll be open on the fourth, if so, short of a room, some of the pressure will be off. Normally, I'd take a zero there, but with the holiday, a lot of what I'll need may be closed. As you can see, I'm fretting since I don't have the answers—some of the big city habits are obviously still within me. A phone call or two will provide the missing info.

One thought is to use my arrival in Harpers Ferry as the time I see the folks, my sister's family, and my cat, which by now surely thinks I'm dead. Maybe that's the best solution to all these conflicting timetables. I was going to wait till Pennsylvania.

What was interesting today? Well, as I mentioned, meeting One Leg Wonder. He did a funny Linda Blair-exorcist impression by keeping his artificial leg still and him walking around it at his high-tech joint pivot. He has a great sense of humor. I don't think of him in any other way than as a thru-hiker, which I know he liked.

The other was seeing my first fully grown skunk in the wild, much more significant than that little pint-size stinker the other day. I spotted it when I was no more than four feet from it! I quickly gave myself a wide berth from the big stinker. And like yesterday, I saw another four to six deer. Of course the birds are everywhere, I even heard an owl this morning, my first since North Carolina.

Well, its getting dark and as of right now, I'm the only one here in the hut. Will tonight be the first solo night for me since I begun? Only two more days and I celebrate my second-month anniversary on the trail—and tomorrow I walk through nine hundred miles. Boy are they flying by—oh wait, son of a gun, looks like another hiker just showed up tonight.

You get many opportunities for vistas of the Shenandoah valley.
Another rainless, low humidity perfect day.

Location:	Alive, thankfully, at Rock Spring Hut
Today's Miles:	23.9
Total Miles:	912.4
Date:	June 29, 2004

If I wasn't wide awake by the time I hit the trail this morning; what happened in the first hour would correct that.

Today would offer me easy town food *twice*, thanks to my planned distance, so my stride had a bounce and I was moving swiftly. After all, breakfast was just eleven miles up the trail at a camp store.

For some time now, I've started just carrying my hiking poles snapped together in one hand on gentle terrain. I move a bit quieter, and my stride seems a bit longer. Well, as I approached a particular trailside tree, a huge commotion came from above me and about twenty feet to my front. It seems a black bear had sought a high perch on that tree as I approached, but as I neared, it panicked. Apparently, it decided I was too scary, and it wasn't high enough. Its action was to execute an emergency fire-pole slide drill down the tree with no regard to all the noise it would make—and noise it most assuredly did make. This tree slide started with me only twenty feet away. Naturally I looked quickly and when comprehension finally spoke to my scaredy-cat genes within me, I jumped back saying the only calculating, dignified thing that came to mind: holy—! I immediately raised my hiking poles to prepare for the charge that was seconds away. The bear was the size of a large elephant with giant, flesh-ripping, foot-long claws. It had fire in its eyes and smoke venting from its nostrils. To my amazement, this vicious beast upon touching ground hauled butt away from me—Yea, *away* from me. As it powered through the trees and thicket, giving my dilated pupils a nice look at its quickly disappearing rear end, I then realized it wasn't as big as an elephant, nor did it appear to have the foot-long, flesh-ripping claws of a T-Rex as I first thought. It was just a young adult about the size of Winnie the Pooh, which I had scared the honey out of; and it, in turn, scared the Gatorade out of me.

I regained most of my composure but continued to yell "Hey, bear" as a reflex for the next six hours, which was sort of inappropriate since one of those times was inside the camp store. One never knows what may be on the other side of the cookie shelf. After breakfast, I hiked north another eight miles to the Big Meadows lodge where I went to the tap room for chili-and-pepperoni pizza—two of them!—and a beer. The Shenandoah hiking sure is tough, isn't it? I counted that meal as dinner and then moved on to this hut for a strong twenty-four-mile day. I also saw my second doe and fawn together in the trail—they let me move right up on to them, very relaxed they were. It's been another great day of animal spotting.

The night is clear and without cloud cover, the temperature is dropping. It's going to be another brisk night. This *is* summer, right?

With the second-largest population of black bears on the AT,
the Shenandoahs have a variety of ways to make sure you're awake in the morning.

Location:	Gravel Spring Hut
Today's Miles:	28.4
Total Miles:	941.3
Date:	June 30, 2004

June 30 is my second-month anniversary on the trail. To celebrate, I decided to hike a few miles to breakfast at one of the park lodges—Skyland. I had Belgian waffles with eggs and bacon, not unusual unless both were entrees. The waitress just giggled. Then I hiked another chunk of miles to another wayside area where I ate lunch. Then I hiked yet another chunk of miles to the final park wayside where I had two bacon cheeseburgers with two blackberry milkshakes—they were yummy. Then I got sick from all of it. This out-of-control gluttony was raising its ugly face.

At this point I had already covered twenty-three miles, but more were ahead before I could rest. It was my second-largest mileage day—an appropriate achievement on my second-month anniversary. After four big days, tomorrow will see me walk through Shenandoahs' northern boundary and to a road where I'll hitch into Front Royal, Virginia, and a motel. I need it; my shirt is covered in salt stains.

I've enjoyed the park and its abundant wildlife and views. And unlike the Smokys, I've had outstanding weather. Although thrilling, it will be nice to relax my thinking that a black bear is right around the corner ready to pounce—boo!

142

Location:	Front Royal, Virginia
Today's Miles:	13.5
Total Miles:	954.7
Date:	July 1, 2004

A nice thunderstorm moved in after midnight to dump a load of rain. I love the sound of rain, especially when it's significant and especially when I'm snug as a bug in a shelter.

It was a nice half-day conclusion to four big days. As I neared the road, I had my "Hiker to Town" bandana ready, but I noticed someone at their van by the trailhead. It was the owner of one of the hiker hostels: Terrapin Station hostel. He gave me and two other hikers—Cliffdancer and Bear Bait—a lift. We all went for lunch at the Mexican restaurant on the spur of the moment. Why I even got to swing by the post office to pick up my mail drop—lucky number 13. Then after several platters of gooey, cheesy, mushy Mex, they dropped me at the Quality Inn. It would be my first shower in five days of hard sweating; my clothes needed a wash more than I think I did. Maybe not. I spent the rest of the night sequestered on the king bed watching TV. Yep, I'm a slug.

Leaving the gentle mountains of Shenandoah National Park
and edging ever closer to the next state line.

Location:	Rod Hollow Shelter
Today's Miles:	24.1
Total Miles:	978.8
Date:	July 2, 2004

What an emotional roller coaster today was. Just yesterday one of the hikers who went to lunch had said that Belle had left the trail. I knew she was going to hike out of Pearisberg, but that was weeks ago. I had assumed she was back there taking her time, being patient with her ankle. So hearing that she'd come off was sad. She had such true grit to hang in there so long, hoping for a strong recovery. I felt bad for her. Today would be the first of two long days, which would have me positioned for a short mileage day into Harpers Ferry the morning of July 4.

The miles were clicking off fairly fast and in no time I reached the second of what would be a four shelter day. To my shock and pleasant surprise, the shelter register had an entry from Belle just two days earlier. I was stunned. Figuring a best guess, I imagined that if I hiked long and hard, I had an outside chance of catching her either this very day with a thirty or thirty-six-mile day. Or most definitely by midmorning on the next—the game was afoot! I kicked the legs into high gear covering the 4.4 miles to the next shelter in an hour twenty. The register entry from her showed I'd closed the two-day lead by half a day. I could tell from her writing that she wasn't enjoying being alone and apparently the foot pain was still there. On to the next shelter which was nine miles and over more difficult rocky terrain. I did it in two hours and fifty minutes; it had now been 24.1 miles, and I was exhausted. But I figured if I could find the strength for yet another eight miles I just might close the distance, then I opened the shelter register.

Belle had made it here last night and was here this very morning. But the news was bad. Her hiking was really putting her in pain. All I can say is that it must have been considerable, she's no wallflower. The register's morning entry announced that the swelling and pain were too much in conjunction with the loneliness of missing her trail buddies. She had decided, sadly, to come off the trail she had grown to love and fly home. I couldn't believe what I was reading. To go from the joy of having my new friend so close to having the deck of cards fall. I just sat there on the shelter's edge overwhelmed with those words, my eyes filled with tears. I couldn't help but think if I could have gone faster, got to her sooner, maybe I could have reversed her sadness from being out here by herself. I closed nearly two days in one long twenty-four-mile day, and it wasn't enough. Nobody knows better than me how easy it is to get down or depressed out here, it has happened to me on other attempts. If it wasn't for Belle and others like Carp, Goose, Dave Underfoot, Dharma and Greg, and so many others, my hike may have been very different.

I am strong this year because of the strong fellowship I've found in others out here. My faith and these friendships have given my legs wings. Belle wanted to hike the Appalachian Trail and hike she did, more than three hundred miles. She did it on her first ever foray into backpacking in nasty, cold, wet weather that constantly whispered in her ear to stop, to quit, which she would not. Eventually the trail stopped her the only way it could, through injury. It knew her willpower would never give in. Belle, you hiked the good hike, I'm proud of you; and you should be proud of you too. The trail just won't be as musical—ding, ding.

I'm renaming Rod Hollow Shelter, Firefly Hollow: the light show was magical and helped soothe the sadness of learning a friend had come off the trail.

Location:	Blackburn AT Center
Today's Miles:	17.8
Total Miles:	996.6
Date:	July 3, 2004

The plan was to attack the next fourteen miles of trail hard. It was the infamous section called the Roller Coaster. A series of thirteen ups and downs which are covered in rocks and ask for your full attention. On top of the roller coaster was the lingering thought that I might still catch Belle at the hostel just ten miles north. The roller coaster was rather like being back in Georgia with its quick ups and awkward rocks, but with nearly a thousand miles on these legs, my nimbleness of foot is at a pretty high level. So the miles, although strenuous, were not as bad as I was expecting. I reached the hostel at 10:45 a.m. only to find all the rooms empty. The caretaker informed me she'd caught a ride to Dulles airport near Washington DC at eight.

So there it is, three lousy hours late—I felt I was living a Hollywood movie. Once again, I was sad for her, we all help each other by just being out here. Many don't like hearing about others when they come off the trail—it weakens them in a way I guess.

I collapsed into an Adirondack chair on the porch to comfort my soul with a Diet Coke and a pint of Cherry Garcia. The caretaker asked me if I was going to the BBQ. "BBQ?" I asked. Seems another seven miles north, there's a fabulous place called the Blackburn AT Center run by the large Potomac Appalachian Trail Club. Since I was tired and also tired of doing twenty-mile days, a stop there would shorten the day and just might put a smile on what up till now seemed like a pretty sour twenty-four hours.

I arrived about 4 p.m. after all the roller coaster was behind me and immediately got a beer put in my hand. Things were lookin' up. Burgers, chicken, and wonderful salads followed soon thereafter. I was meeting an entirely new group of hikers again. The conversations with the hikers as well as the club members were engaging. As darkness fell, the picnic tables were cleared and loaded up with fireworklike objects and lit. Not quite on the level of our nation's capital celebration or as naturally enchanting as last night's firefly show, it was still wonderfully festive; and it reminded me there was much to smile about. For today, yours truly walked across another state line. Virginia is in my past, and West Virginia is my present. And if that weren't enough, in just 3.4 miles tomorrow morning, I walk through the *one-thousand-mile* mark. Then it's in to historic Harpers Ferry and the office of the ATC to get my picture taken. Wow, one thousand miles!

The Roller Coaster explained. Feel free to scream.

Location:	Harpers Ferry, West Virginia
Today's Miles:	12.6
Total Miles:	1009.2
Date:	July 4, 2004

Happy Independence Day, everyone, and happy halfway to me!

I hit the trail my usual time, only this morning it was socked in fog. Thunder was rumbling everywhere on the ridgeline, but Harpers Ferry was a scant twelve miles away. With my rain gear on and strengthened by the emotional accomplishment that lay just hours ahead of me, I hiked with an air of invincibility. The rain came in buckets and then dump trucks, but I continued. At 8 a.m., I guesstimated that I had hiked, carried, and survived my way across one thousand miles of rock, woods, weather, and mountains. There were no neon lights in the wilderness to announce my achievement. As I neared Harpers Ferry, my heart swelled with pride. My legs and feet were on autopilot delivering me as a casual bystander to the fabled trail town. I reached the ATC by eleven where Rachael, a worker/volunteer captured my skinny new self on a Polaroid. I was number 534, which was marked in red Sharpie, signifying that I was a northbounder. If reaching Mt. Katahdin is anything like this morning, only greater I suppose, I'll be a puddle of tears and joy and pride and smiles.

Along the way, everyone has been commenting on my pace, which at two months and four days is exceptionally quick. Many have misjudged my age as being midthirties, which those of you who know my true age also makes me raise my head a bit higher. There is still much more to hike, but for today I will pause and cherish what is and leave what will be for later. My folks arrived a bit before one. It was wonderful to see them and take this smallish break at their house. A quick look at their scale reports that I've lost thirty-three pounds. I'm stronger in more ways than I've ever been in my life—and I don't mean just muscle.

I got some news from another hiker of Dave Underfoot's whereabouts. It seems that rainy day out of Pearisberg, when we would be meeting up at the shelter; Dave severely hurt his knee and stopped at the shelter before. In a lot of pain, the next day he hiked back to Pearisberg and eventually had to end his hike. With both of us in Harpers Ferry, it'd be nice to reconnect, but he was at a hostel north of the town across the Potomac. And with my folks about to arrive, we'll most likely miss each other. Maybe he'll e-mail his whereabouts. He's a great guy and fun to hike with. I'm losing hiking buddies, and its only halfway. I guess that's to be expected. (Knock on wood.) I'm injury free, so it will be on to Maine soon. Despite today's deluge and being soaking wet, life is fun, fun, fun.

Stopping to smell the evergreen pays dividends in ways we can't even imagine.

1009.2 miles and 33 pounds lighter.

*Hello from Harpers Ferry, the psychological halfway point and the headquarters
of the Appalachian Trail Conservancy (new name). It is here our hike gets documented with a photo.
When I started down in Georgia, more than 1,500 other hikers had begun, but here I'm no.534.
This feels unbelievably incredible, does it show?*

GeorGIA to MAINe

Part Two

Location:	PA 16
Today's Miles:	43.2 (two days' total)
Total Miles:	1052.4
Date:	July 6, 2004

We leave Harpers Ferry in grand style by way of an enormous railroad bridge over the Potomac River. The majority of the hiking for the next two weeks will be flat ridgelines that go on for ten to fifteen miles at a time. Only the loose rocks and boulders will slow our pace. The big ascents and descents south of here won't appear again until Massachusetts. Or so I've been informed. I'm familiar with this area of Maryland and Pennsylvania since it is here that I actually learned the joy of the journey. As a result, crossing the bridge out of Harpers Ferry and the state line into Maryland didn't have the same impact on me as others. It won't be until New Jersey, some two weeks away, that I'll feel the excitement of new territory again.

Reaching Harpers Ferry has been by far the most joyful destination thus far, but leaving it means that I now face an even longer second half. It's been said that when you reach the White Mountains of New Hampshire, 80 percent of the hike has been completed but only 20 percent of the effort. Well, we'll see on that. For now, I'll keep doing what has been working for me—staying in the moment and only concerning myself with today. Tomorrow will take care of itself.

Just a few days ago, word on the trail was that someone died up on Katahdin last week. Seems a rockslide injured two, killed one, and another escaped any injury. It reminded me that despite the good quality of the trail, when we're out there, our only protection is our wits, common sense, and physical abilities. It's fun, but its no cakewalk. And as we move north into the Whites, it becomes even more dangerous. Umm, I meant to say, thrilling.

The temperatures will be higher now due to the low elevations and sunken valleys that seem to hold the breezes at bay. Maybe wrongfully, I just want this chunk to be behind me. I've seen it, hiked it. So with my folks near this area, I'm planning on hiking to meet them many times at road crossings instead of my normal shelter-to-shelter hikes. Some do this as slack packing, which means not hiking with their backpacks. The ATC has no problem with this style, but for me personally, I just like the idea of Georgia to Maine with a backpack. Nutty, but it makes sense for me. I certainly won't be carrying a lot of food or my stove, but I like my backpack; and it's sticking with me all the way to Mt. Katahdin. And I'm of the mind that one needs to be prepared if things do turn sour. Having your stuff gives you options. But more important than that right now is saying good night from Maryland. Yep, state line no.5.

Leaving Harpers Ferry by crossing the Potomac River and
another state line. Welcome to Maryland.

Location:	PA 34
Today's Miles:	43.9 (two days' total)
Total Miles:	1096.3
Date:	July 8, 2004

Carrying only what you need helps to heighten your appreciation for the wonderful surprises of the trail. In the case of food, despite our ever-present hunger, I still will only carry what is needed not wanted. If I followed the latter, my pack would be such a burden no joy would be possible. Been there, done that!

This allows me to share an early trail tale. It was my longest section hike, a nine-day one-hundred-and-forty-mile hike that involved no resupply. The food I was carrying would eventually lead to my distaste for dehydrated camp food I now experience. A good week into the journey, the sun had finally graced me with a shadow. The consecutive days of pewter skies was getting a bit tiresome. However, the sun appeared and reintroduced me to my shadow on a small clearing. At first, distracted by my shadow, I almost didn't see it or maybe it was that I didn't believe it at first sight. The trail, as if on a silver platter, was presenting me with an apple! Oh, it was beautiful. Ruby red and chartreuse green with touches of pink, why it even had a perfect stem and a single elegant leaf as if some food stylist had readied it for a photo session.

Being from the city for so many years, I was naturally suspicious. Being a fan of Disney, I also assumed that a wicked witch was hidden waiting for me to bite the poisoned gem. Fortunately, the AT and its powers to relax you, even your bias, overcame my raised eyebrow and had me bending down to pick it up. It was perfect, not even a blemish. But how? I raised my head, and the riddle was solved. A big mature fruit-loaded apple tree dangled its treasure just over my head. I lengthened one of my hiking poles to reach a particularly loaded branch and with one tap, the tree surrendered lunch. I didn't even have to enter into a Wizard of Oz tree fight. They were chilled to a glorious forty-two degrees. There's nothing better than a fresh apple off the tree, one of life's truly great pleasures.

The trail is full of surprises and magic, all we have to do is walk it. As for that same apple tree, the fruit still had some growing to do for we northbounders. But it's sure to make quite a few southbounders happy in another month or more. Timing can be everything at times, can't it?

The gifts of the trail.

(This is the small drawing pad I carry along with an assortment of color markers. Nearly every night after I've gotten water and have had dinner, I rest and draw and write these stories. Most times by headlamp.)

Location:	PA 225
Today's Miles:	44.9 (two days' total)
Total Miles:	1141.2
Date:	July 10, 2004

After much thought, I've decided to share the secret of my youthful skin and appearance. Got your attention, didn't I? As I recently mentioned, one source of flattery for me is how many hikers have been shocked by my true age, which I'm keeping quiet on. Only the other hikers will know for sure.

Billions of dollars are spent each year on antiaging creams, wrinkle elixirs, and miracle overnight masks. Why some have even resorted to injections that paralyze parts of the facial muscles just to have the face in the mirror appear more youthful! It should be noted that I'm in favor of self-improvement. If something about yourself leads to insecurity, then by all means do something about it. Liking what you see can help your self-esteem and in turn your successfulness greatly.

But all those treatments notwithstanding, there is a more natural, effortless way to smooth, younger-looking skin. It is only now making its way from the far, remote mountains of the Mongolian-China border, where for dynasties it has been known. Hollywood tried to capture the legend decades ago in the movie *Lost Horizon* from the book of the same name, where people of advanced years held the complexions of an individual half as young.

Some of us on the AT have stumbled upon this rare treatment by sheer luck and to protect the trail from being swamped by vanity-seeking city dwellers, we've guarded this knowledge. But the need is there and as a result of the countless inquiries, I'll share this newly learned ancient miracle at no profit to me. I do this only as a service to the greater beauty of humanity. It's really quite simple.

Each day when you wake up, take an early morning stroll along the wilderness of the AT. You'll want to be the first one out on the trail to receive the full dosage; this is the secret to experiencing this magical treatment. So enough pomp and circumstance—too late—the secret is cobweb facials.

By being the first out each day, you'll walk yourself, or should I say your face, directly into the full impact of these little eight-legged critters' nightly toil. They're silken webs and strands will paint your face a hundred times over. The only danger is an overly zealous spider that has visions of capturing you whole so it can enjoy you till

Thanksgiving. Most of these strands are invisible and only make themselves known till they lay their sticky filament across your nose or forehead or everything. You can try to remove them, but at best you'll just smear them around. Truly annoying is this treatment, many a hiker will wait to be second or third out in the morning to avoid them. Of course, they don't look as young. But as in so many things that are unpleasant, they produce positive results. So the next time you spot a new wrinkle or can't take your attention off those enlarging crow's feet, slip on some hiking shoes, set your alarm to "too early" and go give yourself a magical morning cobweb facial.

Individual results may vary.

Botox has met its match.

Location:	PA 143
Today's Miles:	47.1 (two days' total)
Total Miles:	1188.3
Date:	July 12, 2004

It poured rain all dadgum day and set a record for the Philly area, so I'm going to talk about something positive. Fortunately, I didn't have to live in it, just hike in it. Hiking to road crossings with a visit home is nice when you're as wet as a tuna. This is another multiple mileage day, the travel back and forth doesn't leave me enough time for daily updates—but the change of pace and family visits agree with me.

I've spoken of my rediscovery of simple things while hiking the AT, but there are many simple accomplishments as well. Said another way, simple victories.

Not unlike getting your sea legs while boating, the Appalachian Trail helps you—requires you—to discover your trail legs. What are trail legs? I would describe it as the ability to wed both balance and nimbleness to your pace without missing a beat regardless of the terrain. Getting your mastery of stride becomes quite useful before entering Pennsylvania. What thru-hikers face in the last days of Virginia-West Virginia, they'll face nearly the entire state, which are rocks the size of lemons, oranges, grapefruits, and Volkswagens. They lay around everywhere and on top of one another and some are diabolically pointed up, ever ready to poke your tender soles. Others have the evil ability to rise up slightly as you approach in hopes of tripping you to the earth so they can get a closer look at your embarrassed face. No really, they do this. At some points, you might go miles while touching nary a molecule of dirt. This geologic nuisance can all be blamed on the ice age that happened eons ago. It is this rockin' trail that has made Pennsylvania the least popular of the fourteen states the AT traverses among many thru-hikers—a surprising distinction since the state is mostly a flat, ridgeline route.

In the book *Walkin' on the Happy Side of Misery* by J. R. "Model T" Tate, he penned this little poem:

> Rocks, rocks, they's hard on your socks.
> They chews up your boots and hurts your foots.
> Dang 'em rocks.

So here's how one of the simple victories happen. You're moving your legs up the trail, left, right, left, right, while your poles are moving right, left, right, left, and your lungs are going in, out, in, out, and it is all rhythmic, smooth, and very Zen. Each is independent and yet dependent on the cadence of the other. There is a harmony and purity and power in it all, but it is also fragile and can disintegrate if one aspect of the triad misses. That's when you come upon the obstacle. It can be rocks or roots, ledges or boulders. It can be a serpentine weave between oaks or pine or poplar or it can be boulder hopping over a rushing stream.

Not unlike the way a pianist just lets go and plays instead of thinking too much, we too let go. What happens next is that our legs and footing gently caress the required surface only but an instant because the other has now taken our momentum on and then its repeated over and over. What happens is step, step, step, hop, step, step, step, hop, step. All you know is that past Olympic champion Nadia Comaneci has nothing on you. The miracle of it all is that the obstacle didn't produce so much as a hiccup in your cadence.

You emerge on the other side of the obstacle still in full stride and rhythm and you know something special just happened. A blush of pride finds your cheeks, and your posture finds a bit more height. Wow! Isn't it amazing how easily I'm entertained?

Give yourself a pat on the back and savor the simple victories of the AT.

Location:	PA 309
Today's Miles:	41.1 (two days' total)
Total Miles:	1229.4
Date:	July 14, 2004

I once asked an authority on rattlesnakes what happens if you're bitten. His answer, "About $20,000 in hospital bills." Gadzooks!

Ever since Duncannon, the famous Pennsylvania rocks have become the norm. The local hiking clubs often write in the shelter registers that they've been out sharpening them for us—the bastards. It's nothing that some tough soles, thick socks, and about five layers of Dr. Scholl's air pillow inserts can't handle. That is if you can still squeeze your foot into your shoe with all that. Surprisingly, it's those little rocks that seem to make your feet ache the most at the end of the day—sort of like walking with an acorn in your shoe. But Pennsylvania has other rocks too. Actually, great fields of them that confuse you as to where you go to follow the trail. Only by wading out into them do you come upon a white blaze. If moving forward a bit puzzled wasn't enough, these boulder fields make just the perfect habitat for rattlesnakes. We hikers do look out for one another though. One person's terrifying encounter can be another's warning, with a note of a snake's territory. Then we can detour and hope it doesn't lead to another snake's home. Boy, these rocks sure are fun, aren't they? Please, before me, really. I'll follow.

Location:	Delaware Water Gap
Today's Miles:	49.6 (two days' total)
Total Miles:	1279.0
Date:	July 16, 2004

I was raised to not say anything if I couldn't say something nice. Boy have I failed to fulfill that teaching. Anyway, I won't say much about this section except Lehigh Gap Mountain is absolutely the wrong name for it. What should you name a fallen, jumble of sun-hot stones that force you to scramble hand over ass risking life and limb? In my opinion I'd call it the Devil's Forehead. You don't follow white blazes up its face, but rather curious triple 6s that somehow seemed etched in the boulders!

No more meet the folks, no more large easy amounts of food, and no more doing laundry daily. It's back to my normal shelter routine and brand new territory. I'm looking forward to getting back out there in a more detached way again. Tomorrow a zero then a glorious new state line, New Jersey, and the third-highest concentration of black bear on the trail. Gulp! It's always something, isn't it?

The Devil's Forehead a.k.a. Lehigh Gap.

Location: Delaware Water Gap
Today's Miles: 0
Total Miles: 1279.0
Date: July 17, 2004

The measurement of a hurricane's destructive power goes by the term category 1, category 2, and up to category 5.

A tornado's destructive power is measured on the Fujita Scale where they're designated as an F1 to a F5.

After two and half months of hiking and exposure to other hikers, I feel it may be in the interest of all concerned to create a measurement on thru-hiker aroma. I'm purposing that this be named the Postcardian Scale of Smell. Designations could be PU-1, PU-2, and up to the very repulsive PU-5. I would also use a graphic icon of a clothespin to further enhance the warning to innocent bystanders.

A hiker with a designation of PU-1 would have an aroma that would cause crinkled nose, flared nostrils, and a turned head upon hugging them.

A PU-3 level might require giving the hiker a five-foot perimeter in a closed room. Any travel in a car with said individual would be with all windows down and your head and nose favoring the opening.

The most destructive and repulsive designation, the formidable PU-5, would pretty much rule out any contact in an enclosed space. A perimeter of fifteen feet would need to be maintained to avoid scorching of the nasal passages and watering of the eyes. Fabrics exposed to PU-5s can never recover; only burning will remedy the stench. Family members of a PU-5 are recommended to perform an intervention with tomato juice. Approaching a PU-5 should be done with extreme caution; the subject could be suffering from *stenchia*, a malady of disorientation. They may try to hug you thinking that you actually want to hug them. Sad but true. You can't hide from the aroma of a PU-5, you can only run, and I suggest you run for all you're worth.

The new scale of smell by yours truly. Let your nose beware.

Location:	Brink Road Shelter
Today's Miles:	24.6
Total Miles:	1303.2
Date:	July 18, 2004

Apparently those famous Pennsylvania rocks do not stop at the state line of New Jersey! I should have taken geology in college then I would have known that the ridgeline the AT follows is the same for both states! Oh well, no bother. Like the mountains we faced down south, the rocks are just something else we move through or over or around.

More importantly is that I crossed my seventh state line of thirteen—and into my eighth state of fourteen. Tonight I'm sleeping in New Jersey, and I'm back to my normal routine of shelter-to-shelter hiking instead of meeting the folks at road crossings. The last ten hours has seen only rain, mist, drizzle, and downpours; and everything is hanging in hopes they'll dry overnight—fat chance! It'll be wet clothing to slip on in the morning. Ah, the joys of thru-hiking.

It's all made a bit more complicated since this tiny shelter is full with seven of us, it sleeps five. One hiker is sleeping on the picnic table that's under the roof's edge since there's no floor space. He apparently doesn't carry a tent or any form of shelter! That's nuts and irresponsible in this hiker's opinion. Another is at our feet sleeping sideways. I don't mind making room for others when it's raining out because someday it'll be me. As we say out here, "There's always room for one more in the shelter when it's raining."

Location:	High Point Shelter
Today's Miles:	19.6
Total Miles:	1323.4
Date:	July 19, 2004

It was another one of those courageous thru-hiker mornings. Yep, had to suck it up and put on wet clothing. It continued to rain all last night and into the morning, the result is nothing had a chance of drying.

The ridgeline was socked in fog and low clouds. Don't ask me what the difference is between the two, and there may not be a difference, but neither allows you to see a whole heck of a lot! But after a short 3.5 miles, I came to NJ 206 road, where a left turn put me in Gyps Pub at 9 a.m. where they made me a breakfast cheeseburger and brewed up some coffee. Another hiker named Amazing Grace was already there, so we waited out the drizzle for an hour while eating. It was an unplanned stop for real food, which are my favorite.

The gray skies gave way to sunshine by 4 p.m. and turned positively beautiful for the rest of the day. The AT was taking us to High Point State Park where you find the High Point Monument, the highest spot in the state of New Jersey. If you don't like the weather in the morning, you can still hike your way into beautiful blue skies, sometimes. I really get to feel the full power of the land and its weather by living out in it for this long of a period. It's unparalleled in my life's experiences, challenging at times but grand.

Location:	Near Long House Road? Maybe.
Today's Miles:	26.0
Total Miles:	1348.8
Date:	July 20, 2004

What a strange ending to a wonderful day. OK, that's the headline, now here's the story.

The morning was beautiful. I headed out at my usual time leaving a full shelter of sleeping hikers. The trail rocks had subsided and eventually replaced with boardwalks. We hiked over many low, boggy, swampy areas; and the only way to get through them was on miles and miles of lumber laid end to end which we step carefully along. Very different from anything we've seen. One boardwalk was quite elaborate; it almost was a pier that stretched a couple of miles through a cattail swamp. I saw a beaver's stick mound house along there.

After a seven-mile beginning, the trail came to the town of Unionville—only Unionville wasn't in New Jersey, but rather New York! Hey, how'd that happen!? I grabbed a pastrami-swiss cheese melt and a whole bunch of other goodies for then and for later at the general store/deli in town. Then it was off for another twelve miles to NJ 94 road. Yea, NJ means New Jersey—somehow I was back in New Jersey!

It's there that a great farmer's market sits ready to sell their fresh baked pies. (Well of course I did—they didn't have apple, so I had an entire peach pie.) What came next was none other than the steepest climb up Wawayanda Mountain. I haven't faced a climb this steep since Albert Mountain back in Georgia. The good news was that it would only be another 5.3 miles to the shelter. That translates for me to less than two hours. Well, two hours came and went—then two and a half. I crossed road after road, none were named, to my displeasure. Then three hours and the hour of 7:30 p.m. drew near. Somehow, after sitting down with the maps, I came to the conclusion that I'd missed the shelter sign and by now was miles past it—wherever it may be. I didn't have a clue, honestly! I knew I was on the AT but nothing else. The next shelter was too far for me—another twelve miles after the shelter I couldn't find.

I will go on record and say that the shelter marking signs in this area are the absolute worst I've come across in the 1,300 miles I've now hiked! The day before, while hiking with Amazing Grace, we both missed the shelter sign we had planned to have lunch at. Both of us missed it. *Couldn't find it* may be more appropriate. These signs are not supposed to be a scavenger hunt! In the meantime, I'm in the woods, somewhere, darkness is coming; and I need to do something very soon.

I pulled out my tent and that is where this is now being written. This is only one reason why it's smart to carry a shelter of some kind, because you just never know. So I'm guessing that today was either a twenty-six or a twenty-eight-mile day. Now if all that wasn't enough to make my day full of texture, just two hours ago I walked around a bend in the trail and right up on a black bear. Yikes! It was a bold sucker 'cause it only ran about fifty feet away and despite my yelling, didn't hightail it away. So if it wasn't going any farther, then I was! Hmm, wonder if it will come visit tonight. It's certainly not boring on the Appalachian Trail. More tomorrow, once I figure out where the heck I am and if I haven't been eaten!

Just me and the silence of the woods tonight—somewhere in New Jersey.

Believe it or not, as well as the Appalachian Trail is marked with white blazes and double white blazes to alert us that a turn or possible trail junction is imminent—hikers find a way to get lost. Really. I met a guy that somehow turned the wrong way back at the Georgia-North Carolina Stateline and was desperately wandering around in the woods for three days before he was found by a park ranger. Despite being rattled and hungry, once pointed in the correct direction, he continued his quest to Maine. At least tonight I can see the AT blazes!

Spooky isn't it?

Is it any wonder why many experience those unnerving feelings that only the silent forests can trigger? We really don't have much history with silence living in the suburbs or cities, do we? Noise, for all its interruptive power, does have an odd way of offering comfort. Do you remember ever turning on a TV or radio to remove the scariness of an empty, silent house when you were a kid? Mountains with their elevation gains may attack our physical abilities on a thru-hike, but it's the emotional challenges that are the real foe. Isolation and loneliness seem to top the list despite the wonderful fellowship that can be found. Hikers invariably find themselves moving in pockets where no one is around; it forces them to confront their own inner strength. It certainly did to me in my first seasons of section hikes years ago. Nighttime only magnifies our frailty, those sounds that go "bump" fuel one of the qualities that truly separate us from all other living creatures, our imagination. The woods are most certainly alive so it's not uncommon to feel you're being watched.

"What was that?" as a chill slivers its way down your spine. During this thru-hike, even with its months of acclimation to silence, I still want, still need, to be at camp before darkness. Even though stopping before dark had practical purposes—drawing and writing my trail journal entries—it kept me from facing the inky abyss and all that lurked within it. I met several brave hikers who thought nothing of hiking into nighttime. Umm, come to think of it, they usually always were hiking with a partner. (Maybe they weren't as brave as I thought.) A few of them shared stories how a particular set of piercing eyes rattled them to the core, and thus ending their nocturnal treks. Others seemed to go out of their way to avoid visiting the woods for those midnight nature calls. Eventually, the unfamiliar becomes familiar. By the time I made Virginia, with calorie deficit in full bloom, many a time I'd get up and walk out into the blackness to eat something without my headlamp on. For me, this was usually a cereal bar or Fritos. I love Fritos, but being quite noisy, moving out into the wooded darkness kept me from waking up the others in the shelter. So often I'd be standing around in the blackness, in the middle of nowhere, with the only weapon being my Spork, grazing like all the other nocturnal wildlife. It's amazing how far a thru-hike can take you!

The photo is real and just one of the many ways nature entertains us on our journey.

Location:	Harriman State Park
Today's Miles:	20.1
Total Miles:	1368.9
Date:	July 21, 2004

Daniel Boone was once asked if he ever got lost while wandering out in the woods. His reply was "No, I was never lost, but I was a might confused for a couple of days."

I packed up the tent this morning and lowered the food bags from the tree and was on the trail early like normal. I had slept really well last night; this tenting thing might need to be done more often. Well, I found that I was indeed where I had reckoned the night before.

Today was an absolute killer. At 8 a.m. I walked into my ninth official state—New York. All of New Jersey is completed. What a glorious morning for the occasion too. At one point on a high rocky out cropping, the pack came off, and I plopped down to gaze at all the beauty; I just hung there doing nothing but looking! Because of last night's extra miles, today would be shorter; I planned to head to town for a motel stay near the trail. By eleven, I emerged from the woods to find a hotdog truck parked and open for business. Its just amazing what you run into out here. So three dogs, chips, and two sodas later, lunch was done. The hotdog truck owner, Joy, let me use her cell phone to call the motel for a reservation. The motel quickly dismissed my inquiry. (Yes, I believe I was snubbed. Later in the day I'd find out that they don't want hikers.) Without the town stop, that added another five miles to the next shelter. Normally that wouldn't cause me much angst, but the terrain of New York was starting to reveal a very ugly side. Remember me describing the Roller Coaster, well that is a kiddy hike compared to what I faced for the next ten plus miles. I'd find out later it's called the Agony Grind. First, there are no switchbacks, its straight up, and then straight down. Deadly! Second, it's totally rock, worse than Pennsylvania. Third, it was ninety degrees with 90 percent humidity. It was miserably hard, the toughest yet by far!!

Halfway through this hell I came upon an ice chest with water at a road crossing. I had already consumed five liters of water and it was only three o'clock. With five-plus miles still to go to the next road and another ten to the shelter, I looked at my profile maps and it showed the terrain would get even harder. Who would want to put a trail here? Anyway, while sitting on the ice chest resting, the water angels left a note saying that if any thru-hiker needed a place to stay, they could assist. They even mentioned that a pay phone was at the road crossing which was just after the trail I was to face. So with their phone number written down, I moved up the trail.

It was so rocky, so steep, so hot, so hard that it was asking everything I had to give. So hostile this day was that as I neared the top of climb four hundred and thirteen, I was startled by a horrific hiss and spitting sound. There eight feet in front of me in this tight rocky space were two six-foot rattlesnakes in full combat mode. They were wrapped around each other and reared up some eighteen inches off the ground. It was fierce! It was at that moment both decided they had something they disliked more than each other—me. One moved down toward me another foot, boy was it angry. I jumped back onto another rock looking for any possible route around the mayhem. Nothing would be easy in this steep slope. I was seriously considering giving up the distance of the climb, but I could see no way to get around this ridge. I stood frozen on that rock for ten minutes more till one of them said uncle and moved off. The champion rattler must have been seven feet, I've never seen anything so menacing!! Eventually, it moved back under a rock, and I double-timed it through the rock pathway with the feeling of heebie-jeebies running down my spine.

Not one of my more favorite moments—literally between a rock and a hard place.

The final decent was practically a gravity fall. It was so steep, my toes were all being smooshed into the toe box of my shoes—painful! What a nutty place for the trail. Totally spent physically and emotionally, I eyed the pay phone and dialed the water angels. I think I sounded a tad desperate—spent, dead—because John and Sue said they'd be there in thirty minutes. They've done my laundry, let me shower, and clean up. We all had a wonderful dinner together in the kitchen and then sat around watching baseball while eating ice cream! Joyful. What a day of contrasts and what trail angels John and Sue are. I sure hope I don't dream of snakes.

Location:	Bear Mountain Inn
Today's Miles:	17.8
Total Miles:	1378.3
Date:	July 22, 2004

Another tough terrain day. Another hot, hazy, and humid day. Are we having fun yet? To cope with the heat, I took my time and took lots of breaks. Fortunately, unlike yesterday, there was a nice breeze. After the harrowing escapade with the two rattlesnakes, I'm afraid I let a harmless five-foot rat snake scare me more than it should; I'm embarrassed to admit. The day also presented me with two big deer bucks. One a ten-pointer, the other an eight. Frankly, I was surprised to see bucks hanging together, didn't know they did that. I seem to be getting wild life in curious pairs lately.

New York seems to be water challenged. It's far from readily available. For the first time since beginning, I had to ration my water for several hours until I found a good flowing brook. I bet I drank close to six liters today, probably close to seven yesterday. This heat in combination with the terrain is tough stuff—if you couldn't tell from my writing. I most certainly will need to dial back the miles or face a horrible, miserable death. The zero I'm taking tomorrow was unplanned, but I know it's the right thing to do. Doing twenty-plus-mile days with no regard to the terrain is asking for trouble, I'm going to slow my pace. This adventure is about fun not misery; it's about adventure not desperate moments. All those days and miles earlier have given me the option to slow down, to linger more. There's time enough to get to Mt. Katahdin, in fact, I think the third week in September is more likely. Accidentally, I glanced at the mileage remaining in this 2,174.1-mile journey, which I've avoided beautifully until tonight. It read 786.8.

Location:	Bear Mountain Inn
Today's Miles:	0
Total Miles:	1378.3
Date:	July 23, 2004

It's called the Lemon Squeezer, and it's bitter! Even with all the weight I've lost, I still had to remove my pack to fit through.

New York isn't all bad as I'm making it out to be, it's just full of texture. This morning I got a great look at the huge Bear Mountain Bridge that spans the Hudson River—can't wait to cross it tomorrow.

It's nice not doing anything, just watching TV in the room. This zero couldn't have been better timed, its been pouring rain for the last six hours. Those rocks and steep ups and downs get a whole lot more interesting when wet!

I want to hike shorter distances through this section, but the shelter distances are way, way far apart. I'd have to do twenty-five-plus miles tomorrow if I want a shelter. Since tomorrow's forecast is rain and the distance is long and the terrain unknown, I've considered another zero, however, I will still hike tomorrow and hope for the best! Making miles is what I do.

Location:	RPH Shelter
Today's Miles:	26.0
Total Miles:	1413.3
Date:	July 24, 2004

The last several days have been challenging due to the heat, humidity, terrain, and trail rockiness. I've noticed how its been influencing my writing, and maybe you have too, I seem to be talking much about the hardships. Well, today that stops because its boring to do so, and besides, the trail was simply glorious all day! The hard rain of yesterday was a cold front down from Canada; it moved all the way through last night giving us hikers sunshine and cool breezes. What a difference a day can make as the saying goes. My timing on that zero was awesome. Say goodbye to the heat and the humidity. On top of that, the trail itself grew smoother, thanks to all the years of oak, maple, and countless other leaves that have piled up to make a nice mulch—wonderful on the soles

Even this shelter is unusually good; it's sort of a house that someone pulled one end off. The water source is a mere ten steps to an old-fashioned water pump; the water though has a lousy taste, most likely from its yellow tint. I have one of the six bunks inside for tonight and if that wasn't special enough, this place even has chairs!! Chairs, can you believe it, one of the great inventions of the civilized world. That alone would make for a great end to the day. However, according to the shelter register, a pizza place delivers. A road passes only one hundred feet from here, so it looks like we'll be eating real food, Yeehaw. Did I die and go to trail heaven? (All we need is a hiker carrying a cell phone, I got rid of mine after week three. Score, a hiker named Space Monkey 2000 has one.)

Before I say good night, I'd share with you one more good fortune. Before the Italian food showed up, a pickup truck arrived and two people got out with lots of bags. It was Socks and her husband, they drove forty-five minutes from their home to bring trail magic to all of us pathetic hikers. (Apparently Socks was recuperating from a broken ankle she got in the Whites of New Hampshire.) They've brought dessert; two kinds of ice cream with various toppings, fruit blend sodas and lots of cookies! So we all gladly ate our dessert before dinner. Kind of makes you feel like a kid.

Can you believe this day? The kindness of great people like them and so many others continue to take the whole adventure to another more special level!

Crossing the Hudson River marks the beginning of the New England area for me.
Not that the motorist would notice, but the AT White Blazes are painted right on the bridge.

Location: Wiley Shelter
Today's Miles: 25.6
Total Miles: 1438.9
Date: July 25, 2004

So much for doing shorter mileage days. It was so nice to head out this morning with the cool weather; there was a definite feel of fall in the breeze.

The highlights today involved some really big oak trees. The first came early in the morning; it had a trunk circumference of about sixteen feet. Guessing it was about 250 years old and right on the AT, come to think of it, all the big ones were right on the AT. The second, pictured here, is said to be the AT's largest. It's so big it has a name—the Dover Oak. Its circumference is larger than that of the Keffer Oak back in Virginia. The Dover Oak is estimated to be around 350 years old; it's massively large, but it didn't look as towering as the Keffer. Later in the day the trail took me past some other large oaks I'd guess to be 150 years in age, just mere pups.

When I arrived here at the shelter I met a whole new group of hikers. Included was a man who thru-hiked two years ago and kept an Internet trail journal like mine. Before I left on this adventure I discovered it, which made for good reading. His name is Big Red. We sat and just talked trail for hours, it was great fun—he's an awesome person. Big Red's been out hiking some sections with his trail buddy Sunset, who's on his second thru-hike. He and Big Red met two years earlier during their thru-hikes. Anyway, before Big Red even introduced himself, I knew who he was from his journal photo.

By keeping my family and friends aware of the hike by posting an Internet journal, I've met others along the journey that upon hearing my trail name say, "Oh my god, I'm reading your journal." It has happened a bunch of times. It's a great feeling to meet those who I've been able to entertain and share the experience. For many, the time in life isn't right to attempt a thru-hike and so they travel along with the hikers through those journals.

The conversation with everyone was warm and wonderful, a nice compliment to the campfire. It was also nice to hang with a group of people who are my age or older. A nice change for once. In the morning, in only a short 1.2 miles, I leave the Empire State, New York, and walk across another state line. Don't blink; they're coming pretty quick.

Connecticut, here I come.

The Dover Oak is estimated to be around 350 years old.

Location:	Kent, Connecticut
Today's Miles:	12.7
Total Miles:	1451.6
Date:	July 26, 2004

I do love this part of the country. The trees are big and mature, the houses are all clabbered board with shutters—and when not painted the traditional white and black, they're all sorts of colonial colors perfectly matched with color accents and trim. This is the land of early America, affluent and very Norman Rockwellian. The towns have village greens and teak wood park benches, which have all turned silver with age. Kent, unlike Sharon, is a bit more bohemian with all the youth running around in tie-dye and body piercing. It is also home of the Kent boarding school for high school years at a nice $32,000 a year!

I crossed the state line in the woods, no marker of any kind, just a mileage reckoning based on my elapsed time and was immediately greeted by the picturesque Ten-Mile River. This region feels different; it has an air of age and history to me, an intangible richness. When I lived in New York City some years ago, most in the summer would head to the famous, posh, see-and-be-seen area called the Hampton's. Not me, I found my compass directing me north along the Hudson River where the hills are rolling and quiet ponds and streams abound. It was here on a day hike in Connecticut that my foot first touched the Appalachian Trail. Little did I know then that the seed and need for more of my childhood outdoor life, and my too long self-imposed imprisonment of living in Metropolis would lead me to this great adventure.

I reached the road into town early, about 11 a.m., and started to walk in rather than hitch. That's when Big Red found me. He'd hitched in from an earlier road crossing to pick up his car and help his bud, Sunset, get the town chores done and back out to the trail. Big Red, as I mentioned before, is just a great, warm human being. I could definitely see myself hanging with him if not for his section hike being over.

The three of us went for cheeseburgers before parting, and then it would be a long drive for Big Red back to Ohio after he got Sunset back to the trailhead. Within a short five hours in town, I managed to polish off eggs benedict with mashed potatoes and vegetables, a cheeseburger, vanilla malt, and then a big salad and a bigger entrée of chicken-and-shrimp picata with rice and veggies. Of course, a beer or two or three also helped to boost the calorie count! Hey, if I don't eat, there might not be any of me left to climb Katahdin. So I must eat, eat, eat because I must walk, walk, walk!

Not surprisingly, the prices of rooms and food in this yuppiedom are higher. But what the heck, I'm working as hard as I ever have—I deserve it!

The Weather Channel is predicting heavy rain with flooding for the northeast tomorrow—great! All this water is good for the skin.

A postcard welcoming us to the tenth state of the thru-hike.

Sharon, Connecticut
16.0
1467.5
July 27, 2004

Despite the forecast, I saw my shadow today several times. It was sort of soft and fuzzy for a shadow, but still there was enough glare from the sun to have one. After a climb up and over a mountain ridgeline, the AT descends to parallel the Housatonic River for nearly five beautifully flat miles. It was a great stroll; lots of children from summer camps were out for day hikes. I think when seeing me they thought I was homeless.

Since I resupplied in Kent, the pack weight was back up a bit, I had planned only a seventeen-mile day accordingly. The next several days would all be twenties. With most of today's journey done by 1 p.m., I started to climb what would be the first of seven mountain ascents that would deliver me to my night's destination. Well, that was the plan.

About halfway up the mountain I was joined by a springer spaniel. She was a sweetheart of a dog and apparently was adopting me as her hiking buddy. After the first mile I was sure she'd turn back and head home, I assumed she must live close by. Anyway, one mile became five or six, and she wasn't going anywhere without me. Her collar said "Kona," and she had tags with a phone number. After she hung with me for a couple of hours, I was pretty sure she was lost. As a result of seeing countless postings on trees for lost dogs from here to Georgia, I was fairly predisposed to recognize one when I saw it. I came upon a road crossing and flagged a car down; the woman understood my plight and lived nearby. I tied my bear bag rope around Kona, and we waited for the woman to go home and call the phone number on the collar. Quickly she returned and said that Kona lived a town or two over the mountain, and she didn't mind taking her over. I was so relieved. I was sure there was a little girl somewhere wondering with sadness as to where her lovely Kona had gone. The delay in the day was enough for me to decide to hop in the lady's minivan and get dropped off in Sharon and out of the rain, which had been falling for the last several hours. Another night of being dry and another dinner in town, two of my most favorite things.

Here in Sharon, there's only one restaurant opened on Tuesday night, and it doesn't open till 5:30 p.m. So for the last hour I've been sitting on the marble stoop of the Sharon Town Hall to get out of the rain, write today's journal entry, and let the time pass till I sit down with a bottle of red wine and eeny-meeny-miney-mull-over the Italian menu. I wonder if anyone else will be wearing rain gear.

So from beautiful Sharon, Connecticut, I'll wish you all a good day, good eating, and a warm bed. I did a good deed today for one of God's gentle creatures, and it has me feeling joyful. Just another postcard from the Appalachian Trail.

Even on rainy days, you can enjoy the splendor of the wilderness.

Location:	Salisbury, Connecticut
Today's Miles:	16.8
Total Miles:	1484.3
Date:	July 28, 2004

I awoke without the normal fretting of rain. The stalled front (stalled, meaning "pain-in-the-ass") was promising hard rain for the morning. But with a reservation for tonight in a dry, quintessential Connecticut inn, I didn't have a whole lot of worries. The taxi service arrived at 7 a.m. and by 7:15, I was back at the road crossing where Kona and I had left the trail. Helping Kona get back to her family yesterday had given me an inner smile—if that makes sense.

The first six miles had several ups and downs, I was careful with my footing all day. Rocks and roots become as slippery as ice when wet. I've gone nearly 1,500 miles without an injury, no reason to get careless now. Sometimes with even the most cautious of stepping, you're going to go down. You can't imagine how slick surfaces can get out here.

All morning I hiked in the clouds with company. My "company," thanks to all the wetness were those little orange-red salamanders I'd met many states ago. First there was one, then two, and three—before long I was counting number twenty with no end in sight. Before I left that mountain section, my count surpassed that record number of forty-six back on Roan Mountain in Virginia. Seventy-one of those little critters came out to hike the wet trail with me, establishing a new tally record.

As the rain subsided, once again I got to see my shadow. The miles flew by, somehow I've lost track of how fast I can now walk this rugged trail. Whether it's up or down or the pleasant flat, and although I'm ever ready to stop at a vista, or pause near a picturesque stream, the distances seem to take less time now. I've always had a pretty good pace to my walk, thanks to working in New York City all those years, but with my newly acquired agility and fitness, I'm even faster without being conscious of it.

These past couple of days I've been shortening the miles to accommodate my new planned four-town escapade. Last night while having dinner in Sharon, I decided to enjoy this area all the more by hiking to these charming townships each night and staying in a B&B or inn. A tad expensive, but it's added a lot of variety to the adventure. I love how the unplanned (finding Kona) has led to a new plan full of texture.

This sure is fun!

Thanks to a rainy morning, the little critters of the forest came out to hike the AT with me today. I counted a record seventy-one on just one mountain.

White Oak

There are trees along the trail that may be taller, but none are as old or with as much girth on their trunk. The Keffer Oak in Virginia is a monster, estimated to be over three hundred years old. Up north, it's the Dover Oak that's said to be larger in trunk diameter, eighteen-plus feet, and is thought to be 350 years old. Regardless, each is massive and majestic in their own right, a wonderful treat to behold.

Location:	South Egremont, Massachusetts
Today's Miles:	18.5
Total Miles:	1502.8
Date:	July 29, 2004

Welcome to Massachusetts! Don't blink or you may just miss another state line.

It was a morning that echoed the feeling of fall. A nice breeze had the low sixty-degree temps hovering near the fifties. It was crisp, brisk, and altogether awesome! The day provided some great views from Race Mountain and Mt. Everett. The climbs as I move north are starting to get higher again. Although we've had many ups and downs, the collection of them has remained at a lower elevation. That now is changing. I left Connecticut on Bear Mountain—a different one from New York. It's their highest point, which also had great views. As I reached MA 41, I whipped out the "Hiker to Town" bandana and *boom*, the first car pulled over. My those words have power.

Had a great dinner at the Egremont Inn and went to bed early. I'll be getting a bit of a late start from here tomorrow since breakfast doesn't start till 8:30 a.m. Then the owner will run myself and another hiker back to the trailhead.

Yesterday's stay at the White Hart Inn in Salisbury. The quintessential Connecticut stop.

Location:	Mt. Wilcox North Lean-To
Today's Miles:	17.1
Total Miles:	1519.9
Date:	July 30, 2004

Never since leaving Springer Mountain have I witnessed such an explosion of mosquitoes. It's as if I crossed the state line into Massachusetts and someone said "Release the skeeters!"

At one area when I stopped to adjust some straps at least fifty or more landed on me. My face and hands were covered in 100 percent DEET, as well as the entire underside of my hat's brim. It helps, can't imagine how maddening it would be without the toxic stuff? I'm sure using it will cause one of my body parts to fall off, but there's not a lot of choice in the matter frankly. And so I'm not guilty of only speaking of hardships, I'll mention how this section of America is so rich and dense in foliage. One of my favorite trees, the bright white birch trees are massive out here on the trail. They, with their snowy white bark, have such purity.

Three months ago today, I said farewell to my folks down in Georgia and began the Approach Trail.

The question that I'm getting most now from strangers is "When will you finish?" The answer to that question is anyone's guess. I still am only focusing on each day, one at a time. I'm not counting down mileage or leaping ahead with calendar guesses. I want to stay in the moment and guard my expectations. It's still a long way and a lot can happen if I shift my thinking.

As I get into Maine, possibly three weeks more, I may have a better sense of it. For now, its northward to Maine and letting this grand adventure grow and grow.

One surprise today just five miles short of this lean-to, that's what they call the shelters up here in New England, I was sitting on the shoulder of a busy road having lunch since that was the only place without biting skeeters. A car abruptly slowed and pulled into the roadside parking area and yelled out his window, "Trail magic!" Yahoo! His name was Skipper, and he thru-hiked in 2001. But today he was sticking an ice cold Bud in my hand and some peanut butter crackers and cookies. That first swallow of icy cold beer on this extremely hazy, hot, and humid day was pure bliss!

Tomorrow I wake to my official third-month anniversary on the Appalachian Trail. *Wow!*

Aside from evergreens, birch trees have been a longtime favorite of mine.

Location:	October Mountain Lean-To
Today's Miles:	22.8
Total Miles:	1542.7
Date:	July 31, 2004

For my third-month anniversary, the trail gave me a present of sorts—a renewed hiker friendship. I was sitting on a rock having a snack when I heard hiking sticks coming up behind me. It was Rainy J, who I hadn't seen since Fontana Dam just before entering the Smokys two and a half months ago. Bilbo came around the corner next, hadn't seen him in over a month—and then good ol' Goose showed up. I yelled, "Goooose," and he said, "Oh my god!" I've been three to four days behind those guys forever. I wasn't trying to catch them; I just figured they always would maintain that distance. Apparently they all took three days off at Bilbo's house and then there they were, like magic!

We were all stunned, they as much as me that I was in front of them! That's an unusual aspect of the trail that does happen a lot. Hikers disappear then reappear like magic constantly. Wonderful trail surprises. Heart-lifting discoveries when you least expect it.

After crossing over the Mass Turnpike, Rainy J's parents had driven up to give out sandwiches and sodas and, well, everything, awesome trail magic. Tonight we're all here in the shelter. Happy anniversary to me!! But tomorrow, Sunday, I head into Dalton to pick up my next mail drop on Monday morning. So I'll be zeroing there to get these seven-day smelly clothes clean. As a result, they'll move on ahead. I may or may not see them again, come what may, it was good to see them today.

Location:	Dalton, Massachusetts
Today's Miles:	12.8
Total Miles:	1554.0
Date:	August 1, 2004

I've heard Maine was dense and dark under the foliage where if you plan it wrong during certain seasons, you'll be eaten alive by all the mosquitoes and black fly. Well, if Maine is worse than Massachusetts, I'll be forgoing food and carrying a gallon of 100 percent DEET! I can't wait to get to higher elevations where the air is colder, or maybe I'll hope for an early cold snap to kill them all off. It's offering a whole new challenge.

Anyway, made it through the bog, swamp, flooded area today on the way to Dalton. Being Sunday, the only thing I can get done is eating and resting, so tomorrow will be a zero.

Location:	Dalton, Massachusetts
Today's Miles:	0
Total Miles:	1554.0
Date:	August 2, 2004

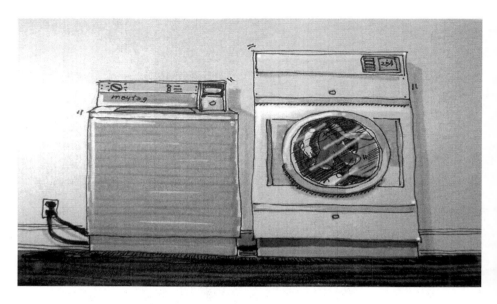

My two new favorite machines: the washer and dryer. The great thing about hiker clothes is that high-tech fabrics dry in a blink of an eye. So a visit to the Laundromat is never longer than forty-five minutes. I never remember laundry being so effortless. It was always something to avoid. You know, with those big baskets loaded beyond full. But now, with so very little that we carry and the promise of clean-smelling, crisp, and strangely stiff garments void of miles and miles of dirt, it is something I always look forward to. My how the trail changes us.

Afterward, it was over to pick up my mail drop and stop in for a visit to the Dalton Public Library for free Internet. I caught up with Carp through e-mail who five days ago was in Palmerton, Pennsylvania—the Devil's Forehead area as I call it. That means I'm about two weeks ahead. Spoke to Belle last night, and she's planning on coming up with her good friends to their house in Franconia Notch, New Hampshire—better known as The Whites—when I get near there. Which is rapidly approaching.

Although I've been hiking solo for some time now, I'm not lonely. The many new discoveries I hike into each day keeps me filled with excitement and smiles. I really like hiking the woods and mountains this way. And besides, its not like I'm by myself, there's quite a few of us out here moving solo. We run into one another frequently. I've actually had a pattern where I seem to meet and then overlap with a new hiker about every two weeks. This overlap in turn, lasts in some cases a week, where I might see them each day. It's a connection, albeit a loose one. But the point that I'm really trying to say is how much stronger emotionally the trail has enabled me to become. It wasn't always that way.

At the time the Appalachian Trail found me two years ago, my life seemed strangely similar to what Tom Hanks's character faced at the end of the movie *Cast Away*—particularly when he was standing in the crossroads, wondering where the tide of life would take him? It was an odd place for someone who always knew where he was going. It's been said that many who hike the AT are misfits or are running away. For me, having been blessed with being able to stand on the top step of the corporate ladder and ask the question "So why aren't I happy?" it would be more accurate to say I was running both to and from something. Running to beauty and simplicity; Running from hype and posturing. Running to fresh breezes and deep forest and running from politics and mediocrity.

Despite being in close proximity to millions of people, I know that for some time I felt terribly lonely. Not too unusual for city living singles I've heard. When I think back now, I can admit that I ran from my own emotional unhappiness. I've met the right woman, but unfortunately at the wrong time. Chasing career during my earlier years was rewarding, however, my priorities were off kilter. More common to most single people though was the scenario of the wrong woman at the right time or the wrong woman at the wrong time. Still with me? It seems that finding the right woman at the right time has been as difficult to find as the treasure of the Sierra Madre. And so, I'm still single.

Additionally, as the years march on, I've found that my core group of friends has been drifting apart year after year. A pretty normal event when new jobs take us to different time zones or children are born and buddies become fathers. Life happens. What somehow eluded me from understanding early on was that the downside of chasing a career is that may be all you'll end up with! So take some advice from someone on the other side and give your soul mate a hug and tell them how lucky you are to have found them.

Continuing along this mental assessment path at the time I decided to first hike the AT, I frankly didn't have a clue to how strong emotionally you'd need to be to thru-hike. My professional ego had misled the rest of me into thinking that all was copasetic. But here's a news flash, an interesting personal dynamic takes place while hiking, one that I never thought would be an issue. Having never married, its not unusual to spend a bit of time with one's self. However, this changes in the wilderness. As I mentioned earlier, when you live in a city, you're single. But when you live in the woods, you're alone. This transformation on past occasions proved to be my biggest adversary. In a way that seems quite obvious now, but wasn't then, my hiking and the solo time it imposed upon me became a glaring metaphor for my life. That is to say, going it alone. Talk about beating yourself up! Just pass me the Raman Noodles with arsenic sauce and I'll boil some water and be done with it. But we get better. Thank you Lord. So I tend to be a bit more empathetic toward others when I detect they're having a tough time of it. Without a joyful spirit, facing the many physically difficult aspects of the trail can play havoc with your will to go on. Its certainly no secret how few actually finish a thru-hike. Things happen. Moods weaken. Some will come off the trail simply because what they wanted to experience has and the motivation has evolved. The ones I feel for are those who come off the trail at a moment of despair, who really didn't want to but they couldn't step outside of the situation they got mired in.

Currently, I'm sitting at the counter in Dalton's Restaurant stuffing my face, the TV in the background just informed me that the rainfall for the month of July was more than double the average. In fact, it was the fifth wettest! Borrowing from a childhood phrase—duh!?!?

This hike has taken me to many a main street. Here I am just hanging out, seeing, feeling, and visiting our land. It's really a unique experience on top of the other entire wilderness ones. Understanding all that the Appalachian Trail is before you begin is next to impossible. Case in point, it never occurred to me how abundant the wildlife would be. Or that hitching into town would prove so easy, or that running around town on foot doing the necessary errands never proved to be a burden.

A true adventure in a modern world, it may be the hardest thing you will ever ask of yourself physically and possibly the most challenging mental-emotional test you may ever face as well. To clearly define all of what the AT is would be quite difficult since it manifests itself on the individual in so many varied ways. It is one thing if not all things. And it is all those things simultaneously and randomly. Simply put, it just is and it is our interaction with it that creates the joys and sorrows. It is for that reason why our true Achilles is our outlook. I find it a terrible shame to know individuals who cannot see the brighter side of life. And frankly, I go out of my way to limit my time in their company.

But beneath all the physical and emotional demands that will be ask of you on a thru-hike, there is the ever-present beauty of nature. Sky's and clouds and trees and valleys and well earned vista's that fill a heart with pride and awe. Your eyes will glimpse the power of this Earth and the breeze will serenade your ears. From sunrise to sunset and every New moon, you'll breathe a freshness that can't be found in the cities. It is intoxicating. If you're not careful, you'll find yourself standing a bit taller, walking with your head angled slightly higher. Once you are truly touched by this grandeur, you will never be the same.

Life is on a level of ten right now, just amazing! I hope you're having as much fun as I am.

Scarlet Tanager

*Probably the most vivid bird on the journey. The one I met was quite brave;
it remained sitting on a branch across the trail in Virginia until
I was only three feet away. Probably couldn't handle my aroma.*

Location:	Mt. Greylock Summit
Today's Miles:	17.0
Total Miles:	1571.5
Date:	August 3, 2004

It's a dramatic night to a surprising day. With the prospect of climbing up Massachusetts's highest mountain—Mt. Greylock—and doing it on a day the Weather Channel forecasts thunderstorms rolling in around 5 p.m., I embraced my "move with purpose" attitude from the start. But when I arrived at the summit with seventeen miles done, most of them up hill by 1:30 p.m., I was still surprised at such an early arrival. I honestly don't know how the miles are clicking off so quickly. A pair of other hikers I met and moved on past on the ascent—"Beagle" and "Moo Juice"— later would tell me that I move very smoothly without effort. I've always been very coordinated, it seems that has benefited my feet. Regardless, I was here early, which offered a lot of quality relaxing time. I even took a nap!

The drama of tonight is coming from that thunderstorm that's moving through. Here on Mt. Greylock, we're on top of the world, so the lightning and wind is unobstructed. We're getting the full force of nature's power. I love it.

Bascom Lodge sits here on the summit and provides rooms and bunk space for about sixty people. But tonight for the lodge dinner, there were only six of us; and one of the guests who comes here often, is sharing his red wine. How nice is that!? Just perfect with the Italian planned menu. The rain and lightning are putting on a great show. Hopefully the force of the front means it may blow on past, giving me cool, favorable hiking weather tomorrow. One can only hope.

Sitting in front of Bascom Lodge is the real point of interest up here. A war memorial by the people of Massachusetts. With its internal spiral staircase, you can climb up this lighthouselike monument to get a 360° view; I was particularly struck by the vast distance to the southern horizon. It was only a few days ago that I was there. It truly was looking back in time. Something not many of us can do. It also allowed me to look to my future and know that there was nothing before me that I could not conquer if I so wanted to. Step by step anything is possible.

In the successful Bill Bryson book *A Walk in the Woods*, he wrote that upon seeing a particular four-foot-tall-by-six-inch-wide map of the Appalachian Trail, he and his sidekick Katz realized that after one month on the trail and only traveling a mere two inches of its four-foot height, they'd never be able to finish. A copy of that very same map which burst their optimistic bubble is hanging here in my room at the lodge. After looking it over, it too left me speechless but for a different reason. Instead of only two inches, it seems I have traveled more than three feet!

The war memorial atop Mt. Greylock, Massachusetts's highest mountain.

Location:	Congdon Shelter
Today's Miles:	20.4
Total Miles:	1591.9
Date:	August 4, 2004

With breakfast served at Bascom Lodge not till 8 a.m., I got on the trail later than normal. Feeling really strong I was able to put the miles quickly behind me. Along the way, I came upon a hiker whose name I'd been seeing in the registers for three months. Her name is "I Need a Hug." A nice woman.

At 1 p.m. the trail led me over the Massachusetts-Vermont state line. That's number 11! So I'm now in Vermont, the land of maple syrup. Mistakenly, I somehow thought the trail would be pleasant—*wrong!* The AT joins another trail called the Long Trail for 97 of its 263 miles. I believe the Long Trail is the first long-distance trail ever made in America; unfortunately, the condition of it in this section is abysmal! Simply dreadful! Not quite a trail so much as a mud bog. The rocks and roots I've whined about in the past now were a blessing. If it weren't for them, there'd be no place to put your feet other than in ankle-deep muck. So Vermont isn't making a very good first impression!

One curious thing I saw today was a rather large hoof print in the mud—a moose. How cool is that? I would love to see a moose in the wild while being on the trail. Moose are so funny looking with their long skinny legs and cute face. And those bull moose with those huge antlers, now that's what I hope to see while on the trail. Tomorrow morning, I make a detour at the next road crossing into the town of Bennington to pick up my third pair of hiking shoes. The first pair lasted six hundred miles. This second pair has lasted one thousand miles. Hopefully my third will be enough to get me all the way to the top of Mt. Katahdin. I'll put them on and ship the old ones back to the folks and hitch out of town so I can still make miles. That will allow me to either make Manchester on Friday or early Saturday morning where I can get my other new item—a new tent. My current tent has a big condensation problem—to use it means having a wet tent by morning, and wet means heavy! Due to poor ventilation, my breathing turns the interior tent walls into a dripping mess of moisture. Not good.

Met some other nice thru-hikers today too; we're all here at the shelter waiting for another big line of thunder showers to move in tonight. Here are April Showers, Alleghany, Don't Mind and Don't Matter, and Speak Up. Twenty-mile days does have a way of introducing you to new people.

Getting sleepy, so I'll say good night. Welcome to Vermont, everyone.

A nice beaver lodge in muddy, boggy Vermont.

Location:	Kid Gore Shelter
Today's Miles:	18.7
Total Miles:	1610.6
Date:	August 5, 2004

The rain came in last night to add wetness to the misery that is the mud-bog section of the Vermont AT.

April Showers and I were first out this morning, and so we were first to come upon the flooded beaver pond. The trail actually went into knee-high deep water. Since we couldn't see the trail, we detoured around, bushwhacking our way through the woods. We made it to the VA 9 road crossing by 8:40 a.m., and April Showers's husband arrived at 8:41! He had driven her winter stuff up from Connecticut since the temps tonight are going to dip toward the low forties, which had her a bit concerned she'd turn into a popsicle.

They drove me into Bennington's post office so I could pick up my third pair of hiking shoes. I did a quick change right there in the post office with everyone in line asking me all kinds of questions about the hike. I had gotten all their attention when I made a public apology to the entire group there in line for my thru-hiker aroma. They all laughed but maintained their distance. Then the three of us headed back to the trailhead, but of course I talked them into breakfast at the diner—my treat. So not only did I get my new shoes effortlessly in a town five miles away, I also got breakfast and a couple of sandwiches to go for the trail in no less than an hour and half. How sweet is that!?

April Showers and I then met Luna for the first time at the trailhead, she's been hiking north since Tennessee for about three months with a large section. Luna has another month before she has to stop and head back for college. She's hoping to get to the New Hampshire-Maine state line. All three of us hiked together to this shelter. Throughout the day the forecasted cold front moved in resulting in some chilllllly breezes. We have others here too, and everyone chipped in to make a nice campfire, just what we needed.

Saw another moose print near the end of today, and Luna just said she heard something rather large over by the privy, but the darkness kept it a mystery. How would any of you like to experience that just before bed? Another unique AT experience.

Luna wearing her purple Hawaiian hiking lei at Kid Gore Shelter.

Location:	Spruce Peak Shelter
Today's Miles:	22.9
Total Miles:	1633.5
Date:	August 6, 2004

Before I talk about today, I need to mention how amazing the location of last night's shelter was. It sits on a hill without trees in front, so you can see the valley beyond—maybe fifty miles. After we all turned in, the temps continued to drop. At one point around 2 a.m., I noticed a glow on the inside of the shelter.

I rolled around to look outside and was given a mighty treat. It was a beautiful moonrise over the valley with thin wisps of clouds. The colder temps had the air so clear, the moons brightness, although at half-wane, still lit up the shelter's interior. But, man, oh man, was it cold! I guess mid-thirties. We hadn't faced temperatures like that since starting back in the springtime. Fortunately, as sunrise came, it too flooded the shelter interior and got us all moving with its warmth.

I planned a long day to get me close to Manchester and its post office's limited hours on Saturday—closes at noon. The mileage was more than Luna and April Showers wanted to do, but I had to get my mail drop and new tent. I didn't want to hike beyond them, but I had to.

By 8:30 a.m. I came upon a perfect picture postcard—a beaver pond. The surface was like a mirror and the morning light ideal. It was a moment! I was riveted to its beauty, just couldn't make myself walk without stopping a dozen times to gaze at it!

It wasn't long before I started up Stratton Mountain; the journey was a rewarding climb through those aromatic balsam fir Christmas trees. The fragrance was like walking around a Christmas tree lot. Once at the summit, thanks to a bright sun, the unusually chilly day was tolerable to have lunch. But when clouds moved over blocking its rays, the temperature plummeted to about forty. I was freezin' my newly acquired boney ass off. I could stay and shiver or hike and get warm. I cut lunch short and moved on to get off the summit. As I dropped in elevation, the warmth returned. With a few miles still to go, I noticed that a moose had been walking the trail quite recently. Its hoofprints were on top of the hiker's boot prints. I started to yell out, "Here, moose, moose!" Why? Beats me? Anyway, it's pretty wild to be walking where there are moose moving around. I mean you see horses and cows all the time, but a moose! Now that's wilderness!!

The trail delivers another picture-perfect postcard.

Location:	Manchester, Vermont
Today's Miles:	2.7
Total Miles:	1636.3
Date:	August 7, 2004

This amazing trail that is constantly delivering surprises gave me the biggest one yet.

It all starts last year, when I went down to Georgia with the intention to hike all the miles on the AT I hadn't already done. This would be a rather large, 1,800-mile section hike, not a thru-hike. On my first day of what would only be a week out, I met Damp Dan. For the entire week, he and I hiked each day to the same location. A nicer guy you will not meet! But issues at home forced me to leave my hike after only the first week. Damp Dan, however, completed what some say was the hardest of years to thru-hike due to excessive rain. He made it the whole way—a huge achievement!

Later that year I contacted him to congratulate him and to ask for his counsel on my own thru-hike this year. Throughout this journey, I've dropped him a postcard or two. While in Dalton, Massachusetts, I answered his e-mail congratulating me on my progress.

Well, Damp Dan and his wife Mary live outside of Boston. He figured with my current pace I'd be arriving in Manchester on Saturday morning, and since we hiked together before, he knew my pattern. So he and Mary hatched a plan.

Meanwhile, back on the mountain, I wake up Saturday morning early and pack up without breakfast to start the short 2.7 miles to the road where I'll try to hitch into town. As I emerge from the woods at 7:23 a.m. and cross the road, I see a man walking over toward me. He says, "I want to ask you a question."

I don't totally know what else he said because the memory banks start processing his voice and then it hit me—holy cow, its Damp Dan! I screamed his name in shock. Mary and he had driven four hours the night before and then parked right at this trail crossing by 7 a.m. because he knew I would be off the mountain early. I was stunned at this incredible act of trail magic and kindness! Damp Dan said he knew I'd need a ride into town with his wry smile. Holy cow, holy cow!

We went into Manchester and had breakfast and just talked and talked. They shared stories of their month hike in France, and I shared stories of the AT. When I asked what they were planning for the day, Damp Dan informed me that they were here for me and wherever I needed to go they'd go. Wow. We all went to the Laundromat, then to the outfitters and supermarket and of course the post office for my food drop and new tent. Later that day they dropped over for wine at the guesthouse I had a room at. With me by now was April Showers and Luna, they made it in midday, and we all shared a room at Sutton's Place.

The five of us laughed and talked out on the back patio before dinner. When it was time to say good night, Damp Dan and Mary offered to take us back to the trailhead. But Luna and April Showers would need to run morning errands early, so I told them it wouldn't be necessary.

As I sat in their car saying good night, I was almost speechless at how to thank them. Damp Dan had been treated so well by others on his thru-hike the year before, he simply wanted to return the kindness. Pass it forward!

I gave Mary a kiss on the cheek and shook Dan's hand. My heart was two times its normal size. If you've not seen the better side of humanity in the world you live in, try hiking the AT. You'll be amazed at what will find you! Thank you, Damp Dan! Thank you, Mary! You both are the best of what this world has. You've filled me with so much joy, I will keep my promise and pass it forward.

To Damp Dan and Mary Dempsey for AT trail magic of the highest order.

Moose

To see a moose while deep in the woods, that's wilderness. Cows are charming, horses majestic, but it's the moose that says I'm out on an adventure. The bulls can exceed 1,200 pounds. April Showers and Luna, who were hiking just behind me, came up on a cow and her calf before the shelter. For me, it's been nothin' but hoofprints. I suppose I'll just have to just keep hiking till I see the real thing.

Balsam Fir

What makes a fir different from other conifers? Their cones grow standing straight up on top of the branch. Their color, being purple-green is also unique in the world of cones.
When the cones mature, they drop both the seeds and scales to the ground, leaving a pencil-like center standing. Legend says these spikes first inspired the Germanic people to decorate their trees with candles or lights. So, that's how it started. Balsam firs reach forty to sixty feet and prefer cool, moist, or shaded places. That's why I always saw them up high in the fog-and-cloud-covered summits.

Location:	Lost Pond Shelter
Today's Miles:	14.8
Total Miles:	1651.1
Date:	August 8, 2004

Due to a large horse show in the Manchester area, obtaining a room, an affordable one that is, was not a simple find. As a result, Luna and April Showers stayed with me in my room at the guesthouse. Sleeping with two beautiful women does sound either quite risqué or terribly lucky of me. But on the AT it happens all the time. Really.

We share rooms, we sleep alongside each other, only inches apart, out in the middle of nowhere; and it's all harmless. Don't get me wrong, there's plenty of romance on the trail, but for the most part, its largely platonic. Since April Showers preferred hiking with someone, her husband actually offered up the notion of me hooking up with her. Wow, what a guy.

Shacking up, AT style, saves motel money leaving more cash for food. As in everything else in life, it all comes down to the chemistry of the individuals.

Having checked out, we all headed to Up for Breakfast with our packs—a great Belgian waffle and double order of bacon for me. Delicious. But with multiple errands to run, Luna and April Showers weren't ready to head back to the trail till 11 a.m. Normally this late of a start might have had me antsy, but I do enjoy their company, so no bother. We hitched up to the trailhead in the back of a dump truck! Hey, whatever works.

Another brisk fall day in August. Every time we'd stop, we'd all start shivering. Tonight, we have the shelter to ourselves, and I managed to get a fire going in spite of all the damp wood. The hike took us up into more large stands of balsam fir trees or what I'm starting to call Christmas Land. The scent is just magical—very holidaylike, and I'm such a big kid at heart. It reminds me of when I was four and the folks took my sister and me to Santa's Village in the mountains surrounding Southern California. It was an enchanting place for a four-year-old—it was the greatest place on earth!

It's cold tonight again, the girls have gone to sleep, and the fire is losing its flame. Time to hop in the mummy. Good night from the mountains of Vermont!

The Green Mountains of Vermont.

Location:	Governor Clement Shelter
Today's Miles:	24.4
Total Miles:	1675.5
Date:	August 9, 2004

The nice campfire I made last night for us kept reigniting off and on all night—nothing like a campfire in the woods. At one point during a nice late night flare-up, all three of us rolled over to gaze and absorb its emotional warmth. The temperatures had once again dipped into the mid-thirties; I had my mummy zipped up so tight, the only thing not covered was my nose. Luna got up first and decided to hustle all her stuff together and start walking without breakfast to warm up. We followed.

Today would have us pass a lot of shelters; they seem to be very close to one another, giving us many options for lunch and night camp. Later at the top of White Rock Mountain, we came upon the coolest area. At the summit where another trail intersects the AT, were hundreds of rock cairns. They were everywhere. Some small, some large, all interesting and artful. We dropped our packs and went to creating our own rock masterpieces.

Living in the area was Luna's cousin, which she'd be making a stop at about the fifteen-mile mark. April Showers decided to join her and not hike the longer miles I was planning. Since I wanted to experience the Inn at Long Trail (an AT tradition), I pushed on to make it a longer day now, giving me only a short one tomorrow into the inn.

The shelter tonight isn't recommended in our guide books, apparently the "towners" come up here and raise hell since a backcountry forest road comes right to it. They don't have to carry their beer far that way. But another hiker named "Patton," whose hiking the Long Trail is here with me. We've made a nice fire, and now both of us are enjoying some hot chocolate. Since it's a Monday night, we think it should be all right.

Thanks to a nice opening in the tree canopy, we're both gazing up since there's supposed to be meteor activity all this week. Cool, huh?

Whizzzzzzzzz. "Hey, there goes one," Patton exclaims. If y'all excuse me, I have to put this pen down and start focusing on the heavens, don't want to miss the show.

Just a sample of the hundreds of rock cairns hikers have made at the top of White Rock Mountain. They give the small area a mystical quality.

Location:	The Inn at Long Trail
Today's Miles:	10.6
Total Miles:	1686.1
Date:	August 10, 2004

The night was uneventful, a good thing since it was a questionable shelter.

The entire day's miles would involve climbing then descending Mt. Killington. Killington is also a township, known as a winter play land.

As I started my climb, the forest grew tighter and denser. That's when I heard four bellowing snorts from the trees about one hundred feet away. I guess it could have been that moose I haven't been able to spot yet—or big foot! Once again the summit was like Christmas Land filled with thousands of evergreen trees. Just over the summit on the descent sits a shelter. I dropped in to sign the register and ran into Neon Leon and Stumpy. I hadn't seen them since we first met at High Point Shelter back in New Jersey. We chatted and caught up a bit, but since they weren't planning on the detour to the Inn, we wished each other happy trails. The inn is .9 tenths off the trail once you hit US 4, with the cars hauling by at Interstate speeds, a hitch seemed unlikely, so I walked it.

I arrived at 11:29 a.m. to pleasantly find out they not only had space for me, but the kitchen would open for lunch in one minute. What timing!

It's now some nine hours since arriving, I've done little other than eat. My hunger over the last several days has been getting quite significant, I'm always hungry it seems! I must be getting down to the last reserves of body fat by now. That may explain the almost constant growling my stomach keeps making. I did watch the movie *Babe*—quite mindless and charming. My choices were limited to action-packed explosion movies or a talking pig. There's nothing like a talking pig to relax you, I always say.

I've been getting really lucky on the weather for the last month now, or so it seems. Most of the storms have been coming in during the evening when I'm all tucked in, cozy, and dry. It's late now—8:45 p.m.—or at least that is for me, and a nice big thunderstorm is putting on a show. I love the sound of rain at bedtime, I only hope Luna and April Showers are dry, they're still out there, due in to here tomorrow. Judging by my planned miles tomorrow, it looks like I'll move past the 1,700-mile mark and that also means an early start. I may not see them as a result. Out here, one short mileage day by them or a long one by you and you just might not ever see familiar faces again! I'm afraid that our one-week trio may have come to an end. If that's true, I'm going to miss them.

But, before that, breakfast!!

The Inn at Long Trail.
A hiker's refuge with great Irish pub food and beverage.

Cirrus

Thin wisps, these clouds usually dissipate as the sun burns off their ice crystals.

Altocumulus

Rain may be a half day away. The cumulus pile up on top of each other leading to overcast skies.

Cumulonimbus

Expect heavy rain and soon. Known by their more common name Thunderheads, they form on warm days, usually in the afternoon. Lightning, hail, and tornados are all possible.

Location: Wintturi Shelter
Today's Miles: 19.9
Total Miles: 1706.0
Date: August 11, 2004

What happens to you after 1,700 miles of backpacking? Well, you not only lose thirty-five pounds of baggage and build muscle fiber that laughs at twenty-mile days, but you get a flexibility you may have never experienced. Flexibility has always been a weakness for me, well not anymore! The two diagrams would at one time have hospitalized me for a month. Now I do them as stretches in the shelter each night. What a long way I've come!

The athleticism that also comes along with 1,700 miles allows you to actually run with your pack on, even though you've already hiked sixteen miles. Of course, thunder and lightning all around while you're on a ridgeline will most certainly give you some extra motivation to put a bounce in your step.

At 3 p.m., while taking a short break, I heard thunder. I still had four-plus miles to the shelter, and the trail was on top of the ridge. You don't think, you just haul. Every downhill I ran, every uphill I dug deep and lunged hard on the poles. The thunder was closing in from the side and behind. I pushed for all my lungs were worth. As I reached the blue blaze side trail to the shelter, the rain started with me in a dead run! The lightning cracked a big boom just as I ducked under the roof of Wintturi Shelter. I collapsed against the back wall as the heavens opened up. A dramatic entrance for certain to the three others who were already here.

THE IMPOSSIBLE IS NOW POSSIBLE!

Location:	Hanover, New Hampshire
Today's Miles:	26.2
Total Miles:	1732.2
Date:	August 12, 2004

Apparently Vermont didn't want me to forget her. The switchbacks that help us climb, which are the standard for most of the trail, were strangely absent! Maybe the students of the Dartmouth Outing Club who watch over this section of the AT, have been too busy with classes. The trail moves straight up the mountain stretching every muscle in the back of my legs. I suppose the trail is preparing us for what lays just over the horizon—"the Whites" of New Hampshire.

Like yesterday, the rumbles in the sky started only miles from reaching Hanover. And once again I felt compelled to hike fast and hard! Fortunately, the closer I got to the Connecticut River, the state line of Vermont and New Hampshire, the easier the terrain became. And so I can now say hello from New Hampshire! This is state number 13 and zero day number 14 or 15? My third month and fourteenth day.

Being here in Hanover echoes feelings of reaching Damascus early on. It too represents a big psychological town stop since Hanover is the last big stop before we enter the Whites. So that means we need to swap out our summer stuff for our winter gear again. Yes, I know its only August 13, but the Whites mean going above tree line, it means climbing up extremely steep mountains that offer no protection from the weather! People die every year in the Whites from exposure. They're serious stuff, and they sure have my attention. I got my winter jacket sent to me but have held off on my fifteen-degree sleeping bag, and thus the extra pound it weighs over my thirty-five-degree bag. I hope that decision won't make me shiver.

Today has been spent at the post office, grocery store, and the barber. Yep, got a shave and a haircut, but it wasn't two bits. I also have to rig some rope tie-downs that can attach to my tent if I need to use the tent platforms used in the Whites. The alpine vegetation is so fragile that camping can only be on designated wooden platforms. A bit unusual but necessary I suppose. So I paid a visit to the local Ace Hardware.

It's been raining a lot thanks to Hurricane Bonnie moving northward and now with Hurricane Charlie, it seems, even way up here, even more rain will power its way up soon. Great! That's all I need—more angst to add to entering the Whites. Oh, well, I fret too much. I have about two days before I face them, maybe by then the wicked weather will have moved on leaving superclear skies and warm bright sunshine. Hey, it could happen!!

As a treat, I finally was able to satisfy my month-long craving for Indian food. Hanover has a couple restaurants which did the trick.

Raspberries left, raspberries right. Raspberries everywhere since entering New Hampshire.

Porcupine

These living pincushions have quite a reputation of nuisance on the trail. They eat the wood that's attached to the shelters, specifically the front edge of the floor. We hikers sit and hang our legs there which rubs our salty sweat into the wood. Porkies are also known to eat your hiking boots for their accumulated salt. What I was shocked to learn from other hikers, who saw them, was that they are tree climbers. Who'd a thunk-it?

Location:	Trapper John Shelter
Today's Miles:	16.7
Total Miles:	1748.9
Date:	August 14, 2004

A very easy day out of Hanover. The trail reenters the woods here at this gas station. I'm having coffee and a chocolate croissant, while sitting on their curb. Yes, nothing but the most posh of places for me.

I spotted three hawks flying with each other today, they were definitely eyeing me over. Most likely looking at my skinny carcass and saying, "Skip him, no more meat on those bones."

The views were great in the afternoon; yesterday's rain had the skies so clear. Here with three others, all section hikers. I made a nice big campfire, we've all been entranced by it for the last two hours. Gotta love it! Hurricane Charley's remnants should find us starting after midnight and will make tomorrow a windy affair. For now, all is right with the trail!

Living the simple life and loving it. If you consider a fancy coffee and croissant the simple life.

217

Location:	Ore Hill Shelter
Today's Miles:	19.3
Total Miles:	1768.2
Date:	August 15, 2004

Worrying accomplishes nothing. Remember the weather forecast for today? Rain at midnight followed by hard rain and high winds all day, compliments of Hurricane Charlie. Well, its so nice when they miss the mark completely. I woke to gray skies, but it was dry. No rain, it didn't even feel like rain.

Do you also remember me mentioning that the mountains were getting bigger? I had to tackle Smart Mountain right out of camp. Even as strong as I've become, it took me two hours and forty-five minutes to reach the summit. I then faced Mt. Cube after I got down the other side of Smart. Somewhere in the middle of that, the sun decided it had had enough of all the clouds and started burning them up. Yea, you go, sun! What a mood changer. The views were awesome almost from everywhere you looked. So the lesson learned is, don't fret over stuff you have no influence on. It's wasted energy!

Today was gorgeous; a trail blessing that was totally unexpected. Sometimes those are the best! Darkness has come, and I have another campfire going. Great ambiance.

Tomorrow holds some real excitement. It's called Mt. Moosilauke, and it officially begins the Whites. Some say it as Moose-a-lock and then some say it as Moose-a-lock-key. The latter feels better to me since it's probably a Native American word. But who knows, even the locals debate it. Regardless how you say it, to climb it will leave you speechless judging by the profile maps. It will be the first four-thousand-foot ascent of the entire journey. It will also be the first time I hike above tree line. This takes us up into an alpine environment, so there should be much to talk about tomorrow night. Stay tuned.

And so tomorrow I hike into the Whites.
"Many have died there from exposure even in the summer," it says.
Are we still having fun?

Location:	Kinsman Notch, NH 112
Today's Miles:	16.9
Total Miles:	1785.1
Date:	August 16, 2004

Today I learned why the "Whites" are infamous! The trail was quite tame for the first eight miles, despite the rain. It led me across the border of the White Mountain National Forest.

What was waiting for me after the tame part was a mountain called Mt. Moosilauke. Moosilauke was the single highest ascent I've faced since beginning. In fact, its the biggest thing I've ever faced in hiking—ever! It's huge and as I mentioned before, it takes me above tree line where nothing but lichens can grow, the conditions are too harsh. What determines tree line is elevation and geographic latitude on the hemisphere. Only evergreen trees, mainly spruce, exist up here and even they cease to grow at some point, thus creating the void called tree line. So stunted are the trees at the line in their growth, they're no higher than your waist and yet one hundred years old.

Moosilauke had my full attention from the start! Two hours of straight up ascent got me to the edge of where the trees disappear. The winds were at 25 to 30 mph; and with my body and clothes soaked in sweat, it got cold fast. Clouds were blowing over the summit as fast as cars on an interstate. I yanked my hat down hard onto my head and continued into the zone where it was only me, the rocks, and the cold howling wind. (At least all that anxiety I had earlier was justified!)

The white blazes we've followed on trees and rocks since Georgia are now replaced by cairns of rocks. I could see the summit when the clouds parted, so I just kept going. I could also see that I was alone, no one else in sight—it was all quite haunting to be on such a huge mountain with all its raw power despite its stillness. The moment grew all the more dramatic as I neared the summit. The closer I got, the higher the wind speed. The rain had stopped, but the sun's warmth was sorely missed. I was inside a void in the clouds' cover when I touched the summit sign. Click, I took my picture, and then I looked for the way off this howling frigid tundra!

If that weren't dramatic enough, the descent would be unlike anything I've had as well! It's sort of like a four-thousand-foot gravity fall with just a smidge of control. Maybe smidge is overstating it. It's about a mile down at a seventy-degree angle. To make things more exciting, all the rocks, roots, and wooden steps were wet. Slippery wet. Icy, slimy, slippery, mossy wet!

I don't want this to sound cocky, but since leaving Springer Mountain in Georgia, I've only fallen three times, that's 1,780 miles on foot. Well, today, I fell three times just trying to get down off this monster.

It wasn't without its beauty though. In all that harsh, raw power, there was great beauty. Pure, untamed wildness. The power of the Earth that we take for granted so frequently is on full display up here. And as far as the descent, it was along the longest cascading waterfall I've ever seen. It must fall some three thousand feet, all the while, no more than just feet away from where you're stepping carefully, hoping upon hope you won't slip and never stop falling!

Like so many times in this adventure, I met two hikers the day before and again today who offered me a ride into town to a motel. I had decided earlier that a warm place to dry out would be a good idea. They were "Loco Motive" and "Navigator," and they've hiked everything I've hiked, only they've done it a section at a time over thirteen years. We ended up having dinner together to share trail stories.

Mt. Moosilauke is now to my south, for which I'm thankful! I am most certainly in a place I'm not familiar with. The Whites have lived up to their reputation and this is only day 1.

Mt. Moosilauke summit in the distance, my first above tree line hike.

Location:	Franconia Notch
Today's Miles:	16.3
Total Miles:	1801.4
Date:	August 17, 2004

With this cool front down from Canada and the higher geographic latitude of New Hampshire, it's fairly chilly when the sun is covered in clouds. This morning, however, the sun was forecasted to win the battle despite the low dense fog, you could just feel it would be a gorgeous day.

Loco Motive, Navigator, and I all met at the hotel's continental breakfast and quickly loaded up to head to the trailhead. By using two cars, they dropped one at the trail where they'll finish or so we thought, and then we all rode over together where we'll begin—which is where I came off yesterday.

The hike over Mt. Moosilauke had offered me a warning that sixteen-mile days here in the Whites was pushing it.

My hike today was a planned 16.3 miles over the south and north peaks of Mt. Kinsman. There didn't appear to be any areas of flat walking. Boy, did it deliver! I started up the first climb and truly had some concerns for my companions, if the hike was to be like this all day, sixteen-plus miles would be too far to attempt in a day for them. We wished each other well and said our farewells on a small rest break and then I climbed, climbed, climbed. It would be a theme that would dominate the day!

At two hours I took a five-minute break by a brook to check mileage. Normally, I would have completed about five and half to six-plus miles in two hours. I had only gone 3.3! This was going to be a long slow day apparently. This caused me even more concern for my new friends. Thankfully the sun did come out bright and strong. What a mood machine the sun can be, seeing the sunlight through the dense trees makes the forest so beautiful. Gives me a smile that reaches down deep inside.

Even though I'd been heading up in elevation since morning, I now came to the ascent up Mt. Kinsman's south peak. Hiking poles aren't much help here since it's about a 1,500-foot rock scramble up a steep jumble or chimney of rock. The tree roots and trunks are your best friend on this climb acting as handholds. The summit was breathtaking! *Wow!* The whole world lay in front of me. *Wow!*

It was now 3 p.m., and I'd only come a little over halfway. I hoped Loco Motive and Navigator would amend their plan and take a side trail down sooner and not try the whole distance. I then pushed on over the north peak and got an amazing look at Mt. Lincoln and Mt. Lafayette in the distance. They were huge—and they were to be the next section. But fortunately not today.

At thirteen miles I came upon Lonesome Lake, it was 5 p.m. Simply stunning! The surface was mirror smooth with the sun's golden hour making for the ideal lighting conditions. And in the background, Mt. Lafayette. What a Kodak moment!

I reached the road at 6:30 p.m. and was totally confused as to where this was in relation to where the car was parked from this morning. I wasn't planning on seeing the guys again, but I wanted to leave a note hoping them all the best. I started walking the interstate toward town some six miles away. For the first time, the "Hiker to Town" bandana failed. The speeds of the cars were just too fast, and frankly, I wouldn't stop on an interstate either. As soon as I packed it up and committed to walking the distance, a car pulled over. He was doing some trail work up north; he is "Hot and Sweaty." I laughed at his trail name. Anyway, by 7:30 I was at the Woodstock Inn in North Woodstock and hoped my friends were not still hiking the mountain. I would later learn through e-mail that the day was indeed quite an ordeal for them. It took them seventeen hours that day which had them making it off the trail at some point past midnight. The Whites are tough, and too many underestimate them. If given the opportunity again, I'll be more forceful with my opinions if it can help avert a bad situation for someone. The past two days' experience in the White's has said loud and clear, that my mileage expectations have got to be reduced! From here on, ten to thirteen miles will be more realistic—and that may even be too ambitious!

Lonesome Lake with Mt. Lafayette and Mt. Lincoln in the distance.

Simple Pleasures

Part primal, part hypnotic, a campfire in the woods is a joyful experience. It speaks of escape and wilderness and yet offers security from the many unknowns that the darkness hides.
This comfort has the power to transform a night's destination into a home. It helps strangers to gather and share in their fellowship of nature. It's a good thing.

Location:	Franconia Notch
Today's Miles:	0
Total Miles:	1801.4
Date:	August 18, 2004

Belle drove up from Cape Cod to pick me up in North Woodstock. Her friends Nat and Terry Bull have a wonderful home in Franconia Ridge. Wonderful because its wonderful—and wonderful because they built the entire thing themselves! What an accomplishment! This was the first time I'd actually seen Belle in "normal" clothes, it had always been hiker stuff up till now. Wow, too bad I'm like a big brother. She's been resting her ankle ever since she came off the trail and what better place for rest than the beach. So although she wasn't completing what she set out to do, she wasn't suffering by any means.

After dinner, I met Nat and Terry who drove up later, really, really nice people! They hike regularly and are close to completing a quest of the tallest mountains in the region. We all just hung doing nothing the next day, it was nice to have a double zero before climbing the Franconia Ridge part of the trail. And just goofin' off, good food and conversation sure beats fretting over the Whites. But of course I did. I am also entering the AMC system of huts. These are not shelter/lean-to objects, but wilderness lodges that sleep forty to ninety paying guests. A bunk in these places is almost impossible since the city folks have long booked them. It adds an amazing amount of uncertainty and forces us into long hikes off the trail to campsites or we have the option of doing chores with the huts staff called the "croo." Then we can sleep in the dining/common room. The whole thing has me on edge, so hanging out with Belle and The Bulls is helping me to relax. Sort of. They call this nirvana, this escape house "Paradise North"—and indeed it is!

Paradise North

Location:	Galehead Hut
Today's Miles:	13.0
Total Miles:	1814.4
Date:	August 20, 2004

After two lazy days hanging with Belle, Dougy, and Nat at their wonderful home, the weather forecast for Franconia Ridge was favorable. The Franconia Ridge is said to be the most beautiful, dramatic section of the AT. The forecast called for sunshine all day—that should have left me suspicious.

Dougy and Nat were celebrating their sixteenth wedding anniversary with a hike that would take them over the last few four-thousand-foot peaks—giving them all forty-eight in the region. They would be camping where I'd be heading to if all went well.

Despite the early morning fog and low clouds, it felt like it could improve for the spectacular above tree line ridge walk of the many summits in today's hike. Belle like a true champ got up early to drive me to the trailhead. The trail started with a big climb up Liberty then onto Little Haystack Mountain—it's not little, I assure you! Then over Mt. Lincoln and Mt. Lafayette which reaches up to 5,200 feet. The ridge walk was indeed spectacular! More dramatic than anything thus far! On Lafayette, the clouds arrived quickly on the 30 to 40 mph wind, erasing all the views. The mist and rain would then follow shortly making everything cold and wet.

The next mountain was Mt. Garfield, which apparently decided I was moving to smoothly and felt I needed to slip and pound my knee on one of its oh-so-hard rocks. "Son of a—!!" Although OK, I hit so hard it rattled me. My planned—all be it a crazy plan—16.4 miles needed to be revised. The Galehead Hut at thirteen miles had space for me there, but only if I did so on the "work for stay" arrangement. This means that with no bunks available, thru-hikers are allowed to help the hut crew for an hour or so cleaning up after dinner and then we, or I in this case, can sleep on the dining room floor. I had a crazy notion this would add more texture to my journey and decided to do it. It meant I wouldn't have to walk another three miles today, which was wise since I slammed my knee awfully hard! The only worry was not meeting up with the anniversary couple—they might worry. But we had discussed "plan B" scenarios.

The rain stopped and gave all of us lounging around Galehead warm sunshine and clear skies. Oh well, so much for forecasts. It's now 6:15 p.m., and all the guests with bunks are eating together at the set dinnertime of 6 p.m. Later at 7:30, I'll join the hut crew for dinner and duty. I think this is going to be fun.

It was really nice to stop early and draw, linger, and soak up the sunshine. The end is drawing closer and closer!

Franconia Ridge is one of the AT's more dramatic sections. Why?

Here it is just five minutes later.

AMC Galehead Hut, a welcome stop.

Location: Crawford Notch
Today's Miles: 14.7
Total Miles: 1829.1
Date: August 21, 2004

Last night after a meager amount of cleaning, the alarm was sounded to alert us of a great sunset. The crew started yelling, "The roof, the roof." We all hauled up the kitchen stairs and out a window onto the shingle roof and grabbed a seat—being with the crew last night, I got a front-row seat. Brilliant pinks and orange lit the clouds as the sun gave its final show. A great unexpected treat. The policy in the AMC Huts is lights-out at 9:30 p.m. That's when I spread out the mummy and visited the sandman.

The morning had the guests a bit quieter than they were last night. It was raining, windy, foggy, and harsh! I headed out at my normal hour only to find it wasn't as cold as it looked. I started shedding clothes immediately to cool off. The terrain was as hard and awkward as yesterday, it would be slow going. By 11 a.m., I was completely soaked despite all the rain gear. In fact, there were fish in the ocean drier than I was! As a result, I just started walking down the middle of this ever-forming Appalachian lake. At some point you just say uncle and embrace the wet. That was today!

Location:	Lakes of the Clouds Hut
Today's Miles:	11.2
Total Miles:	1829.1
Date:	August 22, 2004

When I got off the mountain yesterday, I gave Belle a call. She drove out so I could have a reprieve from the cold, windy rain. The anniversary couple would also be returning from the mountain. It would be my last night with them, for the next week I'd be facing the rest of the Whites and the chief big dog mountain named Mt. Washington.

Like the great hosts they all were, they woke up extra early so that I'd be able to get out on the trail early. Belle compromised and went to the trailhead in her robe, we all said farewell. Natty was particularly encouraging saying that I'd have no problems, that Maine was to be mine. He'd make a great hiker coach.

It was a chilly forty-two degrees, as I moved on up the steep Webster Cliff. The day was clear, and the sky filled with sunshine. It was to be the most perfect of days for hiking here to Lakes of the Clouds Hut—just at the base of Mt. Washington's summit. Once I rose to the ridgeline up Webster Cliffs, I saw it! Although ten miles away, it rose above everything, Mt. Washington was enormous. The day would see over six thousand feet of rugged ascent. Mt. Washington is the second-highest mountain on the AT, but as mentioned before, its latitude puts it above tree line. It is famous for having clocked the highest wind speed ever recorder—231 mph. Hurricane force winds happen over one hundred times a year. The wind today was a meager 15 mph. It was a perfect day indeed, other than not knowing where the heck I'd be able to sleep tonight.

A trail angel, out with her beautiful Australian shepherds gave me a lemon-poppy seed cake just to be nice. She and it were wonderful. At the early hour of 2 p.m., I was here and with the next possible place to sleep being another seven miles, the decision to stay and do another work-for-stay was ideal.

The visibility was ninety miles today, that endless rain yesterday sure did clean the world!

"Stumpy" and I played tag team on washing dishes for an hour and had the entire day to enjoy with that behind us. Sitting and hanging out the rest of the afternoon right in Mt. Washington's shadow was dreamlike. It was transporting me to the alps; it was the best day in two months according to the hut crew. How lucky is that!

Three other thru-hikers are also here tonight: Alleghany, Neon Leon, and Stumpy. We're all sleeping on the dining room tables—yep, lots of variety in this adventure.

Lakes of the Clouds Hut, the best seat on Earth for viewing Mt. Washington.

Location: Pinkham Notch Camp
Today's Miles: 14.7
Total Miles: 1855.0
Date: August 23, 2004

As I climbed up onto one of the dining room tables last night and into my mummy, with all the lights out, I was struck by all the brilliance of the stars. The table I selected for my bed sat in a corner with windows on two sides. It was as close to being in a glass bubble as one could get. And with Mt. Washington in one of those windows, the drama of the moment was all the greater. It would wait there through the night and if lucky, it would allow me to climb her and visit the summit.

I woke this morning to pots and pans from one of the crew members whose turn it was to get breakfast going. It was 5:30 a.m. The other thru-hikers were already stirring, stuffing all their gear back into packs so the dining room tables could be set for the 6:30 breakfast. No, we don't get to participate until after the guests are all finished and if anything is left. Feeling a bit like Cinderella and knowing that the Summit House restaurant on Mt. Washington opened at 8, I'd head up early so that when I got there they'd be open.

It was another clear, outstanding morning with a pink glow from sunrise backlighting the mountain. The summit temperature was forty-one degrees with a below-freezing wind-chill of thirty. Gusting wind speeds were up to 50 mph.

At 7:30, I left the security of the hut to climb the last chunk of rock. The higher I went, the higher the wind speed got, and the colder it became. I'm not sure why, but I had the distinct feeling that guests eating breakfast were watching me climb the summit from the dining room windows. Thirty-eight minutes later I was there—almost alone. Seems the place was just waking up.

I called home to share the good news—and then it was off to make some miles on this awkward rocky landscape. I'm not sure I ever got to place my feet on a flat surface until I crossed a road some nine hours later. The terrain is a pile of rocks on rocks, but it's spectacular! Breathtakingly Spectacular!!

A southbound thru-hiker couple said the trail only gets harder north of here— the famous Mahoosuc Notch and Arm. For the southbounders, everything is still new and rattling. With them only covering some three-hundred-plus miles to this point, their descriptions of what lays ahead are a bit dramatic. By the time a northbounder gets here, there isn't anything we can't handle. But everyone enjoys the sharing of trail info all the same.

Near the end of the day or should I say with five miles left, I came upon three young women whose intention was to hike up to where I'd come from. There was no way over that terrain they'd make it by dark, and they were about out of water. I explained how difficult the terrain would be and that they'd need at least a couple liters of water

Mt. Washington at dawn.

each to make it. If they did continue, they most likely wouldn't be there until 10 p.m., and quite candidly, they didn't look to be ready for the hardships that would go with it. I'm afraid I didn't go too easy on them when I learned they had no safe means of getting water. They said the hut would have water, but they got lost. It was clear they simply didn't know how long or hard it would be to get there. They offered to pay me for the usage of my water pump, I cut her off and said, "You don't understand. We hikers look out for one another." I pulled out my water filter and pumped full all their bottles with good water. At least one problem was solved. I strongly encouraged them to amend their plans and either camp or turn back to where I was heading, which would be easier. What echoed in the back of my head was the ordeal Loco Motive and Navigator went through, so here I was able to make a difference. They thanked me for the advice and agreed to go no farther than the campsite a few tenths ahead. I'm sure they had no idea as to the dangers that exist by going above tree line.

I was going to do all I could to keep them from becoming a newspaper headline.

It turns out that an hour and a half later as I made my destination, a thunderstorm moved in fast and furious and hit the ridgeline where the girls would have been. Boy, that was a close one. The AT is a full-color adventure!

Location:	IMP Campsite
Today's Miles:	13.2
Total Miles:	1868.2
Date:	August 24, 2004

Nobody says anything about the Wildcats of the Whites. No warning, no mention at all. The Wildcats have peaks A, B, C, D, and E. Out of Pinkham Notch Camp, Peak E rises first at about 2,100 feet in only two miles. It's hard, and it's steep!

After them I faced the Carters, principally Carter Dome, yet another tremendously steep climb. But I got a surprise reason to rest on the ascent. Heading south was Cliff Dancer! He'd flip-flopped a month ago. I hadn't seen him since Front Royal, Virginia, where we went for Mexican food together. He was amazed to see me and a little shocked at my progress. It was nice to see a familiar face!

Tonight, here at the shelter, there's the most incredible rustic bench that's been placed at the edge of a clifflike drop-off. At over three thousand feet up, this "Bench of Inspiration" I'm calling it, inspired me to have my hot chocolate and cookies from it. Later, over a dozen others around the campsite, all sat, stood, or kneeled silently for the sunset. Truly beautiful! Some were retired, and some were yet to complete high school. They were from the area, while others were from far away. Some knew their mission in life, while others were trying to find a life with a mission. Here on the trail the wealthy and the budget minded will gel. The young and old will find a chemistry that may have never been possible at home. They'll come from every State in our union. From the plains and farmlands to the modern cities. The accents of Texas or Minnesota or Massachusetts will be as common as those of Europe. Scottish, German and Australian dialects will add color to the campfire talk. Not everyone was hiking the Appalachian Trail, there are many other trails here too, but all were here to do as the plague back down on Springer Mountain in Georgia stated: to seek out and have a fellowship with nature. And that was our bond tonight, to share in the grandeur and beauty of the land and in the warm glow of God's spectacular show.

Tomorrow, it's a short eight-mile day down the mountain and into the town of Gorham, which will sort of officially mean I've finished the Whites. Yahhoooooo!!

But, the difficulty doesn't stop just because the Whites will soon. I now get to face a mountain range every bit as hard—they're called the Mahoosucs (gulp). And the Mahoosuc Notch and Arm—gulp, gulp—are said to be, without a doubt, the hardest miles on the AT. OK, enough with the drama already. This is the most amazing, incredibly stupendous time in life. I am a walking fountain of energy and joy. To all my friends, you've got to try this someday. It's the most fun you can have with your clothes on. However, I am wondering if I'll ever get a nice, lazy stroll through the woods again.

Sharing the silent beauty of sunset.

Location:	Gorham, New Hampshire
Today's Miles:	8.0
Total Miles:	1876.2
Date:	August 25, 2004

Well, I have a confession. I've been getting a bit tired of all the extremely strenuous ups and downs as well as my own anxiety involved with the Whites. There, I said it, moving on. It dipped fairly cold last night on the mountainside, at about 1 a.m. I put on my silk long johns and gloves, then zipped back deep in the mummy. As a result of all the fatigue, I ignored my 6:05 a.m. wrist alarm and snoozed to the irresponsible hour of 8 a.m.! Yep, I'm a rebel, completely irresponsible. When I did poke my head out of my cocoon, it was sunny again. Wow, that's four days in a row.

It was a surprisingly gentle descent that brought a big smile to my face. Finally, an easy trail in the Whites. I started singing the "Do Re Mi Fa So La Ti Do" song from *The Sound of Music.* And right at the particularly loud section of my solo, another hiker from the other direction appeared to embarrass me. Man, oh man, is there nowhere in this huge park where a person with no voice talent can sing? Oh well, the lady hiker giggled and hiked on—most likely to get out of earshot before any eardrum damage could happen. I continued to sing, happy to be on smooth trail again.

Now, I'm here in Gorham, New Hampshire, running all the necessary chores: post office, grocery store, and outfitter. Yea, the outfitter. The Whites played heck with my hiking poles. Not only did one get bent like a banana, but both tips were bent at extreme angles as well as one had its tungsten tip severed. Both are back to normal and ready for duty tomorrow. I considered taking a zero until I saw the forecast—sunny tomorrow, followed by sunny and sunny. Gotta love that! In all, I was able to traverse the whole of the Whites in seven days and four hours. A feat due to good weather—only two bad days—and my willingness to push my legs and lungs to their full measure. I fell only five times; I'd only fallen three times in the first 1,700 miles. And now as a reward, I get to edge ever closer to that last state line.

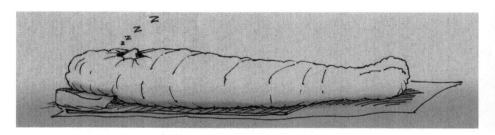

On those cold nights, only my nose can be seen.

236

Location:	Maine! Yahoooooo! (Carlo Col Shelter)
Today's Miles:	17.0
Total Miles:	1892.7
Date:	August 26, 2004

Today, the trail nearly brought me to tears. Not from its difficulty, not from its emotional challenges. No, today it was from jubilation! At 4:14 p.m., I walked into the state of Maine. It was three months and twenty-six days ago I started heading north.

It's really hard to comprehend the huge achievement, the vast distance involved, let alone the enormous demands along this journey! Although the adventure has plenty more to challenge me with, a sense of completeness and joy has found me. Like yesterday, I was singing during parts of the trail. Being surrounded by fir and spruce trees had me feeling I was once again in Christmas Land, so I was singing "Oh, Christmas Tree." Since my memory was inherited from my mother, all I could remember was the first verse, so I actually do more humming than singing. But it's still just as joyful!

I'll now say something I've never ever said, "Good night from Maine—the way life should be according to the state line sign!!"

Location:	Speck Pond Shelter
Today's Miles:	9.5
Total Miles:	1902.7
Date:	August 27, 2004

One look at today's mileage could lead you to calling me a slacker. But another look at the total mileage and you get a whole other impression. So why only 9.5 miles? Well, because of a little thing called the Mahoosuc Notch and Arm. Imagine if you will, a canyon of sheer granite walls some two thousand feet. Then take about one hundred thousand rocks the size of refrigerators and drop them from up on high along a one-mile section to the bottom of the one-hundred-foot wide gorge. OK, got that pictured? Now, lets take about fifty thousand boulders the size of Volkswagens and drop them on top of the first group. And then finally, lets take a few thousand granite chunks the size of a bus and let them scatter on top for kicks!

Cover with moss and throw some ice down in the deep caves for texture, and presto, you've got Mahoosuc Notch. Now, the Notch wouldn't be so bad if left alone, the problem is someone came along and painted AT white blazes here and there, in the most diabolical nasty places. To go into this labyrinth means slivering, squeezing, crawling, sliding, shuffling, jumping, and everything that is best at covering you in filth! Sometimes you're in a cave and the temperature will drop thirty degrees from ice pockets that stay year round. Sometimes you're stripping off your pack so you can fit in and out of a rock hole. Other times I'd just start laughing my head off at the comedy of it all. I found sliding on my ass off an angled rock to the edge of another particularly effective. I had heard that three hours to wiggle through this befuddling labyrinth wasn't uncommon. How I emerged out the other end in an hour is anyone's guess!? Triumphant in my passage, I now got to face the Mahoosuc Arm, which is nothing less than what seemed like 1,700 feet of 70-degree angle ascent. Whatever happened to a nice relaxing stroll in the woods? Jeez Louise. So I rewarded myself with a short 9.5-mile day.

A word about the trail in Maine. The land here is the most wild I've seen on the journey. It's dense, and everything goes steeply up or down with an occasional flattish rock walk on the summits. Everything is covered in spruce and fir evergreens—love it. In many parts it resembles a wildlife path that wiggles up these mountains other than the cliché idea of a walking trail. The roots and trees serve as handholds and in some cases, as stairs. Beautiful lush mosses are everywhere. There's an unusual bird—spruce grouse—that will not run or fly from you when you come up on them. They just look at you as if you're from Mars.

They have a red crescent above their eye, which looks pretty cool; other than that, they are a model of camouflage.

The recent cold spell last week did a good number on the majority of the flying pests, and the weather keeps cooperating by giving us pathetic hikers sunny skies! Tomorrow it's Andover, Maine, and 14.5 miles.

Known as the hardest mile on the Appalachian Trail, the Mahoosuc Notch is really just an adult jungle-gym, labyrinth of rock.

Location: Andover, Maine
Today's Miles: 14.5
Total Miles: 1917.6
Date: August 28, 2004

I really enjoyed stopping early yesterday at Speck Pond. A nice breeze freshened the air all evening, and the temps didn't dip any lower than the low sixties. I woke to thick fog—or low clouds—still haven't figured that one out. Today is Saturday, which means the post office will close at 12:30 p.m., which also means there's no way to pick up my mail drop box. So I think a zero day will be in my future here in Andover. Then Monday morning, I'll pick up the box and get what I truly need out of it—my maps.

The last several days I've felt strong but not powerful as I had the last several months. I'm wondering if calorie deficit is the reason. At some point my body fat is going to become so minimal that there won't be much to draw from. Some of the other hikers here—Smack, Critter, and Caterpillar—have made the same observations about themselves: feeling good but a tad less strong.

When I arrived here at the Andover Guest House, I found a bath scale to check out the situation. I now weigh 166 lbs! I started in Georgia at 207. Forty-one pounds have fallen on to the trail over these last 1,900 miles. I think taking a zero day to eat myself silly sounds like a strategic idea now. Word arrived from the hiker grapevine that April Showers broke her ankle in the Whites. She's got to be crushed. I feel so sorry for her. She hiked over 1,800 miles and was getting so close. It's yet another reminder of how much more difficult the journey has become. And Luna who hoped to make it all the way to the Maine border had to stop just short and head back to college, so she's gone too. I did get an e-mail from her that said she visited the Mt. Washington Visitor Center by car early one morning on the way back home. When she checked the hiker register at about 9am, my name was the last one signed—at 8 a.m. We just missed each other. Damn that timing thing.

The Maine terrain continues to be awkward, dense, steep, and beautiful. I can now also add enchanted. For some reason, a chipmunk, which usually hightails it away from you as you approach, today actually ran over and sat looking at me. No more than three feet away. I mean, it saw me coming and ran right over to me! Magical! Still no moose today. Drat! Just lots of hoofprints. Smack, whom I've mentioned before, however, woke up this morning to chewing sounds. She stuck her head out of her tent to find a huge bull moose, antlers and all, just feet away. It stared at her and went back to chewing. Wow! Something new each day.

Tomorrow, Sunday, I'll sit and eat, eat, eat!!

Speck Pond during a quiet afternoon.

Location:	Andover, Maine
Today's Miles:	0
Total Miles:	1917.6
Date:	August 29, 2004

I'm sure many of you get the impression that my journey with the frequent motel stays is taking away from the adventure. But a hike of the AT can be more than just rocks, trees, and mountains. It's also a stroll down Americana Lane. Here at the Andover Guest House, the owner will not let us bring our backpacks in or our shoes. We can use the kitchen but not the phone. If a call to our families is desired, we have to walk across the street to the payphone, which has a convenient folding chair. Nothing but the finest in accommodations! There's no plan B either if it's raining.

Main street here is one hundred yards long, which includes a restaurant, two general stores, and a post office. You can get breakfast as early as 4:30 a.m., and you can pay for your groceries by simply having them "put on your tab." There are also two gas pumps, an empty baseball field, and a lot of maple trees that are starting to show some orange and red. There is a clock tower opposite the church; however, it's stuck at 9:19—I don't know if it being stuck keeps the bell in its tower from ringing. That's about it for Andover, other than the people are charming, treat us hikers with respect, and all talk with that wonderful Maine accent. I'm seeing the USA the AT way!

Location:	South Arm Road
Today's Miles:	10.1
Total Miles:	1927.7
Date:	August 30, 2004

Hiking the AT presents you with many opportunities to be flexible. My plan was to get my mail drop when the post office opened and then leave Andover. Another hiker, "Alleghany," was doing a slack-pack for ten miles and then would return here to the guesthouse. Alleghany and I met in Vermont, and then again about every five days since then. Our pace is very similar, so we started kicking around the idea of hiking together the rest of the way to the Big K. So I changed my plans and did the ten miles with Alleghany. Coming back to the guesthouse did have its advantages, since last night it had rained all evening. The trail turned out to be a muddy mess; our clothes weren't much better after ten miles in those conditions. It continued to rain off and on throughout the day meaning another muddy mess tomorrow and another good reason to use this place as home base again. I'm still carrying my pack, as I mentioned I'd be doing early on. It's just too comfortable; and I like having my stuff, in case I need flexibility.

You may have noticed how I've reduced my daily miles—finally! It sure is helping me to savor the final chapter in this grand adventure. And once again, I saw moose prints in the trail. Some really huge ones actually. But alas, still no Bullwinkle sighting! It's only a matter of being in the right place at the right time. This is Maine, and the moose outnumber the two-legged residents of Andover.

Location:	ME17
Today's Miles:	13.3
Total Miles:	1941.0
Date:	August 31, 2004

I called the folks tonight to ask if they knew what today was. "It's your fourth-month anniversary on the trail," Mom replied. Yep! Four months! That alone is hard to comprehend, let alone the miles I've covered on foot.

Two hundred years ago—1804 to 2004—marks the bicentennial of one of the most famous American adventures in history: the Lewis and Clark expedition with the Corps of Discovery. Ken Burns made a nice documentary on it. I like that my journey falls on their two hundredth anniversary. The post office issued some awesome stamps commemorating the event—that is, the Lewis and Clark adventure, not my thru-hike.

With the purchase of the Louisiana Territory from France in 1803, then president of the United States, Thomas Jefferson, felt compelled to have their new land explored and mapped. This huge tract of over eight hundred thousand square miles that almost doubled the country, encompassed everything from present-day Texas and Louisiana up to Montana and North Dakota.

The main purpose of the expedition was to find a water route west to the Pacific Ocean. It was believed this Northwest Passage, this fabled Passage to India, could be a boon to commerce through trade with India and the Orient. Up till now that meant sailing around the southern points of Africa and South America, each a long and dangerous journey.

Thomas Jefferson commissioned his trusted private secretary, Meriwether Lewis—how about that for a first name? You can just imagine how many playground fights came about from that moniker!—to command the Corps of Discovery. Lewis in turn recruited his friend William Clark to share equally in the command of the expedition. The forty-plus men who joined them were soldiers whose missions purpose would be one of peace—exploration and mapping, diplomacy and science. Lewis and Clark were to make contact and befriend the Native Americans where possible in this new land. They'd travel by keelboat, canoe, horse, and on foot some 3,700 miles without a single white blaze to guide them. Frankly, most of what was believed about the territory west of St. Louis was based on rumor, legend, Indian information, and some wishful thinking. The United States was primed for expansion and fortunately; a few individuals had the imagination to seek out what lay beyond the horizon. On May 14, 1804, the expedition started moving west from St. Louis along the Missouri River, a feat made all the more difficult since it was upstream.

Averaging only twelve to fourteen miles on a good day, they'd meet many Native American tribes, including the Sioux, Blackfoot, Omahas, Lakota, and the Shoshone. It will be a Shoshone woman named Sacagawea, who will become a highly valued member of the corps—thanks to her talent as an interpreter.

The fundamental belief at this time was that the Rocky Mountains were nothing more than a single ridgeline, and that upon reaching their summit and the headwaters of the Missouri, one could make a single day hike to the other side reaching the headwaters of the Great River of the West, which flowed to the Pacific. They couldn't have been more wrong. The "ridgeline" would last over a one hundred miles including the savage, snow-covered Bitterroot Mountains where for eleven days the group nearly starved, forced to eat their horses to survive. It was at this most desperate of hours that they found the Nez Perce Indians who befriended *them* with food, shelter, and kindness. Could it have been the Nez Perce who first created trail magic?

Animals never seen before were documented such as prairie dogs, bighorn sheep, buffalo, wolves, and the ferocious grizzly. (Give me a black bear any day, if we had grizzlies on the AT, I'm afraid a great many of us wouldn't be hiking solo.) In November, a year and half after setting off from St. Louis, they emerged to a coastal area of the Pacific. Unlike us, where our families often come and pick us up for the trip home, the Corps of Discovery would have to yo-yo. A yo-yo is a thru-hike where upon reaching the end, they turn around and hike back to the other end. Lewis and Clark would wait out the winter before heading back, still with an eye toward discovery and mapping.

Following in the footsteps of Lewis and Clark two hundred years later. Only I have white blazes.

The hoped-for water route across the continent simply did not exist, but the journey marked the turning point for western exploration of North America. The men were welcomed back as heroes when they finally returned in September of 1806. They had been gone so long that much of the nation feared they were dead. Dead tired would be more accurate!

I started back in Georgia four months ago in hopes of living my own adventure. The Appalachian Trail hasn't disappointed me.

Something special presented itself today as a gift. A classic Maine vista! As the rain lifted and the sun broke through, I was given this vast fifty to seventy-mile view of mountains and lakes like none I've seen. It simply looked like Maine, unspoiled, untouched, and limitless. These last two-hundred-plus miles are going to be special indeed!

Location:	Rangeley, Maine
Today's Miles:	13.1
Total Miles:	1954.1
Date:	September 1, 2004

It was Moose o' Plenty Day. First, while en route to the trailhead we saw a momma and her calf. Then another moose, on the side of the road, as well. So three and I wasn't even on the trail yet. The day held high hopes. On the trail, the hoof prints were just everywhere. Big, small, coming, going—I know they were watching me from deep stands of evergreens. Alleghany needed to go into Rangeley for his mail drop, so he and I each grabbed a room at the Rangeley Inn as well as "Polar" and "Pilot"—two other thru-hikers we met this morning at the trailhead. Both are teachers out west; Polar is from Jackson Hole, Wyoming, and Pilot I believe is from . . . hmm, can't remember. They both started as solo female hikers and bonded early on and have hiked together for months now—more nice new people.

Here at the Rangeley Inn, there on a wall of the lobby, was moose no.4. Only most of that moose was missing, unless of course its body was on the other side of the wall. Word has it that here at the inn, unexplained things happen—unexplained things that go bump in the night sending chills down your spine. Maybe I'll get to see a moose ghost. Would that count as no.5? So Moose o' Plenty Day was fun; however, I still haven't seen one on the trail. Oh well, there's still time!

ACTUAL SIZE

moose PRINT

Location:	Poplar Ridge Lean-To
Today's Miles:	10.7
Total Miles:	1964.8
Date:	September 2, 2004

I planned a shorter day for Alleghany and I based on Saddleback, the Horn, and Saddleback Jr. mountains. The morning was a brisk forty-three degrees, clear blue cloudless sunshine. Fall is in the air. Oh, and no ghost came to visit any of us last night.

My guidebook says on a clear day you can see Mt. Katahdin to the north. It certainly was clear and indeed, I think I may have located the correct profile shape of Katahdin on the far distant horizon. But it was impossible to say for certain since I've never seen it other than in photos. The first time I see it will be from the Appalachian Trail—that seems appropriate. As the crow flies, Katahdin may be 150 miles, but as the AT wiggles, about 210 miles. With the wind and temperature, it was simply too cold to hang out on Saddleback Mountain, it was once again above tree line.

As the sun climbed higher, I reached Saddleback Jr., a mere mile from our planned nights stay, I lounged for two hours on the summit. It was glorious! I just flopped down and soaked up the rays, I think I got a tad sunburned actually.

It feels like a half day. The lower mileage is OK when its tough going, but today it eased up. As a result I got here so quickly I felt guilty not pushing on. Hmm. I wonder if this desire to keep walking will be one of the adjustments after the trail.

Loon

A swimming bird of large size with a daggerlike bill, dives from the surface to submerge for minutes at a time. Its birdsong is my absolute favorite of the trail. A falsetto wail and weird yodeling. At night, a haunting haa-ooooo-oooooo. *Loons are what make Maine feel all the more like a wilderness. I got the pleasure of a loon serenade from Pierce Pond Shelter.*

Location:	Crocker Cirque Campsite
Today's Miles:	14.2
Total Miles:	1979.0
Date:	September 3, 2004

A couple of interesting things happened as a result of today's hike. First, we passed under the two hundred miles remaining mark. Currently from tonight's tent site, we're only 195.1 miles from the northern terminus and the end of the entire Appalachian Trail.

Additionally, out of necessity, I did a plan to determine my finishing date. It all comes down to assumptions that the weather will be good and that the summit of Mt. Katahdin will be open. The rangers close it down during bad weather if human life would be at risk climbing it—it is above tree line.

Mt. Katahdin, being Maine's highest, is also the AT's highest continuous mountain ascent. But I'll save more on that for later, back to my finishing date. I have Alleghany and me on an aggressive schedule, which has us summit on Thursday, September 16. This could adjust longer to the seventeenth or eighteenth since the sixteenth means two weeks without a zero day! We both want to go for it. Alleghany wants to because it will bring him in one day shy of five months. Me, I just like the idea of saying four and a half months. Plus, I miss doing more miles or said another way, moving throughout the whole day agrees with me. I don't want to feel I'm lollygaggin'. But tomorrow its Stratton, Maine, for my mail drop, that is if I can do 7.3 miles and hitch in before the post office closes at 11:30 a.m. Then it will be more good town food—lunches, dinners, and breakfast to load me up on calories and energy and fat. My pants are getting awfully droopy. I'm wavering on the edge of maintaining my power on the climbs. The town food will help me store up what I need to complete these last two weeks.

Holy cow, did I just say *two more weeks?*

Hopping rocks is usually how we get across rivers.
Sometimes though, we're given the luxury of a bridge.

Location:	Stratton, Maine
Today's Miles:	7.3
Total Miles:	1986.3
Date:	September 4, 2004

One of the even earlier risers at camp last night agreed to wake Alleghany and me up at 5 a.m.—so I could get a very early start. The post office on Saturdays has very short hours—9:30 to 11:30 a.m. only. But when the voice came to wake us up at five, I told Alleghany I was going back to sleep. Besides, who wants to hike in the dark? At six, Alleghany woke me and said, "You can still make it if you want to." Yep! My George Patton side kicked in! I had the tent packed and all gear loaded in twenty-five minutes. With me being out of food, Alleghany gave me a cookie, some peanut butter crackers, and a cereal bar. I was off like the wind! I climbed both peaks of Crocker Mountain in an hour-five. In only two hours fifty, I was opening up my "Hiker to Town" bandana on Maine road 27 and was in a car heading to Stratton in less than one minute. I walked into the post office at the amazing time of 9:40 a.m. My next stop was to be the Stratton Motel, only the owner of the motel appeared to pick up his mail. Yep, got a ride and a room before 9:50! How's that for military precision! It's just amazing how all the logistics can fall so neatly into one effortless event. The trail continues to surprise.

It's now only 10:30 a.m.; and I've already had three eggs, two orders of bacon, home fries, English muffins, coffee, the biggest OJ they serve, and a slice of pecan pie just for the heck of it! And guess what, I'm still hungry. Good thing lunch starts in an hour.

Spruce Grouse

*The most tame, feathered friend of the AT. The males have a comb of red skin above their eye,
the females are a model of camouflage. You'll see many hanging out right on the trail
in the northern evergreen forests.*

Location:	Little Bigalow Lean-To
Today's Miles:	15.3
Total Miles:	2001.6
Date:	September 5, 2004

Two thousand miles!

It happened at 4:35 p.m. on this, the fifth day of September.

Isn't it amazing what the human spirit can accomplish? This painted milestone sits right in the middle of one of the last paved roads we'll see for some time. It actually sits at 2,006 miles because of how the AT grows slightly longer each year with relocations. The trail is 99 percent protected; but as more land is acquired, it is relocated on to that land till it reaches the full 100 percent. But the marker is still a great photo opportunity.

As a reward, the terrain will be easing off a bit now. I've gotten past those first one hundred miles of Maine, which are the second Whamy after leaving the Whites. In fact, tomorrow I face nothing higher than a five-hundred-foot climb. The next ten days will see the daily mileage pushed back up a tad. A feat only made possible because Maine now wants to give us a big smile and offer its congrats on our hike with more gentle walks.

The trail is taking us into more remote areas with each passing day. The evidence of this is found by simply looking up into the inky black of space and a field of stars so bright and numerous it leaves you speechless. The Milky Way is clearly visible tonight since moonrise is still hours away.

One of today's big surprises was turning a corner and walking into another hiker named Baltimore Jack. We first met in Hot Springs, North Carolina, and then later in Harpers Ferry. We chatted for a while and then One Leg Wonder appeared! I hadn't seen him since the Shenandoahs in Virginia. He flip-flopped and was now heading south to avoid the winter. His artificial leg was holding up although this was leg no.3. Baltimore Jack and he were heading for the Whites. What surprises the AT brings you.

Well, it's going to be cold tonight, so I'm going to visit the woods once more then zip down deep into the mummy and hope nature doesn't call till morning light. I suspect my down-filled mummy is losing its loft and as a result, its warming powers. The only way to regain it is with a good tumble in a dryer with some tennis balls thrown in. Not too many of those out here.

I've been thinking about my friends in Florida with Hurricane Francis pounding on them and others lurking out at sea. Hope you, guys, are doing OK. Good night all.

Two thousand miles on foot and heart.

My Driftwood Thru-hike Trophy

For the last couple of months, I've been looking for that certain something that would be my main souvenir from this adventure. I have a whole house of rocks and such from all over the globe representing my travels. This morning, we came to Flagstaff Lake shrouded in fog and mystery. We had to take a closer look, and there with thousands of others, was this amazingly shaped skull-like driftwood. Alleghany and I were both amazed at its sculptured qualities; it reminded me of a Georgia O'Keeffe painting. When I informed Alleghany I'd be hiking out with it, he assumed I was suffering from calorie-deficit disorientation. It was out of my character to carry extra pack weight. I strapped the trophy to the backpack and for twenty-five miles it was just the three of us.

(Steve Longley, the ferryman who will canoe us across the Kennebeck River in another day or so, will turn out to be an admirer of driftwood himself and will mail the prize home.)

Location:	Pierce Pond Lean-To
Today's Miles:	17.3
Total Miles:	2018.9
Date:	September 6, 2004

Joy, oh, joy. The trail was smooth, flat, and wonderful. We haven't had such a nice walk in the woods for over a month. Why I actually snapped my hiking poles together and carried them. The most amazing thing happened earlier today and right now at this very moment as I'm writing. I was granted one of my two wishes since entering Maine. Seeing a moose on the trail being one, but I've always wanted to hear a loon in the wild. I've seen them, just haven't heard them. Today at "second breakfast," the shelter was at West Carry Pond and that's where a loon called out five or six times. But as special as it was, this shelter is positioned no more than forty feet from Pierce Pond. Loons have been coming in and out all afternoon and now that sunset has come, they're calling out to one another. It's such a haunting lonely call. Beautiful. Wonderful. What a serenade to fall asleep to. This is Maine. This is the AT.

Here at the pond's edge with the crackle of a campfire and the last wisps of magenta hanging in the sky, listening to the loons is as perfect a moment as one can have. Maine and this adventure are so special. This is why I chose to thru-hike.

257

Location: Pleasant Pond Lean-To
Today's Miles: 9.7
Total Miles: 2028.6
Date: September 7, 2004

The symphony put on by the loons last night was magnificent, and the sunset lived up to the symphony. It was simply the best one over these last four months.

Alleghany and I only had a short three-plus miles to reach the Kennebeck River for the 9 to 11 a.m. canoe/ferry crossing. In the past, fording the Kennebeck was part of the hike until a hiker drowned when the water rose too quickly for the individual. Upstream is a dam that does water releases periodically without warning. Since then, a ferry-person and a canoe have been the official way to cross. The canoe has a white blaze painted on it for the purest. Steve Longley arrived on the other side at nine and came across to pick us up. It was a fun and uneventful crossing.

We headed down the road for a big breakfast just a few miles away. Then it was a brief stop for the needed resupply that it'll take to reach Monson—my last mail drop. Monson will be the last town before we enter the 100-Mile Wilderness. It's one of the most remote areas of Maine and obviously the AT. When we come out of it, we're at the foot of Mt. Katahdin in Baxter State Park. But there will be more on that as it comes. After tonight, there are only eight more days till we summit—according to our plan. Everything is becoming more quiet, more calm. I wonder if this is the lull before the storm, I'm wondering if the AT wants to give us one more big day of drama.

The forecast is calling for several days of rain, thanks to the remnants of Hurricane Francis. This complicates things since the remaining mileage of 145.5 miles has many river fords. We'll hope for low calm water and tall wide rocks for those. I'd cross my fingers if it didn't make holding my hiking poles so darn difficult.

Sunset at Pierce Pond and the splendid loon serenade.

Location:	Horseshoe Canyon Lean-To
Today's Miles:	22.0
Total Miles:	2050.6
Date:	September 8, 2004

Today's hike had a theme! Red and wet. We woke to sprinkles and a forecast that promised hard rain for the afternoon. It would be the first day over twenty miles since entering the Whites; I have to admit to looking forward to knocking off some bigger miles. Of course, there was a good reason other than stroking the ego. A long day would give us a short nine miles into Monson the next day—that means getting in at around 10 a.m., leaving lots of time for eating, resupply, eating, laundry, eating, and a bed. Not to mention finding a whole Dutch apple pie which I can devour solo. But back to red and wet.

The trail has been bringing us farther north with every day, and each day I see more and more trees in full autumn color. Bright reds and magentas. Brilliant oranges and yellows sprinkled here and there. The forest is far from its peak; this is just the warm-up act to the grand show to come.

Now for the wet. The rain last night had every leaf, bush, and tree poised to soak us every time we rubbed against them. Add the light rain and you've got a fairly moist thru-hiker. But that's not the fun part. I had three stream fords. The first was manageable with some creative rock and tree hopping. The second had all the rocks underwater so it was shoes into the water. Amazingly there was no difference in the feeling of my socks and shoes when they were submerged. Obviously my feet were already soaked before wading in, and I didn't even know it.

Now came the third, which was a true ford. I found a section where the rocks came up shallower allowing for a knee-high water depth. Other areas would have required a waist-high ford—glad I looked before I crossed. And I'm glad I crossed before all the rain of Hurricane Francis dumps on the land. Which for the record, is now moving in at this hour of 7 p.m. In the morning, we have another river ford right out of the shoot, so we'll get to walk the last miles into Monson in soggy socks again. Oh boy, oh boy.

Only a measly 123.5 miles to Mt. Katahdin now, I can hardly grasp it yet. Its not that I wish it would be over nor do I need it to continue. For me, there's just a new level of excitement to completing this fantastic adventure. Reaching the finish line has its own rewards. Oh, after 2,050 miles, I've finally lost a toenail. Actually two, at the same time. It—the left foot middle nail—fell off today. The right foot middle nail is dangling by 10 percent. My big left toe still has about 70 percent numbness. My right big toe has about 40 percent numbness. That, my gentle reader, is an amazingly lucky foot care fact. I've known hikers who've lost five nails and have had blisters out the whazoo.

Blisters have been miraculously absent for me. My tally for falling down now is thirteen; I seem to be catching up to Alleghany whose up around twenty-four or twenty-five? Remember I had only three falls for the first 1,700 miles, and then I entered the Whites and Maine. But the worst fall is still when I was in Virginia at the Blackburn AT Center hostel. I was backing through a door with my hands full and forgot about the door jam. *Bam!* Over I went flat on my back. I laid there on the floor laughing at the absurdity of it all. A door jam! Hell, apparently it's safer for me to live in the woods.

One of my more comedic campfires.
Seems the breeze wanted to see if I could asphyxiate Alleghany.

Every person on the Appalachian Trail is different. Some of those differences are vast, and fortunately, some are minuet. I met and hiked with a lot of nice people on my journey north. Hikers like Belle, Carp, Pop Up, Reverend Yukon Jack, Mello Mike, Dharma and Greg, April Showers, Luna, Dave Underfoot, Goose, Rainy J, Bilbo, Waker, Smack, Polar, Pilot, Rowboat, K Bear, Doosie, Cliff Dancer, Neon Leon, Stumpy, Caterpillar, Critter, Speak Up, Megabite, Locomotive and Navigator, Mercury, London, Trail Dawg, Wife and Beater, and of course my buddy Alleghany. Some of these chance meetings might be a shared shelter for a night and some would last a week or more due to similar plans. Seldom did I actually walk with them throughout the day, sharing the land, the views, and the silliness. Doing so was enjoyable but was the exception in my hike. Not for any reason other than everyone had their own pace and plan. When I met Goose, I increased my pace to match his and in turn, Dave Underfoot joined in. When I met Waker, he increased his pace to match mine, and so on. Sometimes matching another's pace means slowing down, reducing your miles. This chain of humanity moved north in a variety of ways.

Some latch on to others for security, and some hike farther and faster to lose personalities they'd rather not be around. The social dynamic really isn't that different from anywhere else, but thru-hikers, since we face the same challenges, have an openness toward each other that takes much longer in the normal world.

Long before I met Alleghany, I knew of him, thanks to the shelter registers. Registers are nothing more than a spiral notebook or ledger that is left in the shelter for hikers to write messages, warnings, tell of encounters, or share a trail joy with others on the trail. It helps us to keep track of one another and makes for fun reading each night. They also serve a practical purpose if an emergency back home arises and a hiker needs to be located. A trail runner can check a register to see if the hiker has signed in or not and then be able to determine if they should move north or south along the trail in hopes to find them.

I'd seen Alleghany's entries in the registers for some time since he was up in front of me. And then there was the news of his rattlesnake bite in Connecticut that moved up and down the trail.

The last place I'd expect to encounter a rattlesnake is Connecticut, the pearl necklace and cashmere sweater capital of the world. But Alleghany did. So after a two-mile walk where his leg was in constant trauma, he made it to a road and an ambulance and then a helicopter and then into an emergency room. Although terribly painful, Alleghany was lucky. He had received what is called a "dry bite." What many of us learned from his experience was that four out of five rattlesnake bites are dry bites. This means bites where the snake doesn't release its venom. Generally the bite is an action of defense and only when the snake is actually hunting for prey will it release venom. But the fangs of the reptile are not exactly void of toxins or other chemicals that don't fair well for the human central nervous system. So Alleghany and his leg had to be monitored closely to see if the tissue around the wound was dieing. Thankfully, it wasn't, meaning it was a nonvenom dry bite.

After three long hospital days, a few newspaper and TV interviews, Alleghany returned to the Appalachian Trail a celebrity. A man of true grit and a big, deep smile that reaches to his toes, a nicer guy would be hard to find. He continued north answering his childhood dream to thru-hike the AT he had carried since age nine. A talented guitar player and vocalist, he hiked with a purpose and knew how to make miles. We met that first night in Vermont, he was moving with a tribe of hikers who for me were entirely new faces. As the weeks progressed, we'd bump into one another about every five days through Vermont and New Hampshire. Then in Maine during a zero day, he came walking into the Andover Guest House. He found me with my feet up, drinking red wine, and enjoying the *Lord of the Rings* movie. I stuck a beer in his hand, and our friendship began to grow. He admitted to me later that when he first met me, he didn't like his first impression. But as he ran into me more, he did. I, on the other hand, told him that when I first met him, I did like him. And now that I've been able to know him better, I don't. We were always heckling each other that way—great fun. Alleghany knows how to laugh.

As strong as he is, the emotional stamina required to contend with the physical difficulty of the Whites and the early parts of Maine had started to chip away at his ever-present smile. Walking into the guest house that day and seeing a familiar face, mine, offered a degree of comfort I suppose. Of course, it may have been the beer I stuck in his hand. The next day, we hiked together for the first time, which turned out to be ten miles of laughter. With him being a free spirit and I being a planner, we complimented each other. And with the prospect of having some company through

Alleghany. Snake bite survivor, comedian, imminent 2004 thru-hiker.

the passage of the 100-Mile Wilderness seemed to make sense. In Alleghany I found someone who could hike every bit as strongly as I could. He experiences the same kind of pride in knocking out bigger mileage days. Together, we're finding the dynamic of what he calls the "push-pull." I push him sometimes to go farther and then sometimes he pulls me to go longer. Even though I'm content in my solitude along the trail, hiking with a buddy makes for a richer adventure. There have been times when I wished I could turn to someone and say, "Wow, would you look at that!" Sharing the trail or any of our life's moments with others is in itself another level of joy. Frankly, some hikers simply are not comfortable being by themselves in the mountains; it can be quite unnerving. Having been out here as long as I have, it's easy to understand. Neither of us really needs the other, we just like the fact we make each other laugh. I hope you're all having as much fun as Alleghany and I are.

Location:	Monson, Maine
Today's Miles:	9.0
Total Miles:	2059.6
Date:	September 9, 2004

Will my shoes ever be dry again?

Thanks to the remnants of Hurricane Francis, the Appalachian Trail was a sloppy, muddy, mushy mess. Any hope of keeping dry shoes and socks today would be futile. Heck, whom I kidding, after yesterday's numerous river fords, my shoes weren't even close to dry. And today's hike into Monson would see more of that. So we slogged our way north getting ever closer to Mt. Katahdin. However, between Monson and Katahdin is the gulf of woods called the 100-Mile Wilderness.

By the time the trail came out of the woods to ME15, the rain was relentless. The wind had come up and temperatures had dropped—this is not a favorable scenario for staying warm. After twenty cars drove by without even slowing, I figured I'd better start walking the 3.5 miles toward town. At least that would keep me warm.

Alleghany emerged from the woods about twenty minutes later and got a hitch instantly. So he and the trail magic couple who picked him up was pulling over to save me from the rain and the rest of the road walk.

Soggy and chilled, we got dropped off at the house of the Pie Lady. It's a guesthouse of some tradition; of course her pies are the main draw. I went to the post office to pick up box no.27. Box no.27 is my last mail drop. Box no.1 was four months earlier back in Georgia. Wow, that was so, so long ago. Was that this year? When you walk every day for hours and hours across a significant portion of this country, you tend to have full, rich in texture days.

My goal in Monson was simple. Eat a whole apple pie. Mission accomplished, I'm happy to say. But heading into the 100-Mile Wilderness means no town stops or food drops, as a result I have to carry a lot more food than normal. In fact, it won't all fit into my two food bags, a small dilemma. The plan for Alleghany and I was to cross this section in bigger mileage days that will have us out five nights, arriving at the foot of Mt. Katahdin around lunchtime on the sixth day—most likely with empty food bags. Tomorrow morning, I head out on the last chapter of this unbelievable adventure. This next week will be a journey within the journey I think.

To complicate it all, it seems I've caught a cold. Gee, I wonder how doing 21.5 miles with a head cold is going to feel?

*The 100-Mile Wilderness warning sign would prove
to be truer than we could have imagined on day 1.*

Location: Long Pond Stream Lean-To
Today's Miles: 15.1 (not counting the multi-mile detour)
Total Miles: 2074.7
Date: September 10, 2004

Jumping Jehoshaphat!

I've had wet days, but this was ridiculous. You know all that rain I mentioned from the remnants of Hurricane Francis. Well, it sure turned our river fords into some high drama for day 1 of the 100-Mile Wilderness.

We had three thigh-high, 10 mph current crossings, and two waist-high even faster current crossings. I must have spent or should I say wasted two hours easy on trying to just find the safest place to attempt the ford. At some points it was crazy and frustrating and exciting and dangerous. The roar of the rapids was so loud and violent it had everyone on edge. With the dilemma of where to cross river no.1, other hikers had come up on us. It was totally insane. The current was close to 20 mph and just raging mad. The depth of this beast was completely unknown since to test it was to literally risk life and limb. These other hikers who joined us while we were reconnoitering said they came out to hike the AT not to kill themselves. One of them suggested that we backtrack on the logging roads and rejoin the AT on the other side. It was the only way, and so off we set on a multiple-mile detour that brought us eventually back around to the other side of the river and AT again. I'd find out later that other hikers who didn't think of the detour, ended up camping at that river for over a day waiting for the rapids to stop raging. If all that wasn't nutty enough, the second river

couldn't be crossed either; but Alleghany, in our divide and scout upstream and downstream, came across an old dilapidated wreck of a bridge. I mean this thing was right out of an Indiana Jones movie. It didn't go all the way across, but the cables were in place, so it was quite "iffy" but our best bet. I went first using one side of the cable, then when the bridge ran out, crossed over to the other cable for the last tightrope walk over the roaring river and a successful traverse.

After we made it across that obstacle—I mean bridge—I started humming the theme song to *Raiders of the Lost Arc*.

The 100-Mile Wilderness was putting on a great show for our first day. It was the longest 15.1 miles I've done since—well, since ever. We made it into the shelter just at sunset after three more swollen river fords. It was a very full, harrowing day. It was a day Hollywood has tried to bring us in countless movies, only this wasn't a movie.

My head cold has bloomed throughout all this. Of course, wearing wet socks and pants and everything with a chilled wind is maybe not the best treatment—but I could be wrong on that. Unfortunately, there aren't too many beds out here and mothers willing to make you chicken soup.

Alleghany demonstrating how we battled the river gods.

Location:	Carl Newhall Lean-To
Today's Miles:	20.8
Total Miles:	2095.5
Date:	September 11, 2004

Carrying thirty pounds on your back twenty miles has never been easy, but do it in Maine's wilderness terrain with a head cold and there won't be any part of you that isn't totally spent. Actually, at nineteen miles I was totally spent, the last 1.8 miles I was the walking dead. When the night's destination is at the top of a mountain, it means a long, labor-intensive climb when you've got no gas left in the tank. You just keep going and hoping you'll see the small sign pointing to the side trail and the shelter. Gazing upon that sign is enough to turn borderline despair into elation. Upon arriving, I unpacked and headed back down to the sign to wait for Alleghany, only I wasn't alone. I brought along my small flask of Captain Morgan Spiced Rum to give him a reward. His eyes lit up when he saw me, meaning he was finally at the shelter. Then seeing the flask I was holding out, well, it seemed the exhaustion and toil of his day evaporated like that of a distant echo. Science has told us that physiologically, the recipient of a kindness will actually produce a chemical, possibly called serotonin, and experience euphoria. That's why we all feel so good when we are given things. Wonderfully, the giver is also rewarded physiologically with the euphoria. So being nice to others has its rewards, just in case you need a reason.

On the summit of Chairback Mountain, we got our first positive look of Mt. Katahdin. Unlike before when we weren't exactly sure, today left no doubt.

Tonight, here in the shelter, the "Greatest Mountain" as known by the Native Americans is a mere 78.6 miles away. In these last two days we've covered a full third of the 100-Mile Wilderness. And although the day started with a very chilly morning, we were blessed with midseventies and bright blue skies that went on and on. We had another river ford this afternoon; only this one didn't hold the peril of yesterday's five. Alleghany and I were discussing how those crossings were the most dangerous, life-threatening challenge of the entire journey. Normally routine, the excessive rain from Hurricane Francis on top of all the other rains had those rivers out of control. It was a day that won't be forgotten easily. Maybe they were the AT's last hurrah, that last bit of drama to wake us up and not let us forget the journey. But I can assure you that won't ever be an issue.

My cold, thanks to heavy dosages of medicine, is a tad better or at least that's what I'm telling myself. The 20.8 miles weren't a lung or shortness-of-breath issue, it was just exhaustingly awkward footing that went on the whole day. Another cold night had me using the silk sleeping bag liner to warm up the mummy as well as wearing extra clothes. *Brrr.*

With today being the anniversary of the 9/11 attack, it makes me more appreciative that I'm on this journey. One should not postpone life if they can help it, because anything can happen as we all learned. Being here has made me more aware of life than at any other time. This is a time more than any other to count what we have rather than what we have not. To keep those we love close and seek out the brighter side of life. Some run away from something to the Appalachian Trail while others are running to something. Whichever the motive, it affords you vast amounts of time for introspection or prayer or rejuvenation.

Would I recommend a thru-hike to someone else? Yes, no, maybe. A thru-hike is a deeply personal experience and so should be a personal decision. Has it been good for me? Most definitely. Hopefully this journal will help others make the decision of what would be best for them.

The wonderful wilderness of awes.

Red Fox

Red foxes generally hunt at night, covering many miles in search of food. Hunting mice is one of their most favorite entrees, which may explain why it was at our shelter in Maine. Not much heavier than fifteen pounds, they actually pounce on their prey like that of a cat. Their strong sense of hearing and smell aids in the hunt where they can detect a mouse squeak from 150 yards.

Location:	Cooper Brook Lean-To
Today's Miles:	18.9
Total Miles:	2114.4
Date:	September 12, 2004

Day 3 in the 100-Mile Wilderness. It started with a four-peak ascent over White Cap Mountain. Of course they named each peak as if each was a mountain. The real show comes when you reach peak no.4, White Cap. That's when you really see it. There before us was a close view of Mt. Katahdin, if you call sixty miles close. It's huge. My wide angle camera lens doesn't do it justice. This was the first look where nothing was in front; Katahdin rises up 5,200-plus feet with nothing else around it. It was the only summit touching the clouds. So powerful. So majestic. Our guidebooks say we are now only 59.7 miles of trail from the summit. It also says we walked through 2,100 miles. Tomorrow looks promising despite a planned 21.5-mile day. The profile maps show flat terrain with no significant climbs. When I say flat, what I really mean is "mostly." Nothing is flat out here.

The first good look at Mt. Katahdin and the finish line.

The annoying head cold seemed to bother me more today for some reason, but I think the medications are winning. Good thing. Here at Cooper Brook Lean-To, we're right on the brook and its loud waterfall. Should be warmer here being down low and by the water. I've been freezing my Mahoosucs off the last two mornings.

Location:	Wadleigh Stream Lean-To
Today's Miles:	21.5
Total Miles:	2135.9
Date:	September 13, 2004

I woke to hearing a wild-hair idea from Alleghany to hike farther than the 21.5 miles planned. It seems some fourteen miles ahead of us is a lodge at a large pond that serves gigantic burgers if you're willing to take the three-mile round-trip detour. "Jeeze, Alleghany, if 21.5 miles isn't far enough for you, how 'bout carrying my pack too?" I said. He just smiled his wry little smile fully knowing he'd wear me down into taking the detour before we got there.

Normally, when we head out in the morning, he sets out at a 2.4 mph pace, but this morning with the promise of a "ginormous" burger on the horizon, he was blazing a 3.3 mph pace. (Got to respect a hiker who loves his food!) Miraculously, the awkward Maine terrain gave way to gentle, smooth, meandering trail. By the hour of noon, we had fourteen miles behind us and the detour to fantasy foodland at our feet. Off we went, hearing the sizzle of burgers like the sirens of the sea.

This hiker paradise in the 100-Mile Wilderness is a relatively new tradition and certainly is eroding "the wilderness" component of this section. It's called White House Landing, and we've been hearing about it for months. The detour led us through the woods to a pond side dock where a note said to use the air horn that dangled from the pole. We did.

To our amazement, we saw someone way across the water walk down to a boat and head over to pick us up. I was still in a little disbelief at all this. Hellos were exchanged, and off we went back across to the lodge where no sooner did we walk in that a *one pound* burger was dropped on the grill. This nirvana, this oasis had it all. A frig with sodas and brownies the size of Texas. Yep, had one of those too. Some hikers stay the night to get the full royal treatment of White House Landing, but our plan called for a five-day passage of the wilderness, so at 1:30, we were ferried back across the pond full and happy.

It was a great break, and I'm glad Alleghany coaxed me into it. Besides, we sure could use the calories. In no time at all we made it to the Wadleigh Lean-To. It was one of those days that make you smile deep down inside. Of course, it could have been that pound of burger. The only bummer of the day was figuring out where my burger went to. One moment I was grabbing on to it, the next moment it seemed to have vanished! Thru-hiker hunger is a power not to be toyed with.

The White House Landing boat ride to a thru-hiker size burger.

Wild Blueberries

Maybe what Maine is most famous for. Every day we get an opportunity to eat along the trail.
The berries are not as large as the cultivated ones, and the bushes are not much taller than my knee
but are loaded with the sweet blessings. Always a treat.

Location: Hurd Brook Lean-To
Today's Miles: 19.6
Total Miles: 2155.5
Date: September 14, 2004

Brrr, who left the refrigerator door open? I figured it was about thirty-eight degrees this morning. Just couldn't get warm in the mummy. I kept waking up through the night putting more clothes on. First gloves, then another jacket, and then zipped so tight only my nose was sticking out. And even it felt cold. Glad I'm not claustrophobic.

I hate to whine, but it sure is hard to get motivated in the morning when you're an ice cube. But I did, and it didn't take but five minutes before I started peeling off layers. Hiking sure warms you up fast. Regardless of the cold, thirty minutes later the view of Katahdin would warm the soul. It just keeps getting bigger and closer and more real. Big K is now an unbelievable short 18.6 miles away. What was most significant about today was my attitude, which was one of slow, no-rush pace. But even when I don't try to rush, I made the 19.6 miles by 3 p.m. How does that keep happening? Two thousand one hundred miles of hiking tends to make you quick of foot I guess. Tomorrow we leave the 100-Mile Wilderness and see Katahdin from Abol Bridge, the crossing that takes us into Baxter State Park.

Location:	Katahdin Stream Campground
Today's Miles:	13.4
Total Miles:	2168.9
Date:	September 15, 2004

Hello from Katahdin Stream Campground at the foot of the Greatest Mountain—Mt. Katahdin.

The sun was just waking up when we headed out at 6:15 a.m. After a short fast hour, I emerged out of the wilderness to a logging road that led to Abol Bridge and the camp store for coffee and supplies. But it is the bridge that's famous because it provides us with the "postcard" view of Mt. Katahdin. Once again the weather was ideal—clear endless skies with a warm sunny forecast. What a blessing.

I stood on the bridge staring in awe. Throughout the last week, I've been inching ever closer to it. Mt. Katahdin has gone from being a bump on the horizon to the massive edifice that rose from the earth before me. Once only known as a word, now, tomorrow, it would be a bigger-than-life end to the grandest of adventures. As Alleghany and I entered Baxter State Park, we were a bundle of giggles and pride. This hike has made me the most joyful I can ever remember. It has brought a childlike glee in seeing and experiencing simple things. Each day brought new challenges and new reasons to smile. It deepened my faith and vanquished my lingering mental baggage. Now, more than ever, my stride has a bounce. Standing there on that bridge, looking at that breathtaking monster, it seemed impossible to grasp it all. I'm amazed at my own athleticism, my ability to climb and descend ridiculously rugged terrain. From fording raging rivers to balancing over bog walks and rock hopping and moving from root to tree to whatever. A new level of ability has emerged. Facing the anxiety of the dangerous and the harshness of weather has given me a greater respect for the power of this land.

Standing there was surreal in ways and a hard-earned reward in others. Each state asked us to master a different aspect of the trail; each in turn prepared us for the next phase of difficulty. Tomorrow is the culmination of all that's been learned. Tomorrow I climb the Greatest Mountain and drop my small stone I picked up at Springer Mountain, Georgia, some four and a half months earlier on the summit cairn. The stone has traveled far. My heart and head have traveled further. I think the distance is the most difficult part to comprehend as opposed to the time investment. I have a greater understanding about the size of our land and the size of our planet. Some say, "It's a small world." Yes, unless you walk it. Tomorrow I walk one of the shortest distances of the entire journey, only 5.2 miles up to the summit of Mt. Katahdin. The journey will officially be over, but it's safe to say the memories will not.

The Abol Bridge "postcard" view of Mt. Katahdin.
One last mountain, a lifetime of memories.

Was today to be a bigger day than that starting one down in Georgia? It certainly didn't hold as much complication. Today held purity, one long climb to a sign that symbolizes the completion of one of this world's single greatest individual achievements. Surprisingly, I was able to sleep, but when I woke, I could feel a building rumble of enthusiasm inside.

I packed up my gear for what would be my last time. The pack wouldn't weigh its full weight since carrying loads of food wouldn't be necessary nor carrying my tent. An abbreviated load, mostly foul weather gear and lunch. One must still be prepared as a thru-hiker.

Months ago I was heard saying repeatedly that I'd make it to Maine and Mt. Katahdin if I continued to enjoy the journey. And enjoy it I have. Hikers had been heading up since sunrise; we weren't feeling any urgency to hustle. At the trailhead was a clipboard, which required us to sign in, later to sign out for safety reasons. From this location, the summit was shrouded in cloud cover, but there were patches of blue around. I signed in "Postcard" and glanced at my watch; it read 7:20 a.m. Alleghany and I moved out with a handshake. We'd see each other at the top. What happened next is still puzzling.

I moved out ahead at a pace that felt comfortable and came upon others who had started earlier. By the time the trail turned vertical into steep rock scrambling, many were behind me. I seemed to be powering my way up. A fact I wasn't aware of.

At a mile from the summit, the entire cloud cover cleared, that's when I saw the sign at the top. The closer I got, the faster I went until the last steps slowed to near nonmotion. I reached out with both arms to embrace the sign and rested my face against it. The puzzling part was the complete absence of time. What seemed like forty-five minutes was in reality two hours and forty-five minutes. Where had that time gone?

I posed for several pictures and sat down to gaze not at the above-cloud views and all the grandeur but at the Katahdin—the northern terminus AT sign. I wish I could say I was fully aware of the moment, but I wasn't. Despite being above the clouds, my heart and head were in a fog.

For me, reaching several landmarks along the way held as much significance. Reaching Harpers Ferry left me walking on air with pride. Making the Maine state line nearly brought me to tears of joy. Although my heart was filled with pride and jubilation, it was more of a silent version of them. I rested and reached for lunch and the arrival of Alleghany, which would happen nearly an hour later. When he arrived, he shouted out a rebel yell, and everyone applauded his achievement.

Only now, days later, do I know what was happening to me. I didn't want it to be over. Yes, I wanted to reach the end, but it also ended my recent way of life, which had given me so much joy. My "job" was now over. The simplicity I'd known for four and a half months, over. Adjustments to the normal world will undoubtedly be normal, and I'll write about those soon. But for now, just three words seem to capture it all—I did it.

Location: Summit of Mt. Katahdin
Today's Miles: 5.2
Total Miles: 2174.1
Date: September 16, 2004

I did it.

My final drawing from the Appalachian Trail, but not my last.

A Dedication

The two champions in my life.

It may be true that no one can walk our miles, but that doesn't mean others aren't with us every step of the way. Wives and husbands and friends all take a keen interest in our hikes. And then some go above and beyond to help reduce the burden and make the journey a bit easier. In my case, Shirley and Glenn, a.k.a. "the folks," set the standard for support.

It should be stated here that no matter how old you become, your parents will always act like parents. They can't help themselves. Worrying is one of the things parents do best. But worrying is also caring, and that bodes well for the son-turned-thru-hiker.

It's fair to say that my folks, especially my mother, lived my hike. Although both made sure that mail drops were properly loaded and shipped out on time, a box never failed to be where it needed to be. It was my mother who also transcribed my Internet trail journal. That alone was a very time-consuming task. A person who embraces growth, ever willing to learn, she had to master the art of the computer. Many her age shy away from such unknowns, but not her, she jumps in. Words like *browse* and *jpeg* stopped being concepts to fear. In doing so, I got to hear a growing pride in her voice on those weekly phone calls. She was climbing her own mountains right alongside the ones I was climbing.

As I moved north, they received my handwritten journal pages, my drawings, and the digital pictures of them on a memory stick weekly. With their arrival, she'd sit down with Dad and read the adventure out loud so they could both live the journey. Then she'd go to work and start the countless hours of typing and loading. As for my dad, short of the morning paper and his checkbook, he's not much for reading. That is, until I started writing this adventure. He would hover around waiting for pages to be added to the binder. He was discovering the joy of the journey in his own way. Seeing him sitting and reading my book as it came together certainly had my mother and me exchanging looks of wonder.

But there are more than mail drops and journal transcribing to thank them for. Since this was actually my third hiking season involved with the Appalachian Trail, all those shuttles and long drives to and from the trailheads can't go unmentioned. Even though it gave my father an excuse to get out his maps and visit AAA for countless directions, it still involves them shuffling their own lives to help. A gesture that always came willingly. I remember one particular November morning during that first year where Dad and I left at 5 a.m. for a trailhead when the temperature was twenty-three degrees. *Brrr.* Or that return drive back to Georgia to pick me up when I realized that a thru-hike that first season wasn't going to happen. During this season's past four and half months, it was impossible for them to not check the Weather Channel each day to see what I was facing. They wrote my checks to pay my bills, mastering the forging of my signature. They garaged my car and fed my pet and oversaw the arrival of all my worldly possessions when the movers loaded everything into my storage units. They even haggled with suppliers in Florida over the carry-over bills associated with the sell of my house.

More important than the logistical support though was the emotional support. After two seasons of intended thru-hikes gone awry, you'd think when I informed them that this season I'd be heading back to Georgia to start the whole darn thing over, forfeiting all the miles I'd already hiked, a few cutting remarks or disapproving intonations in their speech would ensue. Nope. None. What I got instead was encouragement and the acknowledgment that the concept of a thru-hike was inside me and important. In a way, it was inside them as well. This season, all three of us thru-hiked from Georgia to Maine. This season, we all did 2,174.1 miles, only I did mine on foot and they did theirs in their heart. Thank you, Mom and Dad. You are the best hiking partners anyone could ever hope for. May every future thru-hiker find the support and strength you have given me.

REFLECTIONS

Wow! How often in life do we get to use that word and truly mean it?

Where do hiking shoes go after successfully guiding one from Georgia to Maine? Mine got retired and turned into conversation pieces. They were good to me, despite the 17 falls that found me during the 2,174.1-mile adventure. I forgive them. As you can see, it took 3 pair to make it. The first pair lasted 600 miles. The second, a 1,000 miles and the third pair fell apart after 250 miles, but the treads remained sticky on the rocks so I ended up wearing them the last 600 miles. I didn't replace them on whether their seams fell apart, which they all did, but if they lost their grip.

Although only a short time has past since I stood atop Mt. Katahdin, it feels like ages ago. The following morning after I finished, some of the realities started to sink in on all that had taken place. As we packed up my car there in Millinocket, my folks needed this that or the other thing for the road trip back toward Philadelphia. It seems in their heads the journey couldn't begin without certain provisions for the ice chest, so off to the grocery store we went. That's what started the bubbling feelings to rise out of me. By the time they returned and everything was loaded, my eyes filled with tears and my heart with anxiety. At that moment I realized how wonderful the simplicity of hiking the Appalachian Trail truly was—to be cherished. It takes a lot of energy to orchestrate life, it's that energy or complication that makes me sad to have to reenter the normal world. The simplicity of life on the trail is what is most desirable. Only while you're out there you may not know it. So instead of welling up at the Katahdin sign, I chose the parking lot of a grocery store. Yea, nutty, I agree, and far from manly.

Will I be one of the few who do it all over again, another Thru-hike? Hmm? I think, most definitely, the Appalachian Trail will see my smile again someday.

Why wouldn't I want to reunite myself with an endeavor that brought me so very much joy? A Thru-hike is joyful, you ask? What's not joyful about simplicity, or a clear purpose, even if it is just a handful of months? Or to reunite with the camaraderie through shared interests, and huge smiles from vistas proudly earned, or transporting myself to another era with discovery and reveling in the grandeur and breathtaking beauty of this blessed land? If this journal can help just one person to succeed in their Thru-hike, then . . . it will have been a complete waste of time. What I want, what I wish for is that it will help many find the joy in the journey and that's why it includes a How-To component in the next section. With words *and* pictures, as well as a daily account, maybe you and others will have a clearer idea of what to expect. One can always hope.

"Twenty years from now, you will be more disappointed with the things you didn't do than by the ones you did do. So throw off the bowlines, sail away from safe harbor, catch the wind in your sails. Explore. Dream. Discover."—Mark Twain

There have been other adjustments that I've been keeping a list on which I'll now share:

1. A constant need for fresh air
2. Answering to my real name
3. Remembering to use deodorant
4. That my wallet no longer has to be a Ziploc
5. Forcing myself to put on different clothes each day, which leads me to
6. Getting used to the fact I now have a waist smaller than when I was in high school
7. That I can now use more than three squares of toilet paper at a time
8. To stop looking at delis and grocery stores with the mindset of resupply

9.   An astonishment at the impatience of so many behind
      the wheels of their cars
10.   Puzzled how all my expensive dress shoes became short,
      narrow, and tight while I was away
11.   That the normal world is a very noisy place
12.   And certainly not least, anxiously looking forward to the
      day when I can feel all of my big toes again

HAVE MORE SMILES IN *YOUR* MILES.

What Worked and What Failed Miserably

To hike the Appalachian Trail, we all follow the same white blazes. But how we follow them is as varied as the hikers. Having successfully thru-hiked it, I witnessed firsthand the good, the bad, and the ugly of others' gear choices and methods. With over two thousand miles of rocks, roots, mountains, and streams, as well as rain, wind, cold, and darkness, there's no reason your gear needs to add to the challenges. In many, I saw my own naïve self from just years earlier where reaching camp triggered an explosion of gear, confusion, and complexity. Some of these hiker worlds would literally resemble that of a bomb going off with everything everywhere and the hiker bewildered as to where a particular doodad had gone. Many have headed out the next morning without all their stuff because they didn't know another way. I can help.

When I first set out to thru-hike with absolutely no backpacking experience two years ago, I sought knowledge through many of the books that were available. Most, more than a decade old, would tout formulas for the weight one should carry at 25 percent of one's own body weight. As a result, I ended up down at Springer Mountain with a backpack as large as a coffee table but far heavier. This section is for those who'd like to avoid making the decisions that lead me to a fifty-four-pound pack and the thinking that it wouldn't be too much of a burden. Although I had the best of intentions and willing to equip myself properly for my six-month adventure, wrong choices were made. Whether you're a man or a woman, it makes no difference—the mountains and the weight do not discriminate. But thankfully, nor do the awe-inspiring vistas and crisp gentle breezes.

It is because I didn't succeed the first time that I believe this section will be all the more important to those wanting to hike. Mastering long-distance backpacking is easy, especially by taking advantage of the revolution that has swept the gear industry in the last few years. I'll help you to hike rather than trudge. To climb instead of grind. My successful Georgia-to-Maine thru-hike in the previous pages is the proof that you can have more smiles in your miles.

This section is a what-and-how-to compendium of what worked for others and me. Most is common sense and simplistic by design, but after seeing so many struggle, it seems many could benefit. Whether you've never climbed a mountain or have spent a whole life camping, you're sure to find an easier way here, or a "I never thought of that." With the right approach, it won't be a matter of whether you *can* touch the sign atop Mt. Katahdin but rather if you *want* to.

Backpacks Don't Have to Be Back Breakers

The first backpack I ever bought was an expedition-size, six-thousand-cubic-inch monster. I was to use it for a thru-hike of the Appalachian Trail. I had never bought a backpack before, so I didn't know what I needed, but the books told me it needed to be *big*. The outfitter I visited was one of those common chain stores that have lots of nice people but few who had long-distance backpacking experience. Or should I say long-distance experience that was more joyful than drudgery. I didn't even know what I didn't know and neither did the smiling salesperson. I didn't even know to ask if they knew anything about backpacking.

The one I selected was chosen for two reason, neither of them being price. For my adventure, price would be no object. I was convinced that the more I paid, the easier it would be to get to Maine.

The first involved the common sales technique of having me slip on the pack with about fifteen pounds of stuff crammed into it and then I was encouraged to walk around the store—the very flat, very smooth showroom floor. "Wow, that is really comfortable on flat showroom floors!" I thought. Gee, this is going to be easy.

The second reason was because, I hate to admit this, but because it was blue.

If those two selection criteria weren't a formula for failure, then the fact the salesperson decided on a large for me, rather than the more correct size of medium, which I wouldn't discover for two years later after two years of droopy packs and sore shoulders, then I don't know what is.

The largest mistake though by far was that I didn't know enough to care about what it weighed. A pack when empty isn't a big deal, but once all that other gear gets loaded, the ounces become pounds quickly. I was now the very proud owner of a 7 lbs 2 oz bundle of burden. And that was empty! Now I will say that if you want to go out with two weeks' worth of food and not ever resupply, then you'll need a bigger pack than what I thru-hiked with and you'll need to get used to caring sixty or more pounds. But I think few do, and I can almost guarantee you that the first week and half will be miserable until you eat that weight down so you can only be moderately uncomfortable.

Here's another way. Instead of a backpack that can carry anything you can think of taking, let's try getting a pack that limits what we can carry. Or at very least, makes us think about what it will and what load weight we should stay under.

The great thing about the gear revolution is that one lighter, smaller something lets you capitalize on a lighter, smaller something else. How so? In the case of backpacks, let's look at the gear world just ten years ago. The average pack weight on an Appalachian Trail thru-hike then was roughly forty-five to fifty-five pounds. As a result, the hiking footwear selection for the majority of hikers was a full leather boot. They provided the extra ankle support you'd need with that much of a load. However, full leather boots are heavy, so now we're adding heavier gear to help us handle our heavier gear. Whether its on our feet or our hips and shoulders makes no difference, you'll have to move with it on the journey. It's crazy. Your legs will think you've disowned them, your heaving lungs will curse you for all they're worth on those uphills, and your knees may just decide to retaliate on the downhills by making you crawl home. Naturally all this weight will affect your stamina and the number of miles you'll be able to do.

Thankfully, the same axiom is true for lighter gear. The more we lighten some of our gear, the more we can lighten the rest of the gear. As a parallel example, the most common hiking footwear on the AT this year was hiking shoes not boots. Being no taller than a sneaker, their weight is a fraction of a leather boot. This works since what most people are carrying is in the twenty-five-to-thirty-five pound range. With less load weight, your footwear can be lighter and your backpack can have fewer internal braces and straps which make it lighter too. Additionally, with everything being lighter, your stamina will be greater as well as your daily miles. See how it's all connected?

"Counting ounces isn't fanatical, it's practical."

—Me

The backpack that got me to Maine weighed a mere two pounds five ounces and could carry, if fully loaded, up to four-thousand-cubic inches. But I never filled it up. It had all the necessary luxury items like a good padded hip belt and stout load lifter straps. And it was really comfortable walking around an outfitters floor, not to mention two thousand miles of the Appalachian Mountains. Where I went right was seeking out the knowledge of well-experienced long-distance hikers and an outfitter that had individuals who knew their stuff. Along the Appalachian Trail, Mt. Rogers Outfitters

(MRO) in Damascus, Virginia and Mountain Crossings in Neels Gap, Georgia, foot the bill to name a few.

The backpack that won my heart was the ULA P2. ULA stands for Ultra Light Adventure. It's important to say here that I obviously believe in going light on gear but not ultralight. What's the difference? Hiking as an ultralighter means foregoing with luxuries. It means carrying the absolute bare minimum and nothing more. To me that seemed a bit harsh despite the low weight. I did not want my thru-hike to be a foray in deprivation. I wanted to have a few goodies to add richness and to normalize what would be the most extreme of endeavors. I'll speak of those specifics in a later chapter.

The ULA P2 came to me from MRO. It had wonderful pockets on the hip belt and outside mesh sleeves all around. This top loading pack is very simple but not simpleminded. It's designed for long-distance efficiency and proved to not have a single design or quality flaw. Other packs are good as well, but keep them at three pounds or less for a capacity of four-thousand-cubic inches. Remember, start counting every ounce, to save three ounces here means being able to subtract the weight of your headlamp. Save two pounds and you can hypothetically subtract the entire weight of your sleeping bag. Backpacks are a big source of weight. Be choosey, and don't let the color blue sway you.

One of the funnier aspects of those books I read early on were the diagrams that showed you techniques on how to hoist up those heavy fifty-pound backpacks onto your body. The clean and jerk to your thigh or hip, then wiggling your arm and shoulder under a strap, followed by the bend over to let the monster lay on your back as you coupled the hip belt. Good grief, I'm so glad I'm hiking without a coffee table on my back anymore.

With a target weight load of thirty pounds, you'll be able to grab the center top handle strap and just swing the pack up and around while you slip an arm through. It's all very sensible and much easier. Many make the mistake of grabbing one of the shoulder straps and raise the pack that way, but a single pack strap wasn't designed to carry the whole weight, albeit for just a few seconds, put a bunch of those lifts together and eventually they'll cause damage.

Another positive on hiking with lighter gear makes itself known on wet, foggy, heavy dew-point days where the moister just hangs in the air. It doesn't have to be raining either. What happens is that every fabric you carry, from stuff sacks to garments to sleeping bags become clammy, absorbed to a small degree with the moisture. What that means is everything has more weight. A fifty-pound pack could increase several pounds. If you slept in a tent that night, it most likely will be wet at morning pack up and a pound or so heavier all by itself. Lighter gear will reduce even that temporary weight too. Light is right.

Since pictures can speak a thousand words, look back to the prehike story in the front of the book called "What We Carry" and witness the drawing I made.

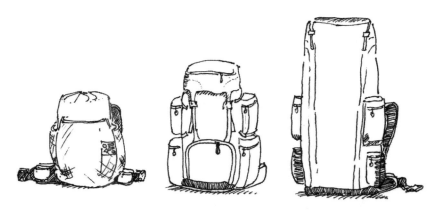

The good.   *The not-as-good.*   *And the "what-was-I-thinking" ugly.*

NOT ALL HIKING SHOES ARE CREATED EQUAL

Since we've touched on footwear a bit, let's look at it more completely and include our feet. If they're not happy, we won't be going very far.

The good news is that with lighter pack weights you no longer need to wear those heavier, less nimble full leather boots. And without them also goes the interminably painful process of breaking them in so that they won't eat up your feet, particularly your heels with blisters.

The bad news is that the lighter, more nimble hiking shoe made of fabric, rubber, and bits of leather, don't have the endurance of those boots. That means for a thru-hike, you'll need to buy two, three, even four pairs for the journey. But having a nimble lighter shoe will pay dividends at the end of every day's hike by reducing your foot and leg fatigue.

The first thing you obviously want is a comfortable shoe. Really, I kid you not. Now, let's talk about how to get one.

Your feet are one size when you're sitting down, like when you're getting them measured to see what size shoe to try on, and then quite another size when you're standing up putting your full weight on them. Most feet will spread and lengthen which will take up that toe box space you really want to maintain. The fastest way to lose your toenails is to have shoes your toes pound into on the downhills.

Usually your foot is measured for width and length, but two other measurements are every bit as important: the shape and volume. Maybe the biggest reason why so many face terribly painful blisters on their heels is because the shoe selected isn't the right shape. Here's my example. Montrail is a very popular, well-represented shoe out on the AT and were the first hiking shoes I bought a few years ago. Even with sock liners and experimenting with various types of socks, those shoes turned my heels into hamburger on six mile, flat walks during break-in periods. They were not full boots or the lower hiking shoe, but were the popular midhigh style of hiking boot. I even sought out custom-lacing techniques in the futile effort to hold my heel still; the laces would be so tight the circulation in my toes would be cut off adding to the misery.

After forty miles of hopeless break-in and trying everything, I said uncle and returned them. That's when I found out that from a different shoe fitter that my foot shape was more of a triangle and that boots heel cup was too wide for me on that brand. I also learned that I had a lower volume foot, which seems to be by my account, less of an issue. What I did next was to inquire at many levels to find a master boot fitter and when I did find one, I drove four hours to have a fitting session with him. Four hours of driving seemed like a small price to pay for the promise of four to six months of happy feet on the trail. Everything that I'll now detail allowed to me to walk from Georgia to Maine without a single blister, without a single day where my feet were screaming at me with ache due to a big mileage day. And I did over forty-five days of twenty miles or more. There was one day in New Jersey that gave me a raw spot after twenty-six miles in wet shoes and socks, I was a bit lost and didn't want to slow down and kept pushing. That wasn't the footwear's fault.

One important design feature to seek out in your hiking shoes is a sole with a "rocker" heel and toe. I know it must sound like I have a PhD in footwear, but I don't. My knowledge comes from the school of hard walks.

A rocker toe and heel is a sole that curves up at the toe and heel. It allows for the shoe to "rock" forward with your stride. This replaces the need for those countless hours of break-in time. Believe me, it makes all the difference. What worked for me was a low hiking shoe by Lowa. Hiking shoes or trail shoes differ from running shoes mainly by having stiffer soles while remaining flexible. Those stiffer soles will be your best friends against every sharp rock and root. When you identify your shoe of choice, buy one pair and start wearing them every day with the socks and insoles that you've selected, which we'll discuss in the next paragraphs. This is how you and your shoes will get to know each other and start what can be a great friendship. If all is OK, then call and get two additional pair and start alternating between all of them in your workouts, errands, everything. If yours fit you the way mine did, you won't want to wear anything else because nothing else will be as comfortable.

ROCKER SOLE

What I learned from the master boot fitter was that the reason most hikers get such massive foot ache is that their insoles are only allowing them to use the front forefoot or ball of their foot and the heel. A custom footbed by Superfeet, which is far cheaper than an orthopedic one but more expensive than their standard footbeds, gives your foot an additional midpoint of support. This midpoint helps the foot from compressing and recoiling all day long and reduces the toil on the other areas. Since I'd eventually have more than one pair of shoes and because I wanted a backup footbed, I had two made at that time. Underneath those I placed Dr. Scholl's double-pillow insoles; but since they retained rainwater like a sponge, I switched to the gel insoles by the same brand. It seems obvious to use some cushioning in your hiking shoes, doesn't it? But in the eighteen weeks it took me to walk the entire distance, I knew of no other who used them. I did, however, have many hikers say that they had never considered it and now would, partially due to my ability to do more miles a day easily. But this is only just a part.

Socks: You'll need socks, a couple pair, and some replacements along the way. I like to use sock liners with my backpacking heavy socks. A liner helps in minimizing moisture and reduces friction next to the skin. For my main heavy socks, I went with Dahlgren's Backpacker. They're thick on the sole, but not on the top giving them a better breathing quality that reduces foot sweating. They truly are high-tech thinking in a sock.

After a month or so, if I felt that the fluff factor of the heavy socks was disappearing, I'd have another set mailed to me in my mail drop box by the folks.

Now, as to method, this is what worked for me, and I'm sure it would for you. Each day when I arrived at camp, I'd naturally take off the shoes and remove my socks. I'd then rub them, my feet not the shoes, in Bag Balm. Bag Balm is a thick lanolin suave that farmers use on the udders of their dairy cow to reduce chaffing and to moisturize. I started using it when its success was revealed by an accomplished three-time thru-hiker. It comes in various sizes, I carried the one-ounce tin. It took two tins for the journey. Then, after you give your foot a good rub, slip on the sock liners you didn't wear that day and put on your camp shoes. Come bedtime, sleep in the liners. In the morning just put the spare pair of thick hiking socks over them and lace up. This has you alternating between your two pairs allowing the hiked-in socks to air and fluff back out.

To ensure your heel is placed fully in the shoes' heel cup at lacing, tap your shoe—heel first on the ground and then with your foot stretched out in front, lace. This eliminates the extra space.

Now, if you've been hiking in the rain, that's a different story. If at the end of the day your socks are drenched, wring them out and hang them in the shelter or try to stretch them over something to increase their chances of drying. Some have used their Nalgene bottles, but since I don't use them, I'd just hang them. In the morning if it's still raining and is going to be wet, do not put on the dry pair. Put the damp ones back on and hike the day until those conditions improve. This is where having liners earn their keep. Anyway, this method will help you have a dry set for camp. Not every aspect of a thru-hike is pleasurable; the morning wet clothing ritual may be my least favorite. Many make the mistake of putting on the dry pair and then have two sets of wet everything. Not good and heavy too. If the next day is dry, but all the plants are laden with water, consider heading out in the morning with the rain pants on to keep the socks dry until things dry out. If its sunny and dry the next day, hike out wearing your dry set and have the wet ones hanging outside the pack to speed the drying.

The small example above is one of the reasons I liked having rain pants, that and I get cold easily when its wet and windy. But as you'd guess by now, not all rain pants are created equal as well. If you buy shoes that are waterproof-Gore Tex like mine, you'll have to get rain pants with straight, stovepipe pant legs. Not ones that cinch with elastic at the bottom. A straight, normal pant cuff will fit over your socks and shoes the way normal pants do and thus will allow the water to run all the way down to the shoe or ground. If you have the cinch, elastic gathered cuff, they'll end up on your ankles allowing all the water run-off to be deposited to your socks. And then it seeps and travels its way into the shoe, and you might as well get used to clammy feet. Waterproof gators would help in the same wet-morning scenario, but I didn't carry them.

Blisters: To avoid them out there is one of your biggest priorities and what I've explained will give you a great chance at doing so. But if one of those villains does find you, what then? Well, many will go into denial that the hot spot on their foot isn't a big deal, or that if they stop to look they'll lose time, or they're tougher than that. Poppycock I say! It's the unaddressed hot spot that becomes a blister that can have you sitting it out on the sidelines for days on end. A short stop is being proactive and thinking of the big picture and joy of the journey. So stop and don't be a chucklehead.

I carried moleskin and Band-Aids, but with all the sweat and friction generated on the skin of your feet, they've never held. Here's what to do. By proactively covering your heels with one long piece of duct tape so that it wraps a good four to five inches on each side of the foot will help blister prone feet to be invincible. Duct tape will be a strategic component in keeping you pain free and foot strong.

Get some of those circular foam corn pads and then carry about six feet of duct tape wrapped around your hiking sticks. Yea, you'll be using hiking sticks, but we'll talk about those later. Anyway, place the corn ring around the hot spot or blister, which more than likely will be on your heel. Then take about eight inches of duct tape and apply it equally left and right with the corn ring in the center. Take another six-inch piece and apply it vertically going up the Achilles and down underneath the heel. That sounds like a lot of tape to hold one small corn ring in place, but I assure you with all the force that's down there and moisture, it'll take that much to keep it all where it's suppose to be. The tape will be tight at first especially at the Achilles due to the joints' travel distance—just take that into consideration when putting on that vertical piece. I'd flex my foot up as to fully stretch the skin as I rub the tape down. Put your socks back on and don't give it another thought. You might want to just leave it on for the next several days unless it became a blister at which case you'll want to get the fluid out of it, let it air out and then reapply another same kind bandage.

As far as lacing, you should customize your approach to meet the needs of your feet. For me, I skipped the third cross over to give more freedom to the top of my foot and at the last two eyelets I would intertwine the laces the way you do before tying a bow. Only I'd double intertwine them so when you cinch it down it stays. By doing this double on the top two eyelets added greater locking power to keep my heel anchored into the heel cup to prevent blisters. If you have midhigh boots or taller, you can use this technique on several of the last eyelets. Of course after you tie your bow, always double knot the laces. Short of water, your shoe comfort may be the most important aspect of the hike.

Should You Use Hiking Poles?

That was the question I asked two years ago of one who had successfully thru-hiked. Their answer was that they didn't start with them, but they got some upon reaching Damascus—450 miles of trail. They then added that they'd wished they had them the whole time.

Hiking poles or trekking poles, whatever you call them, you need one for each hand because they have so very many benefits. Mine have prevented me from falling on my face more times than I can count, and this is coming from one who doesn't fall often. They reduce the effort your legs must bare on the journey. I would guess that with a slight push forward with your arms on an uphill, as much as 20 percent of the effort can be eased. On the downhills and step-downs, they are downright *brilliant* in easing the extreme stress put on your knees. By planting the poles in front of you on big downhills, you can use your arm muscles to soften the step-down impact that goes right to the knee. One of the biggest surprises new backpackers discover is that going downhill is every bit as tough as going uphill—only different.

Whenever I would hear someone complaining that their knees were killing them, more times than not they didn't have two trekking poles. When I'd hear the same complaint and they did have them, I'd ask to see how they were holding them. Oddly, everyone has just enough arrogance that they can't imagine they could possibly hold a hiking pole with its strap improperly. But amazingly they do hold it wrong. Those smart people who make them actually put a ton of thinking into the straps. Hold them right and you can go downhill and really help your knees. Hold them wrong and the downhills will be like you don't even have any. Here's how to hold them so they can help:

1. You want to slide your hand up through the strap coming in from underneath.
2. You then let the fatty part of your thumb joint in your palm rest down on the inside part of the strap.
3. As you hold the grip, both parts of the loop will be in your palm.

1   2   3

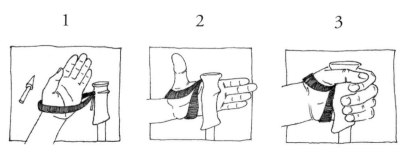

This technique means your thumb is always hanging over part of the loop, which allows you to plant your pole and have control even if you take your hand off the grip! Amazing but true. Do this and your knees will kiss you—if they can figure out how.

What if I only want to carry one pole you ask. I'd say one is better than none, but two is better than one and should be done.

Poles come in handy on uphills, downhills, and awkward terrain such as rocks and roots. They also give you multiple balance points for river fords and rock hopping. I've found in camp that I could thrust both into the ground about a foot apart and hang my shirt over them nicely to dry out. The only time I didn't use them was on gentle terrain when I'd snap them together and hold them in the middle. And if you feel a bit insecure at times, such as in front of a snake or in black bear country, they offer a tad more security. I can actually use one of mine as my tent-tarps front pole. The poles I used were Leki Makalus. They had suspension springs, but after a month I found I liked them in their rigid position more.

YOUR TENT IS YOUR CASTLE

You'll need to carry shelter of some form. To not carry one is naïve and gambling with your own well-being. It also is grossly underestimating the power of weather and the land. Anyone who's thru-hiking or another form of long-distance backpacking must plan for the unplanned.

Some on the AT have forgone any form of shelter because of the hundreds of shelter/lean-tos. They falsely assume that they will be able to make it to one or that room will be available upon reaching it. They make this gamble for a variety of reasons, but most involve the elimination of weight. I have actually experienced one of these hikers arriving just at dark while its been raining for hours with no sign of letting up. The five-person shelter had eight wet hikers crammed into it already, and not all of them were skinny thru-hikers either. It was suggested the individual would need to tent. Well, the prideful, ultralighter didn't carry any form of shelter, what he did carry was a willingness to brag about how little his gear weighed. The person would sleep the night in a cramped corner almost sitting up. A day later the indignant ultralighter would write in registers how *he* was a victim of selfish hikers in the shelter. A warped perspective is a comical thing to behold. Hiking light is one thing, hiking irresponsibly is quite another.

This is, by my estimation, the best example between going light on gear and yet still having the items that allow for options. Not all ultralight hikers are as unprepared as that individual, hiking without the basics is too extreme of an approach for me but not for others. "Hike your own hike" is not the AT mantra by accident. And still others would view my pack weight as forgoing too many necessities. The whole intention is to show how you can be completely prepared with all the right gear and not have a huge, heavy load on your back that robs the joy of the journey from you.

Next to your pack, the shelter you chose could be the heaviest item of gear. Fortunately, the lightweight revolution in the gear industry has been widespread. The old target weight of four pounds for a single person tent as touted by most how-to books ten years ago left few choices. Today, however, finds nearly all the manufacturers offering more than one model that regularly beat that weight. Remarkably, some newer tents, tarps, or hammocks have cut that old weight in half with shelters now in the two pound range. At that weight, going without shelter makes no sense at all. The biggest problem with this category though is the "fudging" of those items weight. It's not lying so much as misleading. Some manufacturers will quote the weight of just the tent but not with its rain fly. Or give you a minimum weight if you just used the poles and rain fly but not the tent. Don't be fooled. Look at the total weight; it's the only true honest measure.

A hybrid form of a tent called a tarp-tent, as well as the advent of the hammock have grown popular on the AT. Many like hammocks since regardless of the terrain, just having two trees, they have a nice banana cocoon complete with rain fly. If you toss and turn a bit at night, it may not be the optimal choice for you though.

The tarp-tent uses only a single wall of high-tech silicone impregnated rip-shot nylon rather than that of a tent that generally uses a second separate rain fly cover. Both offer mosquito netting and floors, but the tarp-tent is a faster, easier setup. A good thing in a bad weather setup scenario. Single-wall construction saves greatly on weight; however, many single-wall tents have significant breathability problems. The biggest strike against them is the interior condensation buildup, which makes them a nuisance come morning pack up. I had a single wall tent that was a marvel of terrific thinking: two pop-up vents, a perimeter of floor mosquito netting to further enhance ventilation, and a small peep window. But to use it was to soak it in condensation.

The one-person tent is not an incredibly spacious home. *Cozy* might be a nice way to describe it, coffinlike might be a less nice way. But a tent offers privacy, avoids the shelter mice and snoring fellow hikers. Since I want you to avoid the mistakes I made early on, I'll share what happened two years ago.

Like the hiker named Kingfisher I wrote about in the prehike section called "Night Zero," I too wanted to avoid the shelter mice I'd read so much about, tenting would be how I'd make it to Maine. Not understanding how weight was so important at that time, and the coffinlike feel of a one-person tent, and that it would be my home for six months, I boldly decided on a two-person-size tent. It all seemed quite reasonable to carry a five-and-a-half-pound tent—six-and-a-half pounds when wet—when you've lived in the flat lands of the Chicago area. But when I discovered what all that weight truly felt like on those beginning mountains down in Georgia, I discovered it was far from reasonable, it was asinine.

On this thru-hike, I ultimately gave up on my single-wall, high-tech tent mentioned earlier and changed to the Henry Shires Tarp-tent. It's actually a two-person shelter even though its weight wouldn't have you believing it. With a front and rear storm beak and a sewn-in floor with mosquito netting all around, it still weighs a scant two pounds! Despite it being of single-wall construction, I've had two people sleep in it and had no condensation issues. And the fact you can have it up in under two minutes is an extra bonus. Sometimes the refinement of the gear for the sake of the journey means pulling out the wallet, fortunately I had that option. For those who don't, getting it right the first time is all the more critical and how this can help. If I'd had this shelter when I started, I might have tented out on good weather days more often since tenting offers the psychological advantage of being a bit freer and more in the wilderness than that of the shelters. But on a rainy day, everyone wants to be in the shelter.

On my journey, I pretty much hiked from shelter to shelter even though I always had a tent with me. I found that the shelters allowed for the most effortless way to get in and out of camp and make miles. And their distance apart actually helped me to go farther than I might have been inclined to do simply to reach them. Even those who loved tenting would use their location as a mileage strategy as I did. As far as mice and other snoring hikers, I found that carrying a tiny radio with earplug headphones solved all that. Not only did listening to some music at night agree with me and getting an occasional forecast, but also it did a remarkable job of blocking out the pitter-patter of little mouse feet and snores. If you don't hear the mice, you don't fret and can find the sandman. The radio I chose was a flat oval sports version by Nike and to my pleasant surprise, automatically turned itself off after an hour of no movement. I used it nearly every night. Recently, post hike that is, I've upgraded to the Highgear Trail Audio MP3. It's water resistant, has a FM radio designed into it, is just as light and can be programmed to turn itself off. The lightweight revolution is a beautiful thing. We'll talk more about how to get in and out of camp later. But if you plan on shelters as well, you'd better be a very sound sleeper or take some sleeping agent at night or carry earplugs. It can be noisy at times.

So a shelter of some kind makes infinite sense, especially now that you have so many lightweight choices. At the bare minimum, some carried only an ordinary rectangular tarp and would rope it off with the help of trees if they needed it. Very basic, but its light and gives them options. The Maupin Field Shelter in Virginia has a resident six-foot rat snake, many tented because they could as a result. What if a skunk has sprayed the shelter, or if the shelter is overrun by drunken towners like the Governor Clement Shelter in Vermont or the Deer Lick Shelters in Pennsylvania have from time to time? Some of the hikers who started in Georgia early March through April, the high season for a northbound thru-hike, found as many as thirty or more at a particular night's shelter. Counting on a space inside a shelter is living in fantasyland. So the point is that things happen, and it's nice to have the luxury of an option.

With igloos scarce, tepees hard to find, lean-tos sometimes full, having a shelter is a good thing.

SANDMAN AND YOUR SLEEPING BAG

Nobody that I know likes being cold. And unfortunately, sleeping bags have been a gear category whose warmth ratings have been terribly inconsistent. Some, downright fictional. So we need to buy a bag that's rated to ten degrees lower than we think we'll need. Inquiring from bag owners is one true way of knowing if the bag lives up to its rating. I'll point out a few here in this section that do. As in all our gear, weight is still a critical concern. You can get two bags rated to equal temperatures, and one can weigh twice as much. Because weight and warmth are both important, your sleeping bag or bags—you'll probably need two—will be your most expensive purchase.

A northbound start in Georgia during prime time, March to April, will mean needing a fifteen-degree-rated bag. If you start as early as February, maybe a zero-degree-rated bag. Then as you move north and into May, you can switch out to a warmer-weather-rated bag, say a thirty to forty degree. I know it seems odd to have one that's rated to thirty degrees while hiking in July, but I can guarantee you that on rainy days when the temps never reach sixty and the winds are blowing, it'll take that bag for you to get warm. Remember, if it gets really warm you can simply leave the bag unzipped or sleep on top of it. If it gets cold, you won't have too many choices since your heavier fleece and gloves will have been sent home with your winter bag. During the summer thru-hiking season of 2003, the rain and gray skies were so nasty, many had to have their warmer gear mailed back out to them. Hypothermia usually catches individuals off guard, say when the temperatures are surprisingly mild. A wet day with a breeze and fifty degrees can really do a number on you. Your bag and eating something will be your defense against the shivers in that kind of scenario. One of your top priorities will be to guard against the sleeping bag from ever becoming wet. Some hikers have used a large compactor thick trash bag down inside the entire backpack as added protection with their pack rain cover. This has long been a good technique, but those bags can be fairly heavy and do tear. I used two Outdoor Research Hydrolite Stuff Sack instead of the factory included stuff sack and never had a wet bag. Of course, remember to put the opening on one opposite the opening on the other as you pull it over the first one.

Because mummy sleeping bags are the warmest, I'll be discussing them. They also happen to be the most compressible allowing them to take up less room. A good thing since your pack will be smaller. The first choice you'll face is whether to go synthetic or down. Synthetic materials can be damp and still offer warmth, but they're heavier. Down bags are useless if wet, so extra attention must be paid to protect against rain as we just discussed. But down bags are light and small and toasty, so that's what I chose.

My cold weather down bag was the fifteen-degree Mountainsmith Vision. It weighs a scant 1 lb. 15 oz. And I can attest to its truthful rating. I've slept in nineteen degrees and was still warm; I did supplement its warmth with a silk sleeping bag liner on that night which gave my bag a possible six degrees of extra warmth. It compresses without a compression sack to the size of a small loaf of bread. Marmot makes a fifteen-degree bag called the Helium that is the same weight but might have a higher down fill weight—this is a good thing—and has received good reviews. The Vision had a bigger girth and foot box dimension and so I went with it. Mummies feel a bit restrictive early on, some can be claustrophobic, but you'll adapt. Personally, I went from having a few anxious moments of feeling trapped with only my face exposed to becoming so comfortable that I'd have everything drawn in so tight that only my nose was sticking out. So speaking from experience, you do adapt.

When the warmer temperatures were just around the corner, I switched out the bags and went with my thirty-five-degree Western Mountaineering Highlite. This baby weighs only one pound! And its rating is a truthful one. I've been warm while deeply zipped in it at thirty-six-degree temperatures. But that measly one pound means there's only a half zipper, and the girth and foot box dimensions are minimal. However, I'd recommend it. When I made the change over in bags, it took me a good week or two to truly get used to the bare bones dimensions. As I lost weight and adjusted to it along the journey, I came to believe it was downright spacious. And it packs down to the size of a softball if you really need it to. By the time I reached Maine and sleeping in it for nearly four months, it lost its loft and hence its thirty-five-degree warmth. You can reloft your bag by giving it a tumble in the dryer on air only with a tennis ball thrown in to bounce into it. It works. Recently, I've tried the Marmot Hydrogen thirty-degree bag and liked it too. It was only 1 lb. 5 oz. and spacious.

Silk Liners: A silk liner adds about six ounces but can be used or not used as the case may be. This year I didn't use it down south since I started so late in the season, but when I got up north and decided to not change back to my warmer, cold weather bag, I hedged my gamble by carrying the liner again. That would bring my thirty-five-degree bag to about a twenty-nine temperature rating. When an early cold front pushed down in late August, I was glad I had it for those three to four days. I had originally planned on carrying it the entire way so I could sleep in it by itself in hot weather, but I sent it home with the winter stuff and never had a regret. The only downside is a minor complication of getting in and out of it for those midnight visits to the woods, but you'll master it. If you chose to sleep in your tent, that will add several degrees of warmth those in the shelters won't have. And your hat, gloves, socks, and fleece-jacket like objects will assist in the regulating of warmth as they are needed too. If it wasn't too nippy at bedtime, I usually fell asleep with my hat on without the mummy's hood. As it got colder, I'd pull the hood over and tighten the drawstrings.

Sleeping Pads: Amazingly, I was totally comfortable on my 5/8 inch thick Z-Rest foam pad. It started as a full length one, but I cut three panels off it for weight, which still made it a tad longer than the standard 3/4 length one. The weight I saved with the absent panels covered the weight of my shelter ground cloth, which wasn't cloth so much as two waterproof paper maps scotched-taped together. Shelter floors get dirty and a ground cloth helped from passing it on to me and my gear. Their nice accordion folds made for a quiet, easy pack up in the morning—just take the folds into account when you're taping them together. A single piece of tape the entire length of the seam on both sides lasted all the way to Maine. One thing I tried a year earlier— because I thought it was brilliant in theory but fail miserably in execution—was to use an emergency space blanket bag as the shelter ground cloth. It weighed a mere two ounces, and I could slip my bag and myself into it if things got terribly cold. So it could have a multiple use, which is another good rule of thumb for deciding on what to carry. It made great sense in theory; however, in the morning when you try to fold or roll it up to get going, it made as much noise as trying to fold up a bag of potato chips! Every tiny movement was an annoying crinkle and terribly inconsiderate of others in the shelter. Etiquette asks you to be quiet for the sake of others at night and early in the morning. This year in Virginia I'd meet a section hiker who had the same brilliant idea and the same annoying result. I pulled him aside and gave him some tough love advice for the sake of others. He seemed to be clueless as to the noise he was making.

The full-length Therm-a-Rest is very popular out there, just remember to look at weight and see what you can get by with. For some, a long thick pad was their luxury item. Only you and your back can decided.

Miscellaneous: As far as your pillow, you won't carry one, but you will have one. Your clothes bag will be your pillow; and you may have to arrange your clothes inside so it can be comfortable or high enough or whatever. I've also used my tubelike, rolled-up tent as my pillow on colder nights in a shelter since many of my clothes were on me. Even a shoe turned on its side can offer some comfort in a pinch. I've never been a very sound sleeper so one thing that worked especially well for me was taking Tylenol PM. Not only did it help to deepen my sleep, it allowed me to wake ache free, fully recovered, and ready to go. I followed that formula all the way north to Katahdin. Getting a good night rest is an issue for many, so experiment.

A Warning: Don't trivialize the fact that one item may only weigh three or four ounces more than another. Once you start down that path you're sure to do it again and again. Before you know it you'll have added two pounds from tiny, extra ounces. Remember to think of everything as it relates to the whole. Saving some in one area allows you to not count the weight of something else. I'll remind you that it's not fanatical to count ounces, it's practical.

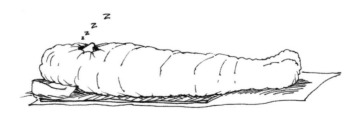

Experiencing a mummy bag early on can be a bit claustrophobic for some, but you'll adjust.
I got so comfortable that I could sleep with only my nose poking out.

Different Day, Same Shirt

Your clothes are every bit a part of your sleeping system and so seems a natural next area to discuss.

Clothes are the one area where you are allowed to buy something because it's *blue* and not be an idiot. My whole pack was filled with so much blue gear that the hiker named Belle, whom I mentioned, used to give me a hard time about it. Oh well, guilty as charged. The heading above is taken from a favorite Appalachian Trail T-shirt. It seems to sum up in four words the essence of clothes and the trail. A thru-hike or a week or longer outing means wearing the same clothes every single day. But let's look at how not to think about a long hike.

Since we'll be walking quite a lot, a lot of socks seem to make sense. Many will try to eek-by with only four pair of heavy hiking socks—that's four ounces per pair and add another six ounces for a few sock liners to have a better chance at keeping the blisters at bay. That brings the sock weight total to 1 lb. 6 oz! Not too unreasonable.

And of course, a nice shirt—or two—for nights in town and several others just because we're civilized and don't live in a cave now, do we? With most collared town shirts weighing about 12 oz and hiking T-shirts at about 8 oz, let's add 2 lb. 8 oz. Pants (20 oz) are always good to have and two pair of shorts (10 oz each) for hot days and a couple of underwear (4 oz each) will naturally be welcome. Really now, one can't possibly wear the same thing day after day, can one? So another 3 lbs. We still have rain gear (32 oz), long johns (12.5 oz), a fleece jacket (16 oz), fleece hat (2 oz), a rain hat or cap (6 oz), glove liners and gloves too (6 oz) and although its not clothing but part of your fowl weather gear, a backpack rain cover (5 oz). Naturally, we'll need several bandanas, say four (4 oz total) and full-length gators (10 oz). That gives us a grand total of 12 lbs 6 oz of just garments. Oh, and I forgot our camp shoes (18 oz)—so roughly, 14½ lbs. Yikes.

Does that sound preposterous? Or too much stuff or too little? I'll tell you the list I just shared with you was my actual clothes count from two years ago when my pack weighed fifty-four pounds. I still have a photo of it and memories of those painful climbs.

Here's what I learned. I like to wear long pants in cooler temperatures; and in the warmer ones, the mosquitoes and biting black fly come out, wearing trousers makes even more strategic sense in my mind. By getting convertible long pants, pants that have zip-off legs, you can have your shorts if you want them. I simply would hike with the zips open and that added ventilation. Many think the idea of long pants is just too hot. I didn't find it the case. Additionally, long pants also eliminate the real nuisances of the trail—poison ivy, poison sumac, thorn scratches—and greatly reduces the chances of a tic hopping on board. There were three, maybe four hikers that got Lyme disease last season and spent time in a hospital or on medication that zapped their energy. I'll stick with my long pants, thank you very much. Long pants also eliminate the need for gators, the pluses far outweigh the minuses by a long shot. I chose the Mountain Hardwear Convertible Pack pant at twenty ounces. They are technically designed with shaped legs and a chamois inner waist. What I liked best though was a simple string and hook sewn into the front left pocket where I always had my knife attached. LL Bean has just come out with a new long pant made of stretchy, water resistant fabric called the Knife Edge hiking pant. They're as light as a whisper, which will be nice, but do not have the zip-off legs or zip cuffs. However, since I didn't need those features really last season, I'm going to be switching mainly because I know they'll dry faster and hence help me avoid those really annoying mornings of slipping on still damp clothes. I did sew a length of string with a hook into the left pocket to keep my tiny knife handy.

My hiking shirt was a silk-weight long sleeve T-shirt by Patagonia. At five ounces it's no heavier than a T-shirt, but its long sleeves once again fight off the bug bites and evil foliage I just mentioned. Almost every picture of me for four and half months saw me wearing the same thing.

Only two pairs of hiking socks and liners will be needed for your thru-hike, and I spelled out how to manage them earlier in the section on shoes. They weigh nine ounces in total.

If I was cold upon reaching camp and needed to change into dry warmer stuff, I carried Patagonia Silk-Weight long john bottoms (5 oz), which also served as my town pants if I was doing laundry. Another lightweight option that I've adapted post hike is to replace the long john bottoms with silk pajama bottoms. I got mine from Winter Silks and at 5 ounces, they're ideal for camp and as town pants. I only wish they didn't have that Hugh Hefner shiny appearance. I'd also use my midweight fleece in the shelters. Mine was the awesome Patagonia R1 Flash Pullover (11.5 oz). Since I almost never hiked in it, it seldom was smelly or dirty, so it too would be my town shirt during laundry time. Importantly, these two garments would be stored inside a gallon-size Ziploc in the clothes bag. You must have your spare set of clothes dry in the event you really need their warming properties.

For colder weather I carried a very compressible jacket pullover by—yea, you guessed it—Patagonia called the Micropuff Pullover (12.5 oz). This piece would be with me the first and last months. Stuffed into my clothes sack at night made for the most awesome pillow. A new addition I've looked into is a 725-fill down ultralight jacket from Mont-Bell. At just 7.4 ounces, what's not to love? So, it might replace my Micro Puff.

My rain jacket was a Marmot Precip with pit zips and a hood (12 oz), and my rain pants are by Mountain Hardwear with straight leg cuffs and full zips at nine ounces. Many forgo the use of rain pants, but I tend to get cold easily in wet conditions, and they can help keep the socks and shoes dry from the rain and early-morning-dew-soaked plants along the trail. For the times when the forecast called for a solid day of rain, I'd head out only wearing the rain pants and the convertible pack pant packed away. This kept things a tad cooler. Also, the rain pants having full zips and duel zipper handles, you can open the top ones to add ventilation to your legs. But make no mistake about it, if you wear rain gear you are going to sweat for all your worth. You are going to get drenched in perspiration from inside. The reason to wear them is to stay warm, and to use them in extremely cold conditions to help hold your heat in. I once walked twelve miles in six inches of snow and twenty-degree temperatures and still managed a sweat from their warmth. Recently Patagonia has introduced the Specter rain pullover with a hood that weighs a scant 6.5 ounces. That's half the weight of my Precip jacket. Yep, I had to upgrade—another 5.5 ounces eliminated. My hat was a wide brim number that I'd wear during moderate rain, but if it rained cats and dogs, I'd pull the hood up over it. However, a baseball cap works better for that use though. The wide brim hat (4 oz) was by Mountain Hardwear, but I added six vent holes around the top for extra ventilation—a trick I learned from Mello Mike back down in Tennessee. And finally, Etowah made my backpack rain cover from ultralight rip-shot nylon at three ounces. They're designed like a large shower cap with small elastic hooks on the bottom to really secure it against strong winds—and it all stuffs back into a tiny pouch that's sewn right into it. Brilliant design.

One extra little thing I brought and used often on chilly morns before my own body heat kicked in was a wind shirt called the Patagonia Dragonfly. Even with a hood, it weighs a scant three ounces and stuffs into its own breast pocket for a size no larger than a lemon. Everyone should have one of these gems.

I had a fleece hat (1.5 oz) and midweight gloves (2 oz) with me always. Both, also from Patagonia. And finally, to avoid chaffing between my legs, I also wore their stretchy seamless shorts, which are similar to a biker-length short that's close to the body. No added weight since they were always on. Second only to blisters, hikers complained about the pain from chaffing. Most do not wear underwear to help with breathability, but the seamless shorts worked so wonderfully that I kept them all the way to Maine. You can take off your pants and get in your sleeping bag without flashing anyone or you can take a swim, they're pretty versatile. There are many fine makers of high-tech garments out there, but none better than Patagonia. They're the tops in my book.

So the sub-total is roughly seven pounds nine ounces. Add in my camp shoes (12 oz) and three bandanas (2 oz), and we have a total winter clothing weight of eight pounds five ounces. That is almost seven pounds lighter than just two years ago, almost a 50 percent lighter load and obviously will take up far less space. We like that. And when we send home the winter jacket, sleeping bag, and silk liner, we knock off another 2 ½ pounds! Wow, no wonder I did so many twenty-mile days.

Nothing demonstrates the axiom "Count the ounces and the pounds will take care of themselves" better than this example.

Now let's talk more about method with our clothes. I mentioned how I'd use the wind shirt for early morning warmth until my body heat made it unnecessary. Or how your spare set is kept in a Ziploc to ensure you always have something dry to slip into. And in the earlier shoe section, how straight leg cuffs are better than cinch cuffs on rain pants. So let's go back to the title of this section, "Different Day, Same Shirt." It says that each day will mean you'll have to wear the same thing. If it's been very damp through the night and your stuff hasn't dried, you'll have to have one of those courageous moments on the trail and put that cold wet clothing on again. Yep, never a joyful experience. Fortunately, the high-tech fabrics warm up on you in seconds. Really. Just make sure to wring out your stuff when you get in camp as best you can and try to hang them in the sun or breeze. Often, after my shirt had a little drying time, I'd actually slip my barely damp shirt back on and go to bed. Nothing guarantees dry, warm clothing in the morning like the heater of your body and sleeping bag. In fact, it was common when my stuff wasn't wet, and I wanted to avoid the brisk feeling of putting on cold clothes, I'd throw them down into the sleeping bag. By morning they're as toasty as you are.

One notion out on the AT was the one about putting your wet clothes underneath your sleeping pad at night and slowly your heat would work its way through the pad and dry the clothes. Horsefeathers, never worked for me. Feel free to try, but don't say it came from me.

With the huge and constant consumption of water you'll be drinking, you're bound to have to get up in the middle of the night and visit the woods. I found that keeping my camp shoes at the edge of the shelter near my head with my headlamp in them gave me the two items necessary for an effortless midnight visit. If you caught that I said near your head, that means you should most likely orient yourself in a shelter with your feet in and your head out toward the open side. I know this sounds backward, but shelter mice, when present, like to run around the wall rafters and the inside floor perimeter. Seldom do they traipse across the very exposed front edge of the shelter floor. This is why you have your head to the opening. Isn't it amazing what one can learn? But since I have gone on record in saying there are mice in the shelters, never was I ever bothered by them. Nor did they ever get into my food since I always hung it properly on the tuna can, string and stick antimouse hangers. I drew a picture of them early in the hike in the section Georgia to Maine. So don't fret. But don't leave food in your pack or leave your pockets zipped up if you've had food in them. They'll chew right though to get a misplaced crumb.

Last but not least are your camp shoes. You really want something light, easy to get on and off and really comfortable for walking around town during errands. Last season I carried Tecnica's PacMoc at 1 lb. 3 oz. But others wore the very popular Crocs made of injection-molded foam. Now that they come with a heel strap, I too have switched. Mine are size eleven and only tip the scale at twelve ounces. That's another seven ounces saved.

Now Where Did I Put That?

After a while on the trail, if you do the same thing and put your gear in the same place, you'll be able to reach for an item without ever turning on a light. You'll become such a finely tuned hiking-living machine, that life out there will be effortless. I kid you not. I got so that I could reach in a stuff sack, open a Ziploc, pull out a spare battery, open the radio, replace the old battery, snap the radio together, put the stuff sack away, and return to listening to music without ever missing a beat or using the headlamp.

Organize your stuff so that life gets easier out there. One funny ha-ha that several of us had was when Pop Up hiked out one morning only to return after a mile when he realized he'd forgotten his sleeping bag. Not funny to him, but definitely a giggle nonetheless.

Here's a simple approach. Get a small light stuff sack, I used an Outdoor Research Hydrolite in the color of green. In it I kept my electroniclike stuff: Petzl Tikka headlamp, Nike miniradio and ear plug headphones, spare batteries in a Ziploc, spare lip balm, and a small foldable flask of Captain Morgan Spiced Rum. Well, not everything was electronic so much as electrifying. The batteries I carried were AAA, and everything that needed batteries took AAA. Very sensible and flexible, very interchangeable. I also kept my sunglasses there in a Ziploc as well. This bag would be used every night, and so it was always next to my camp shoes near my head. It was the only bag I carried that was green. So there was never any confusion as to where a certain something was or what was in the green bag. It always had the items I listed.

I also had another Hydrolite bag of the same small size but the color red. It held my short list of toiletries. A few repair items. A short list of medicines. Minimal first aid. Whistle. Bag Balm. Basically every little thing I didn't use every day other than my toothbrush and Bag Balm, which I did. I knew that nearly everything was in the tiny red bag, but most were seldom used, if ever.

I used two medium stuff sacks for my food, a blue one and a black one. The blue one held my alcohol stove, cook pot, fuel, lighters, and all my dinners, cookies for dessert, and hot chocolate since I needed my stove to have it. Any extra snacks were also there. My bear rope, a fifty-foot nylon string wed to a small pouch I could drop a rock into was also in the blue dinner bag since nighttime meant hanging the food in bear country. It was always so nice and easy to just grab the blue bag and know that my entire kitchen and night's menu was there, even my dessert and hot coco. The only glitch was that the "spork" couldn't be in both places. I suppose I could have had two but didn't.

In the black food bag I had breakfast, lunch, snack foods, and Gatorade packets. I made a high-energy protein breakfast milkshake each morning that only required adding water to a powder. As a result, I didn't carry a cup or mug, but carried a Tupperware milk shaker that also served as my cup for hot chocolate at night. I also kept my "spork" in there since some of my lunches were small foil bags of chicken or tuna.

My clothes bag was another ultralight bag, this one made by Etowah in the color of purple. What was in it is fairly obvious. Don't forget to put your spare set of clothes in a Ziploc. They have to be dry and ready for you.

OK, are you counting? That's five bags, each a different color so far. The last bag was actually another blue one, it was another Hydrolite water-resistant bag I slipped over the sleeping bag stuff sack which we discussed in the last section. That's everything. Doesn't sound like very much, does it? It's nice that even stuff sacks have taken part in the lightweight gear revolution. Just a couple of years ago, the same number of sacks would account for well over a pound of weight. But today all those I've cited wouldn't exceed nine ounces.

The only thing that was left to itself was my water pump /filter. But we'll talk water in the next section. Now, all these bags get put inside the backpack in addition to my camp shoes and sleeping pad. I am of the school of thought that everything goes into the inside. Why, you ask. One thing, stuff falls off. Boy did I find a lot of camp shoes on the trail that dropped without the hiker knowing. Second, a streamlined pack is more maneuverable with all the dodging and weaving that happens. Third, there's fewer things for branches to snag, which can throw you off balance resulting in a fall. Fourth, it just looks like you know what you're doing and you're doing it with style and grace. Remember what Billy Crystal said as Ricardo Monteban on *Saturday Night Live* years ago, "It was more important to look marvelous than to feel marvelous!"

On the outside of our packs, we keep our fowl weather gear: rain jacket and pants, hat if we're not wearing it, the wind shirt, and our rain cover. We don't want to be looking around for those items when the heavens are opening up. My backpack had three external mesh stretch pockets; the biggest was the center and that's where the above was kept.

On the side I kept a Ziploc that had several other smaller Ziplocs in it. One held my toilet paper. One held my vitamins. Another my Tylenol PM. And finally, a bottle of Excedrin Extra Strength. I used these items every day and sometimes during the hike, so easy access, without having to dig made effortless sense. The other side held my maps and thru-hiker handbook, yep, in a Ziploc. The handbook got lighter every few days since as I walked off a page, I'd tear it out. By the time I got to Mt. Katahdin in Maine it weighed a mere trifle of its original self.

The backpack I carried, the ULA P2 had wonderful pockets on the hip belt. One of them is where I kept my bug head net. Outdoor Research makes a nice one that collapses down with a simple twist of the metal ring that holds it out. My DEET lotion or spray was in the same pocket. The other pocket held my digital camera and custom bandana I made that said "Hiker to Town." You want that as handy as rain gear when you're looking for a hitch into town.

As for packing technique of the inside, nothing was too critical except when I once moved my water bladder up to the top. All that water weight up high made the pack wobble. My ULA P2 has a vertical bladder sleeve up against my back. This orientation made the balance phenomenal. I found that during those real gully washer rainstorms, rain water somehow found a way, as water always does, to the bottom of the backpack. So I always kept my camp shoes there and then everything stacked on top. The diagram shows how I packed it every time. And by packing it the same or having a packing ritual, you don't find yourself leaving a sleeping bag or anything else for that matter behind, which would leave you either befuddled or hoppin' mad at yourself.

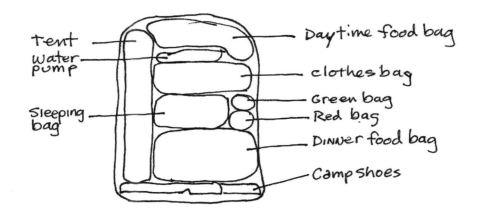

My stuff. Simple but not simpleminded.

The only thing you can't see in the diagram is how the sleeping pad was in there. Logic says to put it against your back side, but because the water bladder was there, my pad was to the opposite. I found the easiest way to get it in the pack was by sliding it down first while the pack was empty and then it was bag after bag until I was pulling the last drawstring tight. Notice how I can pull the tent out if need be without digging or setting everything out on to the ground—a good thing in a bad weather set up. So instead of packing up your tent into a small bundle, roll it up into a hotdog shape. You may want to get a stuff sack to accommodate this if it doesn't already. I've also managed to surround the one item that has to stay dry at all costs, my sleeping bag.

WATER

There are several approaches to harvest it in the woods and much will be dependent on your comfort level. Before I began, I was a major advocate of always treating it, whether through pump filter or drops. But I found I relaxed that strict philosophy once I got to see where some of the water was coming from. Here was my guiding thought: if the water was coming right out of the ground, where I could see its source, then I did not pump it or treat it. Examples of this happen numerous times up on mountaintops where springs would percolate up.

If, however, I could not see its origin, such as a brook or stream, then I used my filter. It is the unknown that you need to guard against. We can't know if an animal has defecated or died up stream from where we would be taking it. I only violated this rule a handful of times when the sources seem particularly pure, but it was a risk—a calculated gamble if you will.

I was amazed at how much water I consumed out there. My average was four liters every day, maybe a touch higher. The most I went through was on a ninety-degrees day with 90 percent humidity and rocks and rattlesnakes were making their presence know. I consumed seven liters that day. Regardless of the heat, mountain spring water, cold and crisp is simply delicious. But in some ways it wasn't enough for me. I discovered in my second week on the trail that when I added Gatorade powder to my water, my endurance was more significant and my power on tough climbs more substantial. I shared this news with several who were hiking and noticed they adapted the approach. Carrying the powder packets means carrying extra weight in your food bag, but the increased physical ability makes it worth its weight.

I always hiked out of town with my water bladder filled with two liters of straight, out-of-the-bottle Gatorade. As it went down I'd just add water to it as needed. Instead of the one packet-per-liter recommendation, I'd use one bag per two liters. That way I didn't have to carry quite as many packets, which averaged about 1 ½ per day. If ever the opportunity of a nearby store presented itself for food, I also always filled the bladder with the full-strength power beverage. I loved the taste of the fruit punch flavor, and I did get a wee bit bored with plain water. Some of those young Turks out there on the trail barely need anything to do twenty miles, but being in my midforties, I found drinking it to be strategic. Because it tasted so good, having sugar and hence calories, I always was drinking. Keeping yourself well hydrated also reduces fatigue and apparently has a whole host of benefits as I've been told.

When it came down to water filters or purification drops, it was a tie out on the trail. My water filter is the MSR Miniworks X—the red one. It works very well, and the ceramic cartridge is very easy to clean in the field. Just wipe off the sediment with a tiny pad that was included and the flow rate increased. Very simple and easy. I splurged and bought two brand new cartridges during the journey. There's nothing like a new cartridge for a fast flow rate and quick fill up. However, it weights one pound, but since having water is maybe the most important thing, it made great sense to me to carry it. Having a pump means getting clean water immediately without the twenty-minute waiting period adding drops requires. Sometimes the water sources are shallow tiny pools where pulling water without a pump is slow and tedious. But using drops is nearly a full pound less in weight. So it comes down to immediate gratification with weight or waiting and less weight. The old days of using iodine drops and having to taste it are over thanks to Aqua Mira's two-bottle drop system. It was the drop treatment of choice for those following that approach by 99 percent. Steripen has introduced a new lightweight UV light. It looks quite interesting, so I may need to give it a try. With batteries it weighs only six ounces.

Many still used the common water bottle by Nalgene out there while others just used an empty soda bottle, which was lighter than a Nalgene. Frankly, after you've experienced the benefits of carrying a water bladder and their bite-valve tubes, I can't understand why anyone would do the other. With a bladder and bite valve, you never have to stop to drink. Your tube exits your pack, my ULA has small exit holes on either side for efficiency and then you simple slide it under your sternum strap of the backpack. You can always see mine in photographs when I'm wearing my pack—usually red, thanks to the Gatorade fruit punch. I carried two water bladders: a four liter and a two liter.

The four liter was my main bladder that sat vertically in a sleeve built into my backpack. But I didn't carry four liters of liquid, that would have been eight pounds and not necessary. Only in the dry years in Pennsylvania would I ever need to use its full capacity to keep from running out. Come to think of it, this season despite all the rainfall, New York seemed to be water challenged, but I just think that's more because sources aren't as readily near the trail. Before I started my thru-hike, I poured a two-liter bottle of Gatorade into that bladder and then marked on the bag with a Sharpie the level line. Then I used that two-liter level as my standard for hiking during the day, refilling if necessary along the way. By the time I made camp, I was usually running on empty, but I always knew the mileage and amount of water I had without needing to look. You just become aware of your pattern of consumption and get a great feel for it. Not being a fortuneteller, I did have to consult my handbook to stay abreast of where sources were.

Upon reaching camp, one of the first things I'd do is get water. The four-liter bladder would get about three liters put in it so I had water to drink for the rest of the day and night and still have enough in the morning—based on my two-liter level mark I put on the bladder—to hike out without having to pump anymore. This allowed me to get moving and make miles early without a lot of morning chores. Just pack and go. It worked brilliantly.

The two liter would also be filled upon reaching camp for the night's dinner, hot chocolate, and morning breakfast milkshake needs. This bag was only for straight water, Gatorade powder was never added to this bladder. Then, in the morning if any was left after the milkshake, I ask others if they needed any filtered water. Once emptied, the bladder was folded up and put back into the same little pump filter stuff sack, ready for the next camp.

Some used the bigger water bag that might hold a gallon of water that they'd hang in the shelter or tree branch. As they needed water, they just pumped some out of the big bag or add drops to whatever they were putting it in when needed. It meant getting large amounts of water quickly from the source, but it also meant treating and pumping water throughout the evening. What worked for me was to do it once when I arrived and use that time as a resting, cooling down period and then put the pump away and be done with it. The bladders I used were the MSR Dromlite, and I liked how the filter screwed into them. I never had a problem with them. Camelbacks and Platypus are also well represented out there. I was aware of several hikers whose bite-value tubes on Camelbacks pulled off while inside their packs unfortunately filling their packs with water. Not good. Both of the Dromlite bags weigh less than one Nalgene bottle and most I know usually have two. Alleghany, to avoid water weight, only carried one but carried a little cup he snapped on to his shoulder strap. I think he called it a Sierra cup, and when ever he'd come upon a good clean spring, he just use the Sierra and drink to his thirst's content. He also carried the Sweetwater pump and seemed happy with it. I believe MSR now owns the Sweetwater brand.

Pliers, Bowie Knifes, and Corkscrews

Since we'll be going out to face the wilds of this planet, a big knife with all sorts of doodads, just to be safe. Be prepared as the Boy Scouts say. The first one I carried was a classic: brushed metal with the ability to fold a hundred and one objects down to the size of an energy bar. A marvel really, but more than a half a pound! Gulp. If the mood hit me to carve a totem pole out there, it would be perfect. But when all you need is a blade to slice salami or something to scrape the dirt out from a fingernail, you don't require very much, do you? The people at Swiss Army Knife make a keychain-size pocket-knife that is the tiniest thing you've every seen. So diminutive in statue that every time I looked at it and thought about the gargantuan size of an AT thru-hike, I had to laugh. At only one ounce, it was all I ever needed for 2,174.1 miles.

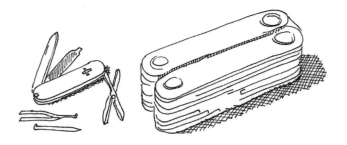

You won't slay any bears with it,
but at only an ounce, you can outrun them.

How to Boil Water

Technology has found the camp kitchen too. You can now boil water in the woods in under ninety seconds, which comes in handy if you're a rushing city person who's got appointments to keep. You can also now simmer smoothly or sauté with sass, or where a campfire is allowed, you can cook Ramen with a rustic flair. How ever you do it, you have lots of lightweight choices.

A long tradition on the Appalachian Trail is the small and light alcohol stove. It's sort of a tuna can with holes really. Anyway, before there was a lightweight revolution, hikers devised these little gems to save a couple of pounds from the large pump fuel canisters and noisy portable burners. Alcohol stoves use primarily denatured alcohol but will also work on rubbing alcohol, though it doesn't burn as hot. These little stoves are terribly efficient and beautifully simple. Just pour an ounce or so from your equally tiny fuel bottle and put a match to it. Wrap a tight windshield around it, and set your pot down. Effortless. Your eating habits will determine how much fuel. One guy I knew would eat two dehydrated dinners a night, then have some tea plus hot coffee in the morning, so he carried a lot more fuel than me. I basically used it for hot chocolate with my cookies after dinner. Yea, I know that sounds just cuter than all get out.

Other alcohol stoves are made out of two soda can bottoms slid over the top of one another with tiny holes for the flames. With most of these, the hiker uses a circular wire mesh that wraps around the stove and the pot is set up on top, while others have tiny legs the pot rests on. So simple is their design that many hikers make them for themselves. Some are real works of art.

Two alcohol stoves and a screw-down canister stove found at most knowledgeable outfitters.

Because the pump liquid fuel, single burner stove is more expensive and hence, has a higher margin, most mainstream outfitters don't sell these little alcohol stoves of simplicity. But things are changing since all of us want lightweight stuff.

The newer canister stoves are light and effortless too and have become very popular on the trail with most resupply points carrying the new canister replacements. One new twist on the canister stove is a complete cooking system called the Jetboil. This little thing includes the fuel, stove, pot, which also is your cup and lid. At under a pound when its canister is full, and able to boil twelve liters of water faster than any other device, it's a marvel of technology. If that wasn't cool enough, it all packs away inside itself. Another small stove is one that takes solid fuel squares called the Espit. But the smell of these things is awful to my nose, so just in case I ever go thru-hiking again, I'm not going to recommend them and hope they all disappear from the earth.

You should only carry one pot, and it should have handles built into it eliminating the need for a separate pot griper. The Evernew titanium ones are ideal and weigh nothing even with their lid—make sure that it's the smallest it can be for your needs and that your stove can fit into it for saving space. My stove, the one on the left is made by Etowah and it, the windscreen and disposable lighters, all fit inside the cook pot with the lid closed. Then they are stored inside the dinner food bag along with your small bottle of denatured alcohol. Most easy dinners require either one or two cups of boiling water, so before you head out, scratch some marks on the inside of the pot for those measurements to make everything brain-dead simple. Additionally, I found that two cups of water in my small titanium pot could get right to the edge of boiling in four minutes with just ¾ of an ounce of denatured alcohol, so long as the lid and windscreen are in place. I didn't need the water to boil since it was filtered and allowing it to boil made the entrée so hot, it took fifteen minutes before it was cool enough to enjoy. So I also took my eight-ounce transparent plastic fuel bottle and with a Sharpie marked off 3/4 ounce lines. As the reverend of my church says, "Fail to plan and plan to fail." With just a smidge of preparation, everything will be effortless.

You can make a windscreen from the bottom of those heavier foil-roasting pans available at a grocery store. Cut it so that it's taller than your stove and comes up over your pots sides for heat efficiencies, but your pots handles don't hit it. Your pot should just fit inside its diameter. Crimp the foil ends of the windscreen together making it circular and leave it that way. For storage, flatten it and fold in threes, that way it'll fit inside the pot with the stove. To use it, just unfold and reshape into a circle. Most all the windscreens I saw on the trail weren't sized to their pot, they were way larger than they needed to be and so heavier than they needed to be.

 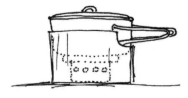

Foil windscreen with lower area for pot handles. Pot sitting on top of stove with windscreen.

A tip: When you pour your denatured alcohol into the stove cup, do so over the ground, not the floor of the shelter, tent or picnic table. I've seen many a burn spot because of spilt fuel. And as far as your tent, don't even think it. The new high-tech fabrics and flames don't get along very well at all.

Hike Your Own Hike

It's the mantra of the Appalachian Trail and should be the philosophy of all hiking. It means that you should not let others influence how you hike your hike. It also means for you to not try to hike someone else's hike.

Some of the younger hikers you'll meet out there will define themselves by how many miles they'll do. Many have limited time between college terms and will need to hike aggressively, while some of them fall into thinking that the hike is a competition. Goose and I met one hiker who bragged to us how he averaged thirty-one miles a day in his first month. He went on to say how he was going to catch so-and-so who he heard was a fast hiker. Well, OK then. Whatever. We asked him if he ever stopped at a beautiful vista or lingered by a brook for lunch. The hiker shifted sort of uncomfortably and shrugged. On the opposite end, I met a hiker who proudly claimed to be the slowest hiker out there.

If you plan on a thru-hike, you'll need to get used to the idea of hiking regardless of how yuk the weather may be. An AT adage states, "No rain, no pain, no gain, no Maine." Every morning I woke to a gray day, I could sense a lack of enthusiasm, and yet I packed up and got going. Many times the morning would clear up presenting me with blue skies and sunshine breaking through the tree canopy. Because I got going, I had a lot of miles done and the yuk of the day all but forgotten. And still other times by just moving on, you can actually walk yourself into better weather. But you've got to hike, that's what thru-hikers do.

On your journey to Maine, or Georgia depending on your direction, you are going to get rained on. So don't fret, become comfortable that it's just another condition. One reason I carried full rain gear is that when I put it on and saddled up with my backpack covered as well, I felt invincible. Sure your feet will get wet. They'll dry. When I zipped up my hood and battened down the hatches, knowing that you've also taken the right precautions with protecting the gear that must stay dry, I could hike without worrying. You just might enjoy the texture of it all. Dealing with rain comes down to your mental outlook, it's a Zen thing. Without the rain you'd have dry springs and a dead wasteland, so embrace the variety.

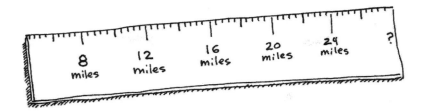

The thing that caused me the most anxiety was rumbling thunder overhead; we walk many a mountain ridgeline exposing ourselves to nature's wrath. If that's the case, stop early at a shelter, or set up the tent and lie down. One thing that worked for me was when the forecast called for afternoon thunderstorms, I made sure I got going early like usual, but I moved with purpose all day with only short breaks until I reached my planned destination. At one point in the hike, I seem to remember the forecast called for afternoon thunderstorms for a good two weeks. More often than not, I avoided the storm from catching me because I didn't lollygag. I can assure you I had my fair share of rain walks, but moving with purpose helped me to dodge a great deal of nature's drama.

You'll also need to watch how many zero days you take. Long about my sixth week, I hiked up on a couple that had already taken more than thirty zero days. Whether they finished I have no knowledge, it didn't seem like they were having much fun. Depending on when you start, the only immovable truth is the closing of Baxter State Park and Mt. Katahdin on October 15. When I began on May 1, which was definitely making me the caboose of the 2004 season of thru-hikers, I had 5 ½ months before the park closed. So I came up with a plan that had me there one week before the closing. You want some buffer days since the summit of Mt. Katahdin isn't always open due to weather conditions. Unfortunately, my plan did not allow for any zero days. But what I discovered, as you will, I was able to do more miles than I thought I could; this was a big discovery as well as a source of pride. The result was I reached Mt. Katahdin three weeks ahead of plan and that was on top of having twenty zero days! Making good miles gives you options and carrying a lighter load leads to making good miles. Zero days agreed with me, when on the trail I pretty much always moved throughout the day putting a higher-than-normal chunk of miles behind me. Although each morning I woke feeling fully recovered, I also felt compelled to proactively give myself body rest about every week or so. Especially in the first half where strength and stamina were being built. Another form of rest called a *Nero*, short for near zero, means hiking shorter miles into a town and getting a motel room and good food and continuing on the next morning. As Alleghany and I neared Katahdin in those last weeks, we both noticed how some of our strength was reducing. So on numerous times we'd hike ten to fourteen miles and hitch into town, stay the night, and eat a lunch, a dinner and then a breakfast before hiking on. We both noticed how the extra calories helped return us to our full capability. The good news is that you control your start date and options on how you can hike your hike.

Some hikers don't actually like taking zeros, they'd rather get into town early, get all the resupply and chores done and head back out. While some simply want or need to save money, taking a zero usually results in pulling out your wallet frequently.

FEELING DOWN

Rocks, roots, and rattlesnakes are wimpy adversaries next to the destructive power of feeling depressed. Even the most stout of heart will confront the loneliness that the isolation of the woods and mountains can present you with. Just because you long for the wilderness experience, doesn't mean you want to be alone. Thankfully for us all, one of the Appalachian Trail's strong suits is the sense of community among the hikers. As thru-hikers move north, friendships and even romance find them. Individuals become hiking partners and tribes. The system of shelters and their registers along the trail become the social hub of this emotional strength. And yet, oddly, despair can creep up on you.

If you find your mood low, I'd recommend getting into town and have a good rest and some good food and relax. Don't think that others won't listen to your plight, we share the bond of the difficulties, an empathic ear isn't that hard to find. Be careful to not let a down mood take you off the trail prematurely. We all get emotionally low at some time in the journey and you will definitely too. Try to guard against making a come-off-the-trail decision when it's raining or when you're down. You may regret it when your mood improves or when the sun starts to shine again. Even if you do come off, you can change your mind. The AT is a volunteer adventure, and it's your journey. Generally the double whammy that causes many to stop is when both the physical hardships and the emotional, no fun, lonely doldrums gang up on them. Carrying a heavy load up and down the mountains or out-of-control blisters or nonstop rain and wet gear can bring on the lows. Despair is a hard thing to step outside of. I once wrote in my journal that when I lived in the city, I was single. But when I was in the woods, I was alone. At the risk of sounding Pollyanna, the sun will come out again, it did for me. Just seeing the sun always had a marvelous effect on me or you might meet someone nice or a vista or stream or deer will touch you and things will improve. But there are things ahead of time that can help you to be less vulnerable to the mental-emotional demands you'll face.

I haven't seen the benefit in thinking of the enormity of the hike. What seems to be an effective way to thru-hike is to stay in the moment and look no farther than the day's goal of where you want to end up for camp. I found that thinking of the whole hike in terms of time and distance to be overwhelming, even destructive. Taking it one day at a time will keep you focused on enjoying the day; the bigger journey will take care of itself. Many I met wanted to get to Mt. Katahdin where I wanted to have fun and enjoy each day. One way isn't better than the other, this is just what worked for me and hopefully it might give you a hike filled with as much joy as mine was.

When you begin, you'll need to be patient with your body to let it get used to the many physical challenges. Be conservative with your mileage, do not try to go out and beat the mountains. You may be the master of the universe in your city world, but out there, they are. I've seen many who thought their mastery would transfer to their hike and emotionally faced a foe they were not familiar with. Don't let your ego mislead you; eight miles in Chicago isn't the same as eight miles in Georgia.

The closer I got to the finish, the more others would ask when I would complete the journey. I went out of my way to not look at the mileage tally countdown, focusing on what was left seemed to be the wrong mind-set for me. I felt the need to keep looking to what was still in front of me, the "It ain't over till it's over" thought; and if I relax my caution, a hike-ending injury could find me. Others have told me that was their main fret the closer they got to the end. I once described myself out on the trail as being a mental cupcake, so when I say stay in the moment, don't fret over the things you can't control anyway and try to see the brighter side of the adventure, those days will indeed string together one by one and you'll find yourself posing for a photo by a sign that says *Katahdin*.

Now that's a bit of a macrolook at the hike, now let's look at the micro. During the hike, I encourage you to be single-minded and only do one thing at a time. Multitasking in the business or normal world may have its benefits, but on the trail it can spell disaster. Looking for radio stations on the radio while walking can have you not seeing the root that's sticking up; turning an ankle is just one wrong step away, so stay in the moment. If you want to drink water and keep walking, make sure you have a bladder with bite-valve tube, otherwise with a Nalgene you might walk off a cliff. What's worse is that nearly every year, several hikers break a leg or ankle despite trying to be careful. The last thing the trail needs help on is tripping you up, which it surely will do. So no multitasking while you're making miles. Watch your step, literally.

MAIL DROPS, MAPS, AND HITCHHIKING

If you're the sort who likes to plan, here's what I did. Before I started, for some reason I was under the impression that getting into towns from the trail would be difficult. With some of the towns being ten miles away, the whole thing seemed daunting. And besides, I've never hitchhiked in my life, so that pastime also seemed a bit scary actually. Well, it wasn't. In fact, it became so effortless I remained amazed at the willingness of those to stop and pick up one wearing a backpack. In my meager attempt to bring some emotional control to the hitch, I made a bandana with those three magic words on it: Hiker to Town. In the corners, I placed Velcro squares and then added some to my hiking sticks so that when I reached the road, I simple attached the minibillboard. My idea of the Velcro on the sticks and corners was one of my better thoughts. Worked like a champ. But let us get back to the plan.

I felt that having mail drops would make it easier on me by reducing my town chores. Which it did until my taste buds started desiring different tastes. The big question about mail drops though is how many, how far apart, and to where. My earlier experiences on the AT had shown me that doing about fifteen miles a day was well within my range once I was in trail shape. And in the beginning, I could just figure on shorter ten-mile days. With that knowledge, all I had to do was to sit down with my maps and guidebook and actually hike the trail on paper. It should be pointed out here that I used two forms of trail guides. First was the very popular book by Dan "Wingfoot" Bruce called *The Thru-Hiker's Handbook*. This is not sold through the Appalachian Trail Conservancy bookstore, and they'll get miffed at you if you ask them for it. The second source was the profile maps that show you the elevation gains and descents plus shelter locations. Without these, it's hard to know if a ten-mile section is either hard or a breeze. If you can see that one section has no significant climbs, then you can plan on a longer mileage day if you so choose. I found it nice to know.

To make my plan, I sat down over a series of nights and "walked through" what I thought I could do with the profile maps. I knew also that I didn't want to carry seven or eight days of food either since it can get so heavy. So about every fifth day I looked to see where a town post office was and made a list. Some were closer than five days and some were farther, but I think they averaged about five. I literally traversed the entire AT over the next several nights while compiling my list of post offices and the number of nights between each so I'd know how much food each box would need. It's not difficult as much as tedious. According to my guesstimated mileage, my calculations led me to having twenty-seven mail drops.

My mail drop boxes contained the following:

Dehydrated dinners—quantity determined by how many nights out to next box	
Powdered breakfast drinks	"
Lunch foods and snacks	"
Daily vitamins	two per day
Tylenol PM	three per night
Excedrin	
Self-addressed stamped envelope to mail home journal pages	
Small bottle of Captain Morgan Spiced Rum to refill my plastic flask	
Next section's profile maps	
Disposable razor	
Extra journal pad (about every four to five boxes)	
Toilet paper (about every other box)	
Extra Ziplocs	
Hot chocolate packets—quantity determined by how many nights out to next box	
Gatorade packets—1 ½ packets per day out	
AAA batteries	

Some hikers have complained that mail drops cramped their style, having to deal with post office hours of operation. Me, I thought it was all part of the challenges, and I enjoyed seeing all the Americana of the towns. And besides, who's to say that being forced into a rest day for a post office to open is a bad thing. My only angst regarding a mail drop came on a holiday weekend when I basically just resupplied without it and moved on as to avoid stopping for three days. So that was once in twenty-seven boxes. And there were only three times where getting a hitch into town took longer than ten minutes, but a ride eventually did present itself. So that whole cramp-your-style argument doesn't hold water as the saying goes.

I did, however, experience a surprising change in my food desires. Despite enjoying dehydrated dinners before the hike, I found myself acquiring an absolute distaste for them, which left me with hundreds of dollars of food I didn't want to eat. I craved the foods I was used to eating such as sandwiches and chips and the like. To hike all day and be rewarded with a meal that held no appeal would have been my undoing if I didn't make a radical change. So I became a bit of a Santa Claus and gave away the meals to other hikers and started hiking out with deli sandwiches and vacuum-sealed meats and cheeses and even precooked chicken tenders or cheeseburgers. All would be Ziploced and the fresh stuff got enjoyed first. During the cooler temperatures, sandwiches kept just fine, for days on end, only they got a bit smashed, but at least they were flavors I wanted.

My mail drop destinations:

1.	Neels Gap—Walasi Yi Center	Georgia
2.	Nantahala Outdoor Center	North Carolina
3.	Fontana Dam	North Carolina
4.	Mountain Momma's	Tennessee
5.	Hot Springs	North Carolina
6.	Erwin	Tennessee
7.	Damascus	Virginia
8.	Bland	Virginia
9.	Pearisburg	Virginia
10.	Catawba	Virginia
11.	Daleville	Virginia
12.	Waynesboro	Virginia
13.	Front Royal	Virginia
14.	Harpers Ferry	West Virginia
15.	Duncannon	Pennsylvania
16.	Port Clinton	Pennsylvania
17.	Delaware Water Gap	Pennsylvania
18.	Bear Mountain	New York
19.	Kent	Connecticut
20.	Dalton	Massachusetts
21.	Manchester Center	Vermont
22.	Hanover	New Hampshire
23.	North Woodstock	New Hampshire
24.	Gorham	New Hampshire
25.	Andover	Maine
26.	Stratton	Maine
27.	Monson	Maine

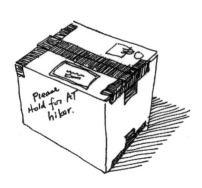

The basics concerning mail drops are, make sure you get the address correct. Make sure if not a post office they still accept packages. Print clearly: Hold for AT hiker—(your real name)—and your ETA date (estimated time of arrival). And on top of everything, send them first class so they arrive at least ten days before getting there. Make sure whoever is handling the mailing of them is aware of your pace, so keep them up to date.

Another box that can help a hiker is what we call a bounce box. This is a box you mail up the trail with things you don't want to carry and won't need till later. Say your bulk supply of vitamins or silk liners or extra socks, etc. By sending it first class as well, it will be forwarded up the trail at no extra charge if you miss it or it you.

BEFORE YOU HIT THE TRAIL, HIT THE HEALTH CLUB

From the time I made the decision to thru-hike the Appalachian Trail, I gave myself a short-term health club membership. For me it was three months. I just didn't want to be a victim of the Approach Trail or any of those early weeks. Throughout all the planning, I was visiting the health club five to six times a week. I was committed to building my leg muscles and my endurance. I hired a personal trainer to help in the development of my conditioning three times a week for two months.

Near the end of January at my first visit to the club, I got on a treadmill and ran 1.5 miles. It was exhausting. I obviously had room for improvement. There's this one saying that some hikers tout about getting in shape that I completely disagree with. The much-touted saying is to hike your way into shape on the trail. No wonder it takes six months for many. Frankly, heading out into the Georgia and North Carolina mountains can be a miserable existence without some strength training and some aerobic endurance.

If you can afford the time to do so, you'll smile more and the likelihood of getting down from the physical hardships will be reduced greatly.

So there I am on the treadmill running one week, then the next week I'd walk with it on an incline. Alternating with walking helped to stretch out those shin muscles since my walking stride has a longer gate. When I run I tend to shuffle with smaller steps. The trainer started me with free-weight machines with the emphasis on my legs.

After two months I was running four miles or a solid hour on the treadmill, five to six times a week. The whole last month I'd run six miles *and* do the Stairmaster for a full hour on level 4. When I was done with my two-hour workout, I was drenched in perspiration. My endurance had grown dramatically because I was pushing myself to be ready for the trail. And all the while, I was doing it in the actual shoes I'd be hiking in (except when running), they and my feet were getting to really know each other. It had to be the chief reason why blisters never found me during the hike.

Do yourself a favor and get busy at getting in shape before your hike. The more you do before, the better you'll deal with the physical hardships. Additionally, start parking your car in the farthest space out from the store or errands you'll be running. It just makes good sense.

THE JOY OF THE JOURNEY

Somewhere over the rainbow is that place called the horizon. A horizon is easily seen but elusive to understand. It's that place where landscape becomes ambiguity. Whether thirty miles or a hundred, it provides our heart and mind with the concept of bigness. It's more right brain than left. I have a feeling that most people take horizons for granted, never really seeing them as something unto itself. Maybe that's the draw for observation decks or why we have special overlooks. Distance is hidden in plain sight from many of us, and these places direct us to look, to experience the grandeur that can be bigness. Many a spirit has been lifted by these vantage points.

A feat that still amazes me is the accomplishment of walking beyond a horizon. I've done it now countless times. Technology may be shrinking the world, but walking reminds me how big it still all is. Horizons challenge us to tear down the fences we've built around our worlds where everything is familiar and safe. They speak to adventure, discovery, and letting go. They ask us to embrace the unknown. They ask us to leap.

If you've felt you haven't done anything special in some time, I'd encourage you to take to the AT or any long trail and go for a walk. While you walk from day to day, pay attention to the sounds of the woods. Pay attention to the trees and sunlight that finds its way through them. Pay attention to the rocks and critters and scurrying fuzzy fauna. Discover how a short period, even an hour of isolation touches your insecurities. Try to see what you look at and to hear what you listen to. After many days with all those experiences, you'll come to a vista that will allow you to look back in time, to see all those yesterdays. Give yourself a pat on the back and tell yourself, "Well done."

But always remember, it's not so much the horizon that is so special as it is all that happens on the way to it. You have a horizon waiting for you on the Appalachian Trail, I hope you'll seek it out, and I hope you'll experience the wonderful wilderness of awes.

Postcard in Maine. X marks the spot of the true two-thousandth mile.

About the Author

I've been described as being equal parts George Patton and Walt Disney.

I've been to all fifty states.

When in a car, even a taxi, you should wear a seat belt. This includes the backseat too.

I believe individuals can make a difference.

I like people who can stand tall when the winds start to blow.

I've had my life threaten three times—all on the same trip. The circumstances involved a very large African bull elephant, a white rhinoceros, and a male lion.

I think we should all look to fix problems instead of blame.

My least favorite word is *timing*—it's why I'm still single.

My favorite word is *effortless*—because it seems the things that are truly great, somehow seem to be that way.

I like being optimistic and trusting.

Nothing brings out the champion in me more than bullies and injustice.

I believe that having principles don't mean much until they cost you money.

I'm fascinated by the drama of weather.

I am a purpose-driven individual.

I love the science channels, particularly the shows about space and our planet.

I'm a fair cook, a good golfer at times, and not too shabby as a watercolor painter.

I believe everyone should see our national parks, but I'm glad they don't since it keeps them quieter.

I don't think big words should be used when small words will do.

I like the old cowboy adage that says there are two theories to arguing with women—neither of them works.

My favorite quotes include "Most problems are simply decisions we haven't made," and "Fail to plan and plan to fail"—both by Robert Schuller.

I grew up in a home where both parents were the breadwinner, and Dad did the cooking.

My other name is Uncle Mark, thanks to my one sister's four kids.

She's older but will deny it.

In my twenty-three years of advertising experience, I've learned that the right decision is not always the popular one.

After carrying a backpack over two thousand miles of the Appalachian Trail, I discovered that simplicity is one of life's truly great pleasures.

I believe the secret to life is to enjoy its journey.

I'd like to hike the John Muir Trail someday because of Ansel Adams's photography.

I love the movies *Casablanca* and *Forrest Gump*.

I'm at my happiest when I'm creating.

And I can't understand why people try to park as close as they can to the front door of the health club.

Hike happy, everyone, and hope to see you out there.

Made in the USA
Middletown, DE
29 June 2015